LIFE
SENTENCES

LIFE SENTENCES

Rage and Survival Behind Bars

||||||

Wilbert Rideau and Ron Wikberg

TIMES 𝕿 BOOKS

All of the articles that appear in this volume were originally published in *The
Angolite: The Prison Newsmagazine,* Louisiana State Penitentiary, Angola,
LA.

*Grateful acknowledgment is made to the following for permission to reprint
previously published material:*

The New York Times: Excerpts from "Very Good Night" by Gilbert
Millstein from the October 15, 1950 issue of *The New York Times.* Copyright
1950 by The New York Times Company. Reprinted by permission.

Charles C. Thomas, Publisher: Excerpt from *Rape in Prison* by Dr. Anthony
M. Scacco, Jr. Reprinted by permission of Charles C. Thomas, Publisher,
Springfield, Illinois.

Library of Congress Cataloging-in-Publication Data

Life sentences : rage and survival behind bars / [edited] by
  Wilbert Rideau and Ron Wikberg.—1st ed.
     p.   cm.
  Includes index.
  ISBN 0–8129–2048–1
    1. Louisiana State Penitentiary.   2. Prisons—Louisiana—Angola.
  3. Criminal justice, administration of—Louisiana.   I. Rideau,
  Wilbert.   II. Wikberg, Ron.
  HV9475.L22L647   1992
  365'.976317—dc20   91–41173

Designed by M 'N O Productions Services, Inc.

Manufactured in the United States of America

9 8 7 6 5 4 3 2

First Edition

Dedicated to fostering a better public
understanding of criminal justice

ACKNOWLEDGMENTS

A unique relationship of trust between individuals of diverse backgrounds and interests made this book possible.

In 1975, Warden C. Murray Henderson, who maintained a keen interest in Rideau's writing activities, assigned him as editor of the prison publication *The Angolite*. In 1976, Henderson's successor, acting Warden C. Paul Phelps, lifted the lid of censorship, allowing the magazine under Rideau to publish anything about the world of prison as long as it was truthful. This journalistic freedom was reinforced and expanded upon by succeeding administrators, Ross Maggio, Frank Blackburn, Hilton Butler, Larry Smith, and Warden John P. Whitley, the current publisher of *The Angolite*. With an enthusiastic nod, Whitley helped to facilitate the production of this book.

This book would still be a dream if not for Random House's Joni Evans and Julie Grau, who discovered us and stuck with us through many ups and downs. Our editor, Ruth Fecych, turned editorial conferences into rewarding classroom sessions in the use of English and language.

To all of them, and many unnamed others, we owe our heartfelt thanks.

On a personal level, there is Kay Smith, for whom I am especially grateful.

—Ron Wikberg

CONTENTS

|||||

LIFE
SENTENCES

THE DEATHMEN

|||||

Ron Wikberg and Wilbert Rideau

*There is just one thing in all this question. It is a question
of how you feel, that is all. It is all inside of you. If you love
the thought of somebody being killed, why, you are for it.
If you hate the thought of somebody being killed, you are
against it.*

—CLARENCE DARROW

Some men hunt animals; others fish. Sam Jones hasn't done either
in a while. He's acquired a more intriguing hobby. Sam kills people.
Nineteen, so far. And he gets paid for it: $400 per death. All were
strangers to Sam. He's never spoken to those he's killed, and they've
all died not knowing the face of their killer. "No, I don't think any
of them ever seen me," Sam acknowledges. It was all impersonal and
done with chilling efficiency. Afterward, he returned to his normal
routine, to await the next phone call informing him that his deadly
services were needed; and he returned to his usual killing place, where
another wretched soul was waiting, dreading his arrival and the com-
mencement of the cold, methodical procedure that would extinguish
the life from his body.

Sam is a nondescript man of average height and build, the guy
sitting next to you almost anywhere. When we met him, he was
dressed casually in T shirt, camouflage pants, and snakeskin cowboy
boots. Piercing blue eyes gazed from a weathered face. His hair was
a dull red; his beard, streaked with gray. He sucked deeply on a

cigarette; when he exhaled, a plume of smoke drifted toward the ceiling.

Sam was born and reared in Louisiana's capital city of Baton Rouge, where he attended school and later served a three-year stint as a police officer: "I worked in a little bit of everything—juvenile, auto theft, wherever I was needed," he recalled. At age forty-nine, he is an electrician but, like many men, he's to some extent a jack-of-all-trades. "I do a little painting, do my own carpenter work," he explained. "I had a lock shop one time, used to be a locksmith, and I got out of that." He likes country-and-western music, and his favorite radio station is Baton Rouge's WYNK. He is divorced, but admits to not playing the night-life scene much. "I do a lot of reading, watching TV," he says. "I don't go out. I don't socialize much." He describes himself as a loner.

Sam defies all of the popular perceptions about those who kill— and he defies them in a disturbing way. "I'm just a normal person that mixes in with a crowd," he once explained to a newspaper reporter, "a normal John Doe that walks the streets every day. I work and I live a normal social life. No, I don't have any horns and I don't see anyone floating around my room at night. No nightmares, and I don't see any ghosts. . . . I go there to do a job, and I do it and leave."

Sam provokes awe and wonder. Nothing in his outward appearance, behavior, or lifestyle distinguishes him from the average citizen or, for that matter, from the people he kills. Yet beneath that surface normality lies a peculiar ability to kill with deliberateness and without compunction. And unlike most people who kill, for whom countless studies have shown the act of murder to be a once-in-a-lifetime incident, Sam kills regularly. But Sam is defined as neither criminal nor murderer. On the contrary, he's licensed to kill. He's Louisiana's official executioner; his instrument of death, the electric chair; his name, an alias.

In an appearance last year on an Australian TV newsmagazine with defense attorney Clive Stafford Smith, Sam provided viewers a chilling peek at the breadth of his peculiar capacity. After he stated that electrocution is too quick and easy for those he executes, the following exchange occurred:

> SMITH: "Let me ask you this then. Say someone stabs somebody 71 times, would you be prepared to go in there and stab the person 71 times?"

SAM: "If it were required, I could do it, yes."

SMITH: "You could? For four hundred bucks?"

SAM: "Well, the money don't have nothin' to do with it."

SMITH: "What is the most gruesome thing you would be prepared to do for the four hundred dollars?"

SAM: "Whatever."

SMITH: "You'd take a candle and sort of drop hot wax on them, pull their nails out and then kill them, or something like that?"

SAM: "If that's what they wanted. If that's what the state tells me to do."

Sam is even a bit of an artist, in a macabre way. As soon as he gets home following an execution, he pulls out a blank canvas and begins painting. When he finishes, he goes to bed and sleeps "like a baby." He's killed nineteen people; he has nineteen paintings. When his collection was described to the Australian audience as "dark, morbid paintings of death," Sam objected: "You calling it pictures of death. I just call it paint on canvas. . . . Some people jog; I draw pictures and execute people."

"It's never bothered me," Sam said of his executions of those deemed unfit to live in society. "There's nothin' to it. It's no different to me executing somebody and goin' to the refrigerator and getting a beer out of it." Even the family bond does not exempt his own son or grandson. "If he did something, they sit him in the chair, he was convicted of it, I'd execute him," he assured us.

And he'd paint another picture.

[February 1991]

BOOK
ONE
IIIII

THE FARRAR LEGACY

Ron Wikberg

'Tis the business of little minds to shrink; but he whose heart is firm, and whose conscience approves his conduct, will pursue his principles unto death.

—THOMAS PAINE

The Crime

It was nearing eleven A.M. as Rene and Lucien Canton exited the large gray house on the corner of Milan and Magnolia. They had just spent half an hour burglarizing the New Orleans residence of Edgar Farrar, Jr., a junior partner in the law firm of Farrar, Jones, Goldsborough & Goldberg and a renowned cotton broker for the region. Farrar, thirty-three, a newlywed of seven months, had married Mary C. "May" Spearing, daughter of a successful tent and awning manufacturer. Spearing had businesses in both New Orleans and Pass Christian, Mississippi, where the Farrars had been visiting on that Halloween day, October 31, 1911. Unknown to the Canton brothers, their departure was being observed by a local black servant and caretaker, Theophile Rodgers, as they headed down Magnolia Street carrying bundles under their arms. Rene and Lucien ended up at 222 Bourbon Street, where Joseph Owen, a dealer in gold and silver, bought their booty for $60. Lucien, twenty, was glad. His half would help toward paying the expense of going to Hot Springs, Arkansas, where he could receive the cure for his syphilis. Rene, twenty-two, also had reasons to be happy. He could get his gun out of the pawn-shop, pay a few bills around town, and get back to Lena Canton, a first cousin with whom he'd lived and "consorted" for several years. The brothers parted, agreeing to meet the next morning.

When Farrar and May returned, Rodgers explained what he had seen. The following morning, November 1, 1911, while on regular rounds, Rodgers saw the Cantons walking down the street and recognized them as the same men. He hurried to get Farrar; they both followed the brothers at a slow pace. May watched her husband leave with Rodgers; she would never see him alive again.

According to Seventh Precinct police reports, Farrar and Rodgers followed the Cantons through five or six blocks of the French Quarter. As the short, slightly built Cantons turned onto Peniston, Farrar, a large man of two hundred pounds, ran up behind the brothers, grabbing both as he yelled to Rodgers to get help. Rene broke away, ran about fifteen paces, turned, and fired a single shot from the Colt .41 he'd just gotten out of hock; then he continued to run away. Farrar eased his grip on Lucien, yelling "He got me!" as he turned Lucien loose; he walked a distance and fell. Rodgers and another man held Lucien till help arrived. Two locals, Bertrand R. Gernsbacher and H. Perloff, a grocer, rushed to the scene. Perloff ran back to his store to get a glass of water; then, returning to the prostrate Farrar, raised him slightly to allow him to drink. With blood coming from both nostrils, Farrar uttered not a word, sinking back to the ground. The young lawyer and businessman, shot through both lungs, died where he lay.

May soon arrived. The *Daily Picayune* described the tragic scene:

> Her husband's face she covered with kisses, while she called to him in most endearing terms to come back to her. Men, grown used to the hard things of the world, with misery, sin and suffering, turned away their faces, and teardrops were in the eyes of many. Kneeling by his dead form, Mrs. Farrar took his hand within her own, and, smoothing it, called to him again and again. And when, after the police, came the hospital ambulance and the doctors and the dead body of her husband had been placed within it, she begged to go along with him. Holding his

hand, while her hot tears fell upon the dead, upturned face, she sobbed his name incoherently in a voice that was a prayer, supplication such as goes straight beyond the eternal skies.

Farrar's body was taken to the residence of his parents. He would be buried the following day.

‖‖‖ The Pretrial Scenario ‖‖‖

Several hours after the shooting, with the help of a streetcar conductor named Ignatius W. Starkey, a former schoolmate of the Cantons who knew many of their friends, Rene was arrested at a house on Derbigny Street. Under interrogation by the district attorney, both Lucien and Rene eventually confessed.

The killing of Edgar Howard Farrar, Jr., on All Saints' Day was the beginning of a criminal case that would encompass two capital trials, spark criticisms of the legal process and criminal-justice system, incite already opinionated news media, and prick the prevailing sensitivities toward socialist philosophies and the politics of the era. It would bring the issue of capital punishment to the forefront of a society that even then grappled with the morality of executing people who commit crimes (though it paid little attention to the lynchings so common at the time).

A member of one of the proudest families in the Southern tradition, young Farrar had been a direct descendant of Jefferson Davis on his mother's side, and of Mrs. Jefferson Davis on his father's. Considered one of the most promising attorneys in the country, his father, Edgar H. Farrar, Sr., had recently completed a term as president of the American Bar Association. The President of the United States had appointed him superintendent of education for one of the nation's recently acquired possessions, the Philippines. Following preliminary schooling in New Orleans, Edgar Jr. went to Sewanee University in Tennessee, finishing his degree in law at the University of Virginia. The younger Farrar deserved the family name. He could speak six languages and was considered a scientist and man of letters. Having an excellent voice, he played an active role in the local music set, singing with the choir of the Trinity Church. His murder at the hands of "hooligans" shook the foundations of Southern aristocracy.

Front-page headlines of New Orleans newspapers described the atmosphere: "E. H. FARRAR, JR., SLAIN TAKING TWO THIEVES," said the *Picayune*. "SHOT DOWN BY THIEF," said the *Times-Democrat*. Both accounts described a brilliant young lawyer bravely pursuing burglars who robbed his honeymoon home. Numerous reporters were present in the district attorney's office as the Cantons made their confessions. Their reports were graphic. "Both appear to be degenerates of the worst type, small of head, with close set, wicked eyes, and cruel mouths. They have been compared in appearance with the Apaches of Paris. Both are said to be afflicted with contagious and loathsome diseases," said the *Picayune*. The mood was clear. The anticipated pace for court proceedings was set.

‖‖‖   The Trials   ‖‖‖
and Sentence

The case was docketed under number 39,386 in Section B, Criminal District Court, and was presided over by the Honorable Frank D. Chretien. District Attorney Adams, along with assistant Warren Doyle, would personally try the case. Finding an attorney to defend the Cantons posed a problem. The case's anticipated notoriety called for an able and well-respected member of the legal profession. Judge Chretien's choice was H. N. Gauthier, a former state judge who was reputed to be an accomplished jurist. Gauthier agreed to defend the Cantons.

The grand jury indicted the brothers for murder on November 4, 1911. Both pled not guilty at their November 9 arraignment and, because of a technical problem, the Cantons had to be re-arraigned on November 13. They again pled not guilty. Judge Chretien set trial for December 14.

Because the first trial would eventually result in a hung jury, its records were not transcribed, and information about it is sparse. However, we know that after a four-day trial, a lone juror refused to vote for "hanging," and Judge Chretien declared a mistrial. "SOCIALIST JUROR SAVES THE CANTONS," declared the *Picayune*. "MISTRIAL FOR CANTONS: ONE JUROR STANDS OUT AGAINST ELEVEN," said the *Times-Democrat*. A deputy sheriff who delivered meals to the jury room told news reporters: "When I went to the jury room to see if dinners would be needed, one juror replied, 'Yes. Eleven dinners and one bale of hay.' "

The lone juror, Henry P. Devlin, a onetime press agent for the Tulane and Crescent Theaters, admitted he was a member of the Socialist party despite the unpopularity of such politics at the time. The newspapers criticized Devlin, saying that his political opinions contributed to the failure to convict the murderers. It "was a most lamentable miscarriage of justice." Devlin, when cornered by reporters, said: "I believe in capital punishment, but I don't believe in capital punishment for both the Cantons. I don't believe in capital punishment for either one."

Devlin's sister, Mrs. Emma Allen, interviewed the day after the trial, told the media she had heard about the trial and the jury situation but had not known it was her brother who caused all the controversy. She told the *Picayune* her brother was a hotheaded socialist, adding: "Last night when I read the paper I thought it was a poor jury to be hung so long. It wouldn't have taken me ten minutes to hang both Cantons. But I did not know it was my brother who was the man who hung the jury."

Fellow jurors also expressed criticisms. "I don't believe Devlin believes in capital punishment," said Charles A. Wettmore, who was manager of the New Orleans Audubon Building. Juror J. W. Wright said, "Man, we exhausted every resource, argued ourselves sick and tried in every possible manner to convince Devlin. He simply wouldn't listen." District Attorney Adams concluded: "I consider the failure of the jury to reach a verdict in this case a gross miscarriage of justice, but it will only nerve the prosecution to greater effort." Just before declaring a mistrial, Judge Chretien asked the jury foreman, A. J. Morel, whether a verdict could possibly be reached. "Not in a thousand years," Morel replied. The final tally: eleven to hang, one for manslaughter on Rene Canton; nine to acquit, three for manslaughter on Lucien Canton. Judge Chretien set January 9, 1912, as the new trial date.

The new trial actually began Friday, February 16, 1912, and was a shorter version of the first. Court records show the prosecution calling five witnesses: Captain George Long, chief of detectives; Warren Doyle, assistant district attorney; Dr. J. A. O'Hara, the coroner; L. T. French, a *Picayune* photographer; and local attorney Henry L. Lazarus, a former state judge. These people had been present in the crowded office of the district attorney during the interrogations and confessions of both Cantons, and their testimony was designed to support the contention that the confessions had not been coerced.

Gauthier cross-examined each witness and attempted to show that the confessions were not voluntary acts. To further support the contention, Gauthier described the intimidating atmosphere of the D.A.'s crowded office, and claimed Rene Canton had been struck in the face by Detective Long while being transported from jail for questioning. The prosecution admitted that the incident had occurred, but said it was precipitated by a misunderstanding: The detective believed Rene was reaching for a police gun sitting on his cell bed. The trial transcript does not show any inquiry by Gauthier as to why a gun might have been on the bed in Canton's cell, and no further interest in the matter was expressed. The lengthy and detailed confessions were read to the jury by Assistant District Attorney Doyle; they included this colloquy between Adams and Rene: "How did you happen to shoot this stout man? Answer: He grabbed me, and I didn't know what he grabbed me for, and I pulled out and shot him." The State then rested its case.

To the surprise of many, when it came time for the defense, Gauthier said: "I have concluded, after consulting with my clients, that it's unnecessary to put any witnesses on the stand." However, he did make an oral motion for a new trial on the grounds that the name of a juror had been misspelled; he told the court that had the defendant known the proper spelling, the juror would have been dismissed with a peremptory challenge. Judge Chretien determined that the matter was harmless error, and at that point the defense rested its case. In less than an hour, the jury returned with a verdict of guilty on Rene Canton and a not guilty verdict on Lucien Canton.

The court minutes of April 15, 1912, reflect sentencing: "Defendant

Rene Canton this date sentenced to be hanged by the neck until he is dead, at the State Penitentiary at Baton Rouge, La., at such time as the Governor of the State of Louisiana shall appoint in his warrant." Headlines in the *Picayune* said, "RENE CANTON GETS DEATH SEN-TENCE," "ERROR IN JUROR'S NAME FAILS TO WIN NEW TRIAL," and "YOUNG THIEF DISPLAYS NO EMOTION WHEN JUDGE CHRETIEN DECREES HIS FATE," adding: "Rene Canton stood up to receive the sentence without visible tremor; in fact, he was as stoical as an Indian, and when Judge Chretien spoke the fatal words which consigned him to the gallows he did not move a muscle, and sat down as unconcerned as if he had received a sentence of five days. Canton was then sent back to the Parish* Prison, and will be removed to the condemned cell."

The appeals process was perfunctory. Gauthier filed a motion for an appeal, and on June 13, the state's highest court affirmed the conviction and sentence. On June 28, a surprisingly short—four-page—request for rehearing filed by Gauthier was rejected.

In the world of crime and punishment, Canton's situation was not entirely bleak. Having a sentence of death, though indeed a serious matter, did not necessarily cause a condemned person to lose all hope of obtaining relief. Between 1892 and 1899, according to Louisiana Pardon Board records, twenty-three death sentences had been reduced to life imprisonment by executive clemency. Another forty-four such commutations were issued between 1900 and 1909. There was always reason to hope. But in Canton's case, the killing of a prominent member of New Orleans society precluded any assistance or plea in his behalf by any official. The news media had crucified him over and over again, and it was highly unlikely that any member of the legal community would rally to his aid. His own attorney, though a re-spected jurist, was not only a friend of the Farrar family but also a member of the same profession as the murder victim. There was no one to come forward and help save Canton's life. Governor Luther E. Hall set December 6, 1912, for his execution.

---

*"Parish" is a Louisiana term for county.

‖‖‖ The First Clemency ‖‖‖

Assistance did come. It came from an unexpected source—the family of the murder victim. On Thanksgiving Day, eight days before Canton's date with the gallows, Edgar Farrar, Sr., penned a plea for mercy to Governor Hall on Canton's behalf. Speaking for the entire family, Farrar wrote:

> This matter has been in our minds for some time, and after mature deliberation, all of us, father, mother, sisters, brothers and widow of my son, have concluded to ask you to reprieve Rene Canton, and to send his case before the Board of Pardons for their consideration as to whether his sentence should not be commuted to imprisonment for life. We feel that this young brute is the product of our society, for which all of us, particularly persons in our position, are to some extent responsible. His father and mother are honest, hard working people. With them the struggle for existence was too bitter and exacting to permit them to devote the time and personal care necessary to develop the good and repress the evil in their son, who thus grew up amid the malign influences that surround the children of the poor in a large city. We believe that he shot my son as instinctively as a snake would strike one who has crossed his path; and while his act was murder in law and in fact, yet it lacked that forethought and deliberation which make a crime of this sort unpardonable. This man is now in no condition of mind to be sent into the next world. We hope and pray that time and reflection will bring repentance and that his soul may be received.

Governor Hall stayed the execution till the state Pardon Board could consider the case. Farrar Sr., wrote a second letter to the board on December 9, 1912, attaching a copy of the letter previously sent to Governor Hall. Farrar explained to the board that the social position and personal feelings of a victim's family should play no part in the extent of Canton's punishment, but that only society as a whole should be considered.

Pardon Board files show that Governor Hall commuted Canton's death sentence to life imprisonment on December 28, 1912, exactly one month after Farrar's first letter to the governor. Canton's would be one of only three death-to-life commutations granted by the governor during 1912.

IIIII   The Penitentiary   IIIII

Prison life has never been particularly rosy, but it is generally agreed that punishment in the early twentieth century was much harsher than it is today. That is particularly true of the Louisiana State Penitentiary, historically known as Angola after one of the original plantations purchased to form what would eventually expand into an 18,000-acre enclave sixty miles northwest of Baton Rouge. Ringed by levees on three sides to protect it from the rampaging Mississippi River, and by the deep ravines and rugged terrain of the Tunica Hills on the fourth side, Angola has not only been one of the nation's most notorious penal facilities, but also one of the most isolated. Even in 1912, its bloody reputation struck terror in the hearts of those destined for it.

That year, the Mississippi overran the levees, requiring an evacuation of the prisoners. An entire crop was ruined. Camps were underwater for two months, and though rebuilding began, disease and epidemics killed many inmates and employees. Angola was expected to turn a profit, but because of the flood of 1912, was unable to do so for years, despite increased pressure from Baton Rouge. Whipping was instituted, and "coming down hard" on the inmates to increase productivity was the new philosophy.

Penitentiary records show Canton was received at Angola on January 13, 1913, and assigned prisoner number 7464. Little information could be found on Canton's life in prison. However, *The Angolite* contacted Roger Thomas, assistant warden for treatment, who for five years has researched and studied the history of the penitentiary, acquiring substantial knowledge of the prison system since the eighteenth century.

Teaching a new convict the ropes, said Thomas, involved first breaking him down by forcing him to do some menial job and work-ing long, hard hours. "Country boys were looked upon better than city boys," he says, "because country boys would adjust faster. They were used to hard work and they were used to manual labor and farm work. The employees were also country, so a city boy coming up here with lily-white hands, the very first thing they are going to do is mess his hands up. It did not matter who or what you were—when you walked into the penitentiary, you were nothing. You were going to work either in the fields or the levee crew.

"The next thing to occur would depend on how quick you adjusted to the system, because you either learned quick, or you died. Surviving depended upon how healthy you were, and then [on your] brains. Now, you got this guy Canton, who could read and write, and he's white. If he served his time in the hard-labor area and he's saying, 'Yes, Boss, yes, Boss,' and he's doing the proper amount of kowtow-ing, and he's got himself adjusted well, they're going to need clerks. They had clerks for everything, and reading and writing was a good skill in 1913. Canton would have gotten a job pretty quick."

The sparse information in prison records does reflect Canton's assignment to Camp E (a minimum security unit) as a trusty under Captain W. W. Pecue. Then, on July 15, 1915, Canton escaped; he wasn't recaptured until July 18. Records show the notation "sent to The Walls [a nineteenth-century maximum security prison] for pun-ishment." Canton's return was made at the time of the first telephone conversation between New York and San Francisco, by Alexander Graham Bell and Thomas A. Watson.

"He probably ran off from some job assignment somewhere," Thomas told *The Angolite*. "Now, he runs and gets caught. When he comes back, his punishment is a whipping. He could get from twenty-five to sixty-five lashes with the 'Bat,' which was a three-foot leather strap about three inches wide, riveted to a wooden handle eighteen inches long. These lashes were administered the same as the former cat-o'-nine-tails, but [the Bat] didn't cut the skin as quickly or easily. The Bat was a more humane way of flogging in those days. Then, after the lashings, you may go to work at some hard labor while you are healing. They wanted you to work while you were sore.

"You see, inmates escaped all the time back in those days. It was no big deal. It isn't like today. The name of the game was to try and get the hell out of here," Thomas adds. He explains that if an escapee could get out of the parish, the chase ended. "If you came out of New Orleans, and ended up in Shreveport, they were going to leave you alone. You could change your name and get away with it." Thomas also says that the state did not start chasing escapees beyond the Louisiana borders until the late 1930s.

Because of sketchy records, it is presumed that Canton spent the next three years at The Walls, in a period during which Louisiana politics, and the penal system, underwent significant changes. The Louisiana legislature was busy abolishing the Board of Control, replacing it with a general manager who would take charge of the state's prisons. The rebuilding made necessary after the great floods of 1903 and 1912 not only took all of the profits made by the prison system, but additional funds had to be appropriated to keep the system solvent. Appointed as general manager was Henry L. Fuqua, a Baton Rouge businessman who, over the course of the next eight years, would set the pace for prison operations for the next forty.

Thomas told *The Angolite,* "There had been fifteen years of the Board of Control, and it didn't work. The biggest thing was that they weren't making any money. They tried whipping the hell out of the convicts between 1912 and 1916. So Fuqua comes along and says, Look, this isn't working. He owns a hardware store. [His idea is to] start using some business practices. Instead of trying to work these people to death and get more out of them, which isn't working anyway, let's cut down on the overhead. This was the new idea, cut down on overhead to make money. What was the biggest overhead? The payroll. So, he comes up with the idea of using inmates to guard themselves—inmates who will . . . understand the plight of the inmates more than anybody else. And it worked." Fuqua fired every guard, except eleven, replacing them with inmate guards. He also eliminated the wearing of "stripes" by convicts, replacing them with white shirts and pants. And he began a system of record keeping, creating a file on individual convicts—a system that would prevail to modern times.

Fuqua also sold the eighty-three-year-old Walls in 1918. "He decided the operations there, hospital and industries, could be moved to Angola's Camp E, so he sold The Walls to the city of Baton Rouge for $45,000," says Thomas. "My guess is that Rene Canton was transferred back to Angola at that time and assigned to Camp E." Available prison records indicate no further incidents of misbehavior or other problems with Canton.

ⅢⅢ   The Second Clemency   ⅢⅢ

The last piece of information available in prison records shows that Rene Canton was discharged from prison on July 7, 1923. Since Canton had been serving a life sentence, he could not have been released from prison unless he received executive clemency commuting the sentence.

Newspaper accounts indicate that Governor John M. Parker, at the recommendation of the general manager and the Board of Pardons, considered Canton for clemency on Independence Day, 1923. But he refused to act on the recommendation until he heard from the family. The governor contacted Mrs. Edgar H. Farrar, Sr., then living in Gulfport, Mississippi. She wrote the governor, saying: "It comforts me to know that there is hope for the man whose act brought misery into so many lives."

The governor then signed the commutation, freeing Canton. According to the *Picayune*, Parker told Canton: "Having served your term and being recommended for pardon, I had declined to grant such until I had communicated with those vitally interested, especially the mother of the man whose life you took. You owe your life and liberty [to] this splendid woman. Your future conduct should be such that it will reflect credit on these actions."

Mrs. Anna F. Goldsborough, the murder victim's sister, who was living in New Orleans, told the *Picayune*:

> We are glad that this man is to have another chance. It wasn't as if my brother had been shot down through a feeling of hatred. And if the murder had been premeditated, we should feel differently in the matter. But, Canton was running at the time he fired the shot, followed by my brother who was a big, strong man,

and it was probably through the instinct of self-preservation that the deed was prompted. . . . Canton has been imprisoned for more than ten years and I believe he has had a stiff punishment. Perhaps he will lead a better life from now on. . . . If Governor Parker has decided to pardon Canton, he must have had good reasons for so doing. The governor is an old friend of my family and wouldn't do anything of the kind without giving the matter deep consideration, I am convinced.

The general manager making the recommendation for Canton was Henry Fuqua, who, shortly after the inmate's release, would resign his position to run for and be elected governor of Louisiana in 1924.

As Canton was being released, he told a *Picayune* reporter at the prison gate that he was going west; he said he owed his freedom to the dead man's heartbroken mother and other relatives who expressed a wish that justice be tempered with mercy. He added: "Without their help, I would still be in prison."

Canton may or may not have realized how fortunate an individual he was, not only to be alive, but to also walk away from prison a free man. Other than perhaps some family members or relatives, whose efforts *The Angolite* cannot confirm, the only persons to come forward on Canton's behalf were his murder victim's family. In clinging to a deeply rooted principle, the Farrars extended forgiveness without proof of redemption, with the hope that Canton's freedom would uncover redeeming qualities in him—just by enabling him to lead a better life.

A year and a half after Canton stepped through the Angola gate, he died of tuberculosis, at age thirty-six, at home in New Orleans. Whether Canton ever redeemed himself in the fashion expected of him by the Farrars, the world will never know.

‖‖‖   Sixty-five   ‖‖‖
Years Later

The Farrars' legacy—the courage of their convictions, their moral beliefs and values—would inspire subsequent generations to touch and improve the lives of others.

A niece of Edgar Howard Farrar, Sr., was Margaret Dixon, who eventually became managing editor of the Baton Rouge–based *Morning Advocate*. Under her leadership the newspaper was a perpetual watchdog over state institutions and the people within them. Dixon was a strong advocate of penal reform and had a keen interest in the treatment of prisoners during the 1950s and 1960s. She had been appointed a member of Governor Earl K. Long's Citizens' Committee, which investigated Angola in 1951. She was recognized posthumously for her contributions and concern for her fellow man by having a state penal facility, Dixon Correctional Institute (DCI) in Jackson, dedicated in her name. Already named in her honor, the front-gate visiting room of the Louisiana State Penitentiary was dedicated to her memory in the mid-1970s.

Dixon's niece (a great-niece of Farrar, Sr.) is Margaret A. Bolton, who, among other things, served as a member and vice-chairman of the Louisiana Board of Pardons under the second administration of Edwin W. Edwards. Bolton, too, was concerned about those in prison deserving of mercy and a second lease on life. Though no longer involved in the criminal justice system, she has also been a substance-abuse counselor with the Department of Health and Human Resources. Bolton's interest in prisons has not waned. When time permits, she makes frequent visits to the prisons to attend functions of inmate self-help organizations, encouraging and assisting those who demonstrate a desire to help themselves. The Farrar Legacy continues.

[December 1988]

THE LEGEND OF LEADBELLY

Wilbert Rideau

In 1934, Angola was a lost and forgotten world to a nation caught in the grip of a depression. The three thousand prisoners housed in ramshackle camps on the sprawling 18,000-acre prison plantation were far removed from the consciousness of the Louisiana public and ruled over by a force of ninety employees who regarded the prison as their own personal domain—much as did the plantation masters who worked their slaves in the same fields before the plantations were converted into the Louisiana State Penitentiary. They had the power of life and death, and many enforced their orders with violence and terror imposed by an army of shotgun-toting convict-guards. With money hard to come by, the prison foremen (called "Mastah," "Boss," or "Cap'n") and their convict-guards drove the "ole thangs" (prisoners) in cane and vegetable fields from the crack of dawn until dusk kissed the horizon, trying to make the prison self-supporting. No one was spared; the 130 women prisoners housed at Camp D had to labor in the fields under the same conditions as the men. Flogging was practiced in epidemic proportions, and laggards in the field were brutally beaten on the spot to spur increased productivity, their haggard bodies pushed to the limits of human endurance, their blood soaking the soil. They died at the rate of forty-one a year.

Money appropriated for feeding, clothing, and housing the prisoners was "diverted" by prison officials, and the inmates had to manage despite the dietary deficiencies of a daily table fare of grits, greens, sweet potatoes, and blackstrap syrup, produced by the prisoners on the farm. The men wore white uniforms (sewn for them by the women) of stiff, unyielding twelve-ounce cotton that chafed them raw—most of them would leave the heavy shirts on the headland and work bare-chested in the hot sun. They wore crude black shoes, made by the Camp E shoe shop of cheap split leather, the uppers nailed to the soles—no fancy sewing. In the summer, they were issued cheap straw farm hats, but nothing else—no socks, underwear, or even belts to hold up their pants. At night they'd lay their stinking, sweat-wet uniforms on the wooden floor of the dormitory, hoping the fabric would dry by morning, while they surrendered their tired, malnourished bodies to the blissful arms of sleep on corn-shuck mattresses, oblivious to the bedbugs and to the mosquitoes zooming in through the unscreened windows. They had only the weekend to look forward to, when they had a day off to rest. They'd lounge around the yards, playing games, gambling, or singing and dancing. Every camp had someone who could sing, strum a guitar, or blow a harmonica, and he was always in demand.

It was a lonely world. In 1933, the legendary Charlie Frazier and a number of other Camp E prisoners shot their way out in an escape that took the lives of five people, including the warden. The gun was believed to have been smuggled in by a visitor, and authorities discontinued all visiting at the prison as a result. Visitors would not be allowed again until late 1937.

One of the few "outsiders" allowed into the prison in 1934 was musical historian John Lomax, curator of the Archive of American Folk Songs of the Library of Congress. Accompanied by his son, Alan, he came to Angola on assignment to track down Southern folk music, and toured the prison in search of prison work songs. But at Camp A, he found more than just songs—he found a black singer-guitarist who fascinated him.

The prisoner's name was Huddie Ledbetter, but everyone called him Leadbelly. He was a big man, about six feet tall. There was no fat on his frame, only solid muscle that told of strength and endurance. Ross Russell, who came to know him well years later, described him: "He was of dark mahogany color, the red hues coming from his mother, Sally, who was half-Cherokee. His face was broad and his features strong, the eyes penetrating and the teeth as solid and as white as a roll of tombstones. A scar, lighter than the flesh, circled his neck from ear to ear, a sinister memento of a knifing fray in which he was left for dead. . . ."

"Leadbelly's voice was not beautiful," author Frederick Ramsey, Jr., would write years later. "It was rough and grainy, and some of its raw tones came up as if scraped out of his throat. It rang out with an intensity because he often shouted with violence. It had a nasal twang. The excitement he engendered came from his understanding of each melody he sang and from a strong, precise sense of rhythm."

With the vibrant strings of his guitar twanging throughout the camp, and his hooting, boasting voice making the walls vibrate, Leadbelly sang for Lomax. He was a natural musician, though he had never had a music lesson in his life. And he loved to sing—once he started, it was hard to stop him. He sang songs that told stories, all sorts of songs that he had either created or picked up along the roads of his life—slave songs, cowboy songs, prison and railroad songs, work songs, spiritual songs . . . all of which he'd, in the most natural way, shout and holler through while making his guitar cry and moan. He sang to suit his mood and action, rarely ever singing a song the same way or with the same music. His music had a spontaneity and reckless sensuality that left Lomax enthralled.

Leadbelly was about forty-five years old, though no one would ever know for certain—not even Leadbelly himself. Various dates have been given for his birth, but he was probably born between 1882 and 1889, on the Jeter plantation near Mooringsport, Louisiana. His parents, both ex-slaves, moved to Texas when he was about five to work as sharecroppers for Henry Simms, a black plantation owner. When they could finally afford it, his parents purchased a small 68½-acre place outside Shreveport, in the Caddo Lake district, for $2.50 an acre. With his father chopping down the trees and his mother clearing the brush, the family built a home and began farming. Leadbelly learned to farm, pick cotton, chop wood, and ride horses at an early age. His chores included having to ride five miles into town to get the mail or the coal oil for the lamps, holding the five-gallon can away from the saddle all the way home so that it didn't touch the horse. As a child, he learned to play the accordion; soon after that, his uncle taught him to play the guitar—and he played well enough to be in demand for the Saturday-night country parties and dances. Those dances, attended by farmers, cotton pickers, mule drivers, and roustabouts, often turned into free-for-all brawls.

Shreveport's Fannin Street was the sin district, a trouble place with whorehouses, gamblers, painted street women, and plenty of drinking and action, a place that his parents admonished him at an early age to stay away from. But it was a place that his father frequented and that Leadbelly wanted to frequent; and just as soon as he could sneak off and go, he went.

The forbidden world of Fannin Street drew young Huddie like a moth to light. It was a rough-and-tumble, honky-tonk wonderland of passion, loud voices, music, pretty women, laughter and fun. His youth often got him kicked out of some of the saloons, whorehouses and gambling dens. But there was no deterring him. He'd stroll down the street or sneak into another joint where he'd hang around soaking in the sights and sounds of this raucous den of iniquity.

Leadbelly had an ear for rhythm and picked up numerous songs. "At fifteen he was old enough to go to the sukey-jumps (parties) and breakdowns," Ramsey wrote. "Setting out after dark and riding alone through the bottomlands in delta country, he would arrive an hour or so later at some lone shanty set down in the wilderness: 'There'd be no white man for twenty miles.' For playing all night, he got all he could drink, all he could handle in the way of girls, and fifty cents in hard cash. At sixteen he was married and father of a child."

But a nameless restlessness had dug its claws deep into his soul. He lived with the girl for a short period, finally leaving her, pregnant with his second child, to live in the Fannin Street world of music, jaded whores, fly-by-night romances, hard liquor, and honky-tonk lawlessness. What for most was nothing more than a weekend escape from the harshness of routine country life became a way of life to him. But even Fannin Street wasn't enough. His restless spirit demanded more, so he headed out to west Texas, where he picked cotton, drove mules, broke wild horses, and worked at whatever would make him a dollar. In Dallas he met Blind Lemon Jefferson, a blues singer and guitarist whose recordings would later become classics. The old man needed someone to lead him around, and Leadbelly volunteered, striking up a friendship with the blind singer as he led him around the rough sections of Dallas for the next several years. They would perform together, with Leadbelly billing himself as "The King of the Twelve-String Guitar." The world that they played in was a lawless and violent one, but Leadbelly was a man in his element. He lived mean, hard, and violently, ready to fight at any time, any place, for any reason, and with any choice of weapons. Sometimes he won, some-times he lost, and sometimes he went to jail. But most of his trouble came from women or jealous lovers and husbands, who came close to killing him on a number of occasions. One of those fly-by-night romances ended in his killing a man in 1918, and he was sent to the Texas State Penitentiary for murder.

He managed to survive the brutal Texas penal system. The grueling, backbreaking labor was something he could handle, and the violence was something he was accustomed to. On the chain gang, he quickly established a reputation as "the number-one man in the number-one gang on the number-one farm in the state," as Alan Lomax wrote years later—and in the prison cotton fields, he worked up to picking a thousand pounds a day; he was "the man who could carry the lead row in the field for 12 or 14 hours a day under the broiling July and August sun and then cut the fool for the guards all evening." His fellow convicts didn't appreciate Leadbelly's readiness to "cut the fool" for their white guards, but he didn't let that stop him. He was as much a con man as he was a musician, and his singing, dancing, and cutting the fool for the authorities enabled him to survive the brutal chain gang, and led to his being made a trusty and becoming a favorite unpaid entertainer of prison personnel—and won him his freedom: After Leadbelly performed for Texas governor Pat Neff, the governor pardoned him a few days before leaving office in 1925.

The prison experience did nothing to change Leadbelly. It only made him tougher, and he immediately returned to playing dance halls and honky-tonk bars, gambling, womanizing, drinking, and fighting. "He had a terribly violent nature," Alan Lomax said of him years later. "When he didn't have whiskey in him, Leadbelly could be a good companion. But when he was drunk or suffering the effects of a hangover, he was unapproachable. . . . I'm positive Leadbelly was guilty of everything he went to prison for, and other things he got away with."

He was known to have been in dangerous situations at least three times in the years that followed his release from prison. According to Ramsey:

Leadbelly never mentioned the first of these three fracases until a skull fracture showed up on X rays taken years later in New York. He said then that he had felt numbness in his fingers for

*Lead Belly among the prisoners at a prison yard at Angola in July 1933
(Photo courtesy The Lead Belly Society)*

a whole year following the night a bottle had cracked his head
open, but he had never gone to a doctor. On the second occasion, he was playing "Mr. Tom Hughes's Town" on his guitar
in a dancehall across the lake from Oil City when a man got a
knife in his neck and had drawn it half around to the other side
before his girl, Era, beat off the attacker. That time, Huddie
reported to the police, "bleeding like a hog," and was told to get
on out of there fast. The third time, he was attacked as he was
coming home from work by members of a gang who said he had
whiskey in his dinner pail. He refused to surrender it, and a fight
began. So, on February 28, 1930, he was sent off to Angola with
a second "assault with intent to murder" against his name.

Here at Angola, the man who had thus far been a failure as a
musician served his time much as he had in the Texas prison—he
worked, he conned, he fought, and he survived—until that day in 1934
when John Lomax discovered him at Camp A. Fascinated by his talent

and potential, Lomax decided to try to get Leadbelly out of prison. Prisoners begging clemency from the governor generally file an application or write a letter. Leadbelly sang his pardon petition, which Lomax recorded at the prison and took to the governor:

> If I had you, Gov'nor O. K. Allen,
> Like you got me,
> I would wake up in de mornin',
> Let you out on reprieve. . . .

For the second time, Leadbelly had sung his way to freedom—Governor O. K. Allen released him. Lomax took Leadbelly north to New York to cut records instead of people, then spent the following year introducing him to the world. Five years later, Leadbelly would be singing in Carnegie Hall, and ten years later in Paris.

"I was born and raised in the country, mamma, but I'm stayin' in town . . . in New York City, what I'm talkin' 'bout," Leadbelly sang in 1935. And he did stay. He made New York his home, giving up his former violent life-style and settling down with Martha Promise, a native of Blanchard, Louisiana, whom he married before newsreel cameras in 1935, following a stormy courtship. From time to time, he'd leave New York to give concerts on the college circuit and to play the nightclubs. He quickly acquired international recognition as a blues folksinger—and, doing better financially than he had ever done in his life, he became one of the best-dressed men in New York. "He hates the days and the nights of the seasons and years that he had to spend wearing old dirty sickly raggedy patched overalls," Folksinger Woody Guthrie explained. Even in Leadbelly's later years, Moses Asch, another friend of his, recalled that the thing that struck a person first about him was his "aristocratic appearance and demeanor . . . his hand-made alligator shoes, beautiful wood cane, gray pin-striped suit, his silver-white cropped hair."

Leadbelly and Martha had a flat on the Lower East Side of the city that was much-frequented by other musicians and singers, and by admiring fans who'd fill the apartment to listen to him sing. His neighbors often complained of the music and noise coming from his apartment. Because he sang the way he felt, his songs were never sung the same way twice. He had an intense dislike for "rehearsing" songs. He relied more on his mood—according to one account, he recorded

*Lead Belly in New York City in 1941 (Photo
courtesy The Lead Belly Society)*

"Big Fat Woman" with a stout woman actually dancing for him in the
studio while he sang in response to watching her.

The dream of all singers and musicians, to have a big hit, eluded
him in his lifetime, despite the hundreds of songs he recorded. On
December 6, 1949, following a highly successful tour of France, he
died in New York's Bellevue Hospital. He was about sixty years old.
After a life of surviving cold, hunger, knives, pistols, chain gangs, and
prison, Leadbelly was finally laid to rest under an ordinary marker in
the Shiloh Baptist Church cemetery north of Shreveport, just a few
miles from the plantation on which he was born. He had been a
violent man and had led a hard and violent existence, much of it in
the pursuit of making a name for himself and trying to be somebody.
He would never know it, but he had earned his place in history,

leaving behind him a legacy of songs, many of which would become classics, appreciated only after his death.

Posthumous renown didn't take long. Eight months following his death, Leadbelly's name was stamped on the American consciousness. The hit song he had long wished for finally arrived. Ironically, it was one that Leadbelly had sung throughout his life, in Texas and Louisiana prisons, and that he had opened every concert with:

> Irene, good night,
> Irene, good night,
> Good night, Irene, good night, Irene,
> I'll kiss you in my dreams.

"In 1934, when Library of Congress Folklorist John Lomax recorded Lead Belly's famed pardon petition," *Time* magazine reported, "he put 'Irene' on the other side. Music-loving Governor O. K. Allen is said to have pardoned the old reprobate as much for 'Irene' as anything. Until Lead Belly died in Manhattan last year, he sang 'Irene' as his theme song."

While other Leadbelly songs ("The Midnight Special," "Rock Island Line," and so on) would become hits long after his death, "Irene," which Lomax had predicted years earlier would "some day be one of the best known American folk songs," swept the nation as no song had ever done before, becoming a "national musical wonder." "The most overpowering phenomenon in the music business these days is a lorn, whining ballad about a marriage gone sour, set in waltz tempo and called 'Good Night, Irene,'" Gilbert Millstein reported in October 1950.

There are 2,563 radio stations, 99 television stations and roughly 400,000 juke boxes in the United States. In one recent month, "Good Night, Irene" was heard about 100,000 times over radio and TV, according to Broadcast Music, Inc., which monitored it. The chances are, in the opinion of *The Billboard,* a trade magazine which bends a large, receptive ear toward these things, that the song may be found in most juke boxes around the country and that it gets played about five times every 24 hours on each one, or some two million times a day in all. There are

1,440 minutes in a day, which means that "Good Night, Irene" can be heard around 1,400 times a minute. Some people in the trade believe that no other song ever sold so fast in so short a time.

During the preceding three months, the song had already sold more than two million records, and close to 500,000 copies of the sheet music had been sold. The song had already been translated into French as "Bon Soir, Lili" and it had even provoked someone to record a song called "Please Say Goodnight to the Guy, Irene, So I Can Get Some Sleep."

Huddie Ledbetter, the man who wanted to be somebody, had finally achieved his wish. Many books and articles have since been written about the legendary Leadbelly and his impact on American folk music, and a movie chronicling his life was directed by Gordon Parks. Parks, who met Leadbelly briefly back in the forties, explained his involvement: "I guess I wanted to do the picture because of what Ledbetter meant as a man and as an artist, and the things he had to go through to accomplish what he did. He wanted to be somebody. The fact that he was a fine musician made it possible. His talent saved him. Without it, he would have rotted in prison."

Contending that he was a native son, Texas made a move following the release of the movie in 1975 to get Leadbelly's remains brought to Harrison County, where a historical marker would be placed over his grave, according him the respect due one of the nation's most famous blues folksingers. The attempt failed, but, according to the New Orleans *Times-Picayune,* "This got the lazy Caddo Parish police jury off their duffs and they voted 14 to 3 to honor Leadbelly with a monument. The nearby *Shreveport Journal* scolded the three holdouts in an editorial saying: '. . . just because they hadn't heard of him [Leadbelly] is no reason to oppose the preservation of local history.' "

[February 1982]

BOOK TWO
IIIII

ANGOLA'S HISTORY

||||||

Wilbert Rideau

Louisiana's first official penitentiary was built in Baton Rouge in
1835. Prior to that time, state prisoners were housed in the dilapidated, vermin-infested New Orleans jail, where one visitor described
them as "chained like wild beasts." There were three hundred state
prisoners, one-third of whom were charged with murder, the rest with
larceny and burglary. Upon its opening, the convicts were transferred
to the new facility, where they spent their nights in solitary confinement and their days manufacturing crude, cheap shoes and cotton,
leather, and woolen products. After nine years, the legislature, during
a period of severe economic depression, concluded that maintaining
the state penitentiary was too costly, and approved the leasing of the
prison and all of its inmates to the private firm of McHatten, Pratt and
Company as a source of cheap labor for use in its profit-making
enterprises. In pursuit of profit, McHatten reduced food and clothing
for convicts to subsistence level, expanded their working hours, and
used brutal force to maintain discipline and productivity.

The Civil War, while a tragedy for others, was a blessing for
convicts in Louisiana. General Ben Butler, commandant of New Orleans, freed all of them. However, soon after the end of the war, the
state reinstituted its convict-lease system. In 1869 the leaseholders sold
out to Major Samuel Lawrence James, who, for the next twenty-five
years, operated the most profitable and brutal prison enterprise in the
history of the state, often in violation of both state law and the terms
of his contract. In his first few months James made a half-million
dollars, a king's fortune in those days. He continued to make incred-
ible profits by working his "state slaves" on the Mississippi River

levees, on railroad construction, and on farms and plantations. Despite criticism and the political power struggles he had to wage from time to time to retain possession of his prisoner-slaves, James was still in complete control of the state's convicts when he died while chatting with his family on the porch of his Angola plantation in 1894. His death changed nothing. The executors of his estate, and his son, Samuel, Jr., continued to work the prisoners for profit. The Prison Board of Control reported that 216 convicts died during the year 1896 alone. And it is estimated that as many as three thousand men, women, and children convicts (most of them black) died from overwork, exposure, brutality, and outright murder during that infamous thirty-year period from 1870 to 1901.

The brutal convict-lease system did not end until the state resumed control and management of its penal system in 1901. But the heinous practice was ended for political reasons rather than humanitarian ones. And, jealous of the huge profits that the James regime had made from the exploitation of convict labor, the state had resumed control of its convicts partly in hopes of pursuing what Governor W. W. Heard termed "the establishment of a great industrial and business enterprise." (Heard was later to become a warden of Angola.) Toward that end, the state purchased the 8,000-acre Angola plantation from the James heirs. In addition, it retained the four levee camps and the Baton Rouge penitentiary; the latter functioned as a receiving and shipping station, a hospital, a maximum-security unit for dangerous prisoners, and a place for executions until it was purchased by the city in 1918. Control and management of the penal system had been transferred to the state—at least on paper: The state retained some of the James people in the new management. However, the more brutal methods employed under the James rule were abandoned, and the convict mortality rate was reduced under Warden W. M. Reynaud. Within four years the state system was reorganized and made self-supporting, even profitable. But the enormous profits envisioned by the proponents of state control eluded it.

Cotton was the principal crop at Angola until boll weevils invaded the plantation, ravaging it beyond remedy and causing prison authorities to switch to sugar cane. The largest sugar refinery in the South was constructed at Angola, and three smaller sugar plantations were purchased, along with four more levee camps (housing for inmates who built and maintained the levees). By 1917, the state had a total of eight camps housing convicts at Angola, four of which still house prisoners today (Camp A, Camp F, Camp H, and Camp I). Additional purchases of adjacent land increased the Angola plantation's size to 18,000 acres by 1922. While farming was always the major work occupying the convicts, the prison later added lumbering and manufacturing to its levee, sugar-refining, and agricultural activities.

In 1912, the angry waters of the Mississippi River overflowed their banks, flooding Angola and causing extensive damage and loss. The prison quickly slipped into financial trouble, which administrative ineptness only aggravated. The prison was finally rescued when Henry L. Fuqua became general manager of the penitentiary. Fuqua was a successful Baton Rouge businessman; the closest he had ever come to penal experience was marrying the daughter of Major James's clerk. But his lack of knowledge was no deterrent to him. He tackled head-on the problems that besieged Angola. In 1917 he fired most of the guards, replacing them with cost-saving trusty convicts. (He viewed the free guards as "brutal bullies with large whips.") He eliminated all brutality that he regarded as "unnecessary," relying on

Convicts at Camp H during the Sugarcane Era (Courtesy The Angolite)

flogging for disciplinary purposes. By streamlining prison operations, Fuqua put Angola on a sound financial footing. He was more like a kindly slave owner than a prison warden, running Angola and treating the inmates in the same paternalistic manner with which slaves had been treated on any well-run plantation before the Civil War. And in doing so, he set a standard that was followed by succeeding wardens until the 1930s. The stability he brought to Angola, however, was only temporary. In 1922, the Mississippi River literally drowned Angola, causing damage so extensive that it brought the prison to the verge of bankruptcy. But that was the next general manager's headache. In 1924 Fuqua was elected governor, dying in office two years later. Newspapers reported that convicts at Angola grieved for the man they called "Marse Henry." It was fitting that they did. There would be very few "Marse Henry"'s in the future.

In 1928 Huey P. Long became governor, marking the start of a nightmare for convicts. A veil of secrecy fell over Angola, a veil that masked mismanagement, corruption, and wanton brutality. A study of prison records revealed that Long's guard captains inflicted 10,000 "official" floggings between 1928 and 1940. It is estimated that a much higher number of "unofficial" beatings of convicts took place in the fields. Under the management of Long's appointee, R. R. "Tighty" Himes, the Louisiana State University business manager, the convict mortality rate reached the highest recorded level since the end of the James regime. And despite the brutality employed by the Long administration to make Angola become not only self-sufficient but profitable for the state, the prison continued to slip into debt.

Himes died in office in 1936, but he left a legacy that would haunt the soul of the state for decades: the infamous Red Hat Cellblock. Himes ordered the construction of the Red Hat in 1933, following an escape attempt. The result was a one-story cement structure containing thirty cells, each approximately six feet long and three feet wide. A solid sheet-steel door closed each cell. The only ventilation was a twelve-inch-square window. Each cell contained a sheet-iron bunk but no mattress. A bucket was provided as a toilet and was emptied each morning. The building was surrounded by an eight-foot-high barbed-wire fence, with a guard tower at each corner, manned twenty-four hours each day. Men confined to the Red Hat were known as Hats or Red Hats because they were required to wear felt hats dipped in red enamel. All Red Hats were required to work in the field, watched by four "high power" guards armed with .30-.30 rifles, plus six ordinary shotgun-toting guards—all with orders to shoot to kill. The Red Hats were fed whatever leftovers remained after the regular Camp E prisoners finished eating. The leftovers would be dumped into buckets and taken to the cellblock in a wheelbarrow. The Red Hat was always kept filled with prisoners considered dangerous—"agitators," belligerents, and the like. And whenever serious disturbances occurred, the Red Hat would be packed with inmates, several to each cell. The cellblock was operated as a "superpunishment" unit until Governor Edwin Edwards discontinued its use in 1973. However, most of the brutal and sadistic methods that were once employed had been abandoned some years earlier.

Himes's management of the prison sparked a revolutionary change in prison policy. During his tenure 194 convicts had escaped. Himes's successors Theophile Landry and Warden L. A. Jones decided there would be no more escapes, and pursued a number of "improved safety measures." They erected twenty-five guard towers around Angola, manning them with marksmen. More and better bloodhounds were secured, and a state police substation was established at the prison. Between 1936 and 1940 there were no more escapes, though a number of convicts were reported shot attempting to do so. For the first time in the history of Angola, "security" became the priority of prison operation, commanding more emphasis than self-sufficiency or profits. Angola was quickly dubbed the Alcatraz of the South.

Under the administration of Governor Earl Long brutality increased dramatically. However, Long, being a lavish spender, pumped some money into Angola. A $1.4-million prison hospital and a camp for women prisoners were built. Long's first superintendent of Angola was Rollo C. Lawrence, who, like everyone before him, was a politician. But there was a difference. Lawrence believed that the first obligation of the prison should be to "rehabilitate" its convicts and, in 1949, he and Angola's first "director of rehabilitation" made some efforts toward that end. Lawrence assigned inmates to prison jobs on the basis of intelligence and ability, with the better-educated inmates assigned to administrative office duties as clerks. While this was an admirable effort, it introduced a new element into prison management: control of the administration and its processes by convict-clerks. Periodically prison operations were controlled and ruled by a gigantic convict-guard and clerk contingent. The prison continued to deteriorate until 1951 when, under Warden Rudolph Easterly, thirty-seven white convicts at Camps E and H kicked off the worst scandal in the state by cutting their Achilles tendons in a protest against brutality, overwork, lack of edible food and decent housing, and continued prison mismanagement by inept political appointees. A massive investigation resulted and Angola was nationally recognized as the worst prison in the country.

Angola and its conditions became a major political issue in the gubernatorial campaign of 1952. Robert F. Kennon was elected and gave improvement of Angola top priority during his administration. Suspending political patronage, he drafted a team of professional penologists from the federal system to manage the prison. A massive construction program was also undertaken to provide better housing for the convicts. Brutality was ordered stopped and many of the old-time employees responsible for many of the prison's problems were forced out of the system via resignations, dismissals, and early retirements. All of the three hundred–odd prison employees were placed under the jurisdiction of the civil service to provide them some small measure of protection from the winds of political change. For the first time in Angola's history, the rehabilitation of the convicts became the official goal.

But the peace, shaky to start with, lasted only until 1962, when politics and a budget slash eroded what few gains had been made. Escapes, brutality, and violence increased and Angola began slipping back into its former barbarity as the penal system increasingly became poisoned with politics, patronage, and the public's revived desire for the prison to show a profit or at least pay its own way. The professionals all left, one by one, and the wardenship changed nine times between 1964 and 1968, a fact that reflected the power vacuum within the system and the fierce struggle between vying factions for control.

In 1968, Governor John J. McKeithen drafted C. Murray Henderson, a former warden of both Iowa and Tennessee prisons, to manage Angola. After stabilizing the political situation, he tried to recapture some of the ground lost during the chaotic period that preceded him. Handicapped by a grossly inadequate budget and a fight on two fronts—forced to find ways for the prison to support itself because of an inadequate budget on one hand, and fighting prison traditionalists who were against all reforms on the other—progress was grudgingly slow. Without money to pay for rehabilitative programs, Henderson encouraged inmates to establish and engage in self-help organizations and programs. Educational and vocational programs were reinstituted and brutality was reduced dramatically. With the ascension of Edwin Edwards to the governorship and of Elayn Hunt to the state directorship of corrections four years later, the fight for reform was carried even further. The backbreaking labor in the fields was ended, the use of inmates as guards was stopped, the notorious Red Hat Cellblock was closed, radical revision of disciplinary procedures occurred, and unnecessary restrictions were removed, giving the inmates a little more freedom of choice. In short, life at Angola became less harsh, a little more humane. But, despite the efforts of Henderson and Hunt, the legislature refused to provide adequate funds to cope with the massive influx of prisoners created by a "get tough" law-and-order movement. The prison became overcrowded; supplies were inadequate to provide for the inmates' basic needs; and the grossly undermanned security force was unable to contain either the tension and violence mounting among the prisoners, or the growth of gangs as more and more prisoners banded together in cliques for self-protection.

By 1973, violence was a brutal, daily reality. Double-bladed hatchets, swords, long steel knives, and Roman-style shields were commonplace. Men slept with steel plates and JCPenney catalogues tied to their chests; even in maximum-security cellblocks, men slept with their doors tied and with blankets tied around their bunks as a means of protection and security. Angola was a lawless jungle, without order or discipline. Fear was the silent ruler of all. From 1972 to 1975, 40 prisoners were stabbed to death and 350 more seriously injured by knife wounds. Gang wars and clique power struggles kept the stretchers rolling; the morbid call "One on the stretcher!" was soon something to be ignored, generally accepted as a routine factor of doing time. Enslavement among inmates was widespread. By 1975 Angola had become the bloodiest prison in the nation.

On June 10, 1975, United States District Judge E. Gordon West stated that the "obviously deplorable conditions" at Angola "not only shock[ed] the conscience" but violated the basic constitutional rights of over four thousand inmates confined there. West declared that the conditions constituted "an extreme public emergency." Acting on a Special Master's Report filed in April by U.S. Magistrate Frank Polozola in a four-year-old civil rights suit lodged by several inmates and joined in by the U.S. Justice Department, Judge West issued a court order instructing the state of Louisiana to end the violence within the sprawling penitentiary and to improve the overall living conditions for the prisoners. Barring the admission of new prisoners until the court-ordered improvements were achieved, West ordered state authorities to relieve overcrowding, take measures to improve the protection of both inmates and employees, hire more guards, and immediately hire necessary competent personnel to provide adequate medical and psychiatric care for all inmates. He also ordered the prison to comply with all state fire, safety, and health standards. Official speculations envisioned that the improvements would cost about $10 million to implement. Judge West's court order would eventually precipitate revolutionary changes throughout Louisiana's penal system for the next fifteen years.

[December 1982]

PHELPS: FIVE YEARS LATER

|||||

Wilbert Rideau

In December of 1975 a small blue twin-engine plane winged out of the wintry clouds to land on the small Angola airstrip. A neat, well-dressed man scrambled out of the pilot's seat and got into a waiting car. He was C. Paul Phelps, the deputy director of the Louisiana Department of Corrections, and had arrived to assume the duties of acting warden of the Louisiana State Penitentiary until a permanent one could be found. Traditionally, an official in the prison hierarchy had always been moved up to assume such duties until a new warden was secured. But not this time. The number two man in the department was taking over the reins, a bold departure from tradition. It was an omen of things to come.

Angola, while officially a part of the Louisiana Department of Corrections, was a power unto itself, traditionally ruled by vested interests and independent of the rest of the state penal system. It obeyed headquarters, its official parent, only if it desired to. It had generally been powerful enough to resist the imposition of the will of headquarters on it.

The prison was a powder keg. It was so jam-packed with prisoners that some had to sleep on floors. Tension ran through the place like unharnessed electricity, exploding here and there in sparks of violence. The prison's small employee force was disenchanted and preoccupied with its own special interests and the struggle for power. In such a climate, inmate cliques reigned supreme, governing human

C. Paul Phelps, Louisiana Secretary of Corrections,
1976–1981, and 1984–1988 (Courtesy The Angolite)

existence and much of prison operations. The strong ruled and the
weak either served or perished. Slavery was widespread. The only law
was that of the knife.

Phelps, a social worker by profession and a correctional bureaucrat
by trade, was a most unlikely man to be assuming the reins of power.
Most of his career had been spent working with juvenile delinquents,
beginning as a probation officer in 1957 with the Baton Rouge Family
Court.

Men taking over as wardens generally do so with the announcement of grandiose plans. Phelps didn't. He knew little about running
a penitentiary and next to nothing about Angola, something he admitted with unheard-of candidness. Soon after his arrival, inmates asked

his plans for the prison; he shocked his questioners by replying matter-of-factly: "I don't have any yet. And I don't know enough about Angola and what it takes to run it to form any. I'm going to first educate myself about this place. After I learn what's going on, then I'll start thinking about what I'm going to do."

And that was what he set about doing—learning. If you wanted to get in touch with him, you'd usually find him roaming around the prison, acquainting himself with the place. He was rarely in his office. A casual, unpretentious man, he'd walk all over the prison, dropping in on inmates and employees and chatting with them.

Phelps was not a physical person, but he paid little heed to physical dangers. Soon after his arrival, there was a minor disturbance in the main prison. As he prepared to leave the administration building to find out what was going on, a prison official stopped him, telling him: "You can't go down there. There's too much danger. You're the warden." Phelps politely thanked the man for his advice, reminded him that he was the warden and that "I'm not going to learn anything sitting on my ass in an office." He went to the main prison and walked unhesitatingly into the midst of the angry prisoners, asking them what their problem was.

Phelps was like that, an inquisitive person, following his curiosity wherever it took him. And wherever he went, one could expect to be asked questions about what one was doing, how, and for what purpose.

He hadn't been in the warden's office very long before Corrections Director Elayn Hunt was hospitalized with terminal cancer. Phelps found himself acting as both warden of the tinderbox maximum-security penitentiary and head of the state's entire penal system.

Phelps utilized his stint as acting warden as an educational period, studying the state penitentiary and its workings. What he saw appalled him, but he made few waves. In his "acting" capacity, he was not operating from a position of power. So he studied things and bided his time. Those who saw him walking around nonchalantly, always asking questions, didn't really take him seriously. They felt that he was harmless, that he didn't know anything, and that once his position was secured he would retreat to a desk like a good bureaucrat.

Phelps surprised everyone by becoming the most demanding corrections director the state has ever had, a director who refused to accept "can't" as a response, or excuses in the place of action. He initiated sweeping changes, unprecedented in penal history. The violence and other problems that had traditionally defeated corrections administrators, he would conquer. He became the most successful correctional administrator in the nation.

Upon becoming corrections director, Phelps declared the situation at Angola "intolerable." When asked what could be expected at Angola, he stated bluntly that the Department of Corrections was going to regain control of Angola, make the prison responsible to the department, and stop the rampant violence in the prison. And that's precisely what happened. Armed with a federal court order, the support of the governor, and almost a blank check from the legislature, Phelps's administration went to work. Angola's entire power structure was changed. Suspected inmate gang leaders were locked up, and undesirable employees were fired, transferred, or forced into retirement. Strict security measures and electronic devices were introduced. Both inmates and employees were put to work and made to do their jobs. While Phelps had the entire state penal system to manage, he took Angola personally, flying back and forth to the prison at least once a week to confer with Ross Maggio (the new warden) and others, making it his business to know everything that went on there. Millions were poured into Angola for expansion and renovation of facilities. Two years after Phelps assumed office, and while the rest of the nation's prisons were racked by violence, Angola was converted into the safest, most secure prison in the country. Phelps achieved something else that no other corrections director in the state had ever been able to do: He had brought Angola under the authority of the Department of Corrections. Headquarters was running the show, and there was no question about it. Angola was no longer a powerful independent entity. Its former lawless state ended, it is now probably the only maximum-security prison in the United States whose operations the federal courts deem constitutional.

During Phelps's administration, Louisiana's penal system experienced phenomenal growth and expansion as it tried to keep pace with the increasing number of people being committed to prison by a get-tough criminal justice system. The Department of Corrections is now a $120-million-a-year operation (with the fifth-largest state agency budget) comprising seven adult and five juvenile facilities. It is responsible for the custody, care, and supervision of 7,700 adult prisoners, 1,000 juvenile prisoners, and 17,000 probationers and parolees. The department's agribusiness operations have expanded from $3 million to $12 million under Phelps's administration, branching out into new business endeavors. "As we acquired more real estate," Phelps explains, "we naturally expanded our operations." As a result of growth and aggressive hiring practices, more and more professional people started joining corrections. Food and medical services were upgraded. Education, prisoner classification, record keeping, legal services, and numerous other operations were improved. Minorities moved into top supervisory positions.

Unlike most administrators, Phelps maintains a continuing personal interest in all aspects of his work—from watching how one inmate progresses through the system, to how an aspiring inmate artist fares while in prison and after he is freed. Phelps is always ready with advice and assistance for those who pursue constructive and meaningful endeavors.

His greatest asset, and perhaps the key to his success in managing the state's penal system, was that he was not glued to tradition or to any particular school of penal thought. He was always open to new ideas, rejecting nothing until its possible applications had been considered. And when in doubt, Phelps was willing to experiment, to learn. That was the way he approached the idea of a free prisoner press at a time when the rest of the nation's penal administrators believe religiously in the necessity of censorship for the security of the institution. Phelps, on the other hand, wanting to create a credible vehicle of information in a place traditionally ruled by rumor, called the editor of *The Angolite* to his office and told him he wanted to equip the paper with the freedom to investigate, photograph, and publish whatever its staff desired so long as they adhered to professional journalistic standards. Told that the idea might not work, Phelps simply shrugged his shoulders: "Let's try it, and see what happens." What happened is now publishing history. Five years later, *Time* magazine called *The Angolite* "the most probing and literate inmate publication in the U.S."

That was Phelps's way—frank, bold, different . . . and accessible; he was perhaps the most accessible correctional administrator in America.

As the penal system grows, Phelps is naturally unable to check on everything happening in every institution around the state; yet at the same time he needs to stay in touch with the "bottom" and to know what is going on there. Assisting him toward that end is a staff of internal-affairs investigators whose job is to investigate every complaint and report back to him. Every letter from either an inmate or employee gets a response. And Phelps demands that all of his institutional administrators leave their offices and spend time roaming around their facilities to learn what is going on.

He has been a most unconventional administrator, nothing like the smooth, professional, executive types found in many penal systems. Given a choice, Phelps prefers to encourage someone to do something rather than order him or her to do it. And nothing is beneath his station. He would just as soon spend his time chatting with an inmate fieldworker as with a sleek politician.

Phelps's basic decency and sense of fair play, which he exercises even when dealing with the cutthroat world of bureaucratic politics, have sometimes driven his supporters up the wall. Once, asked why he didn't move on his enemies as any other administrator might do, he replied: "I'm not made that way. I don't care how the rest play the game. I play fair and, if I can't play fair, I won't play at all." While his practice of being fair with his enemies may anguish his supporters, it is the reason for the respect and loyalty Phelps commands from those who know him. Peggy LaPuma, his executive assistant, has been working with him since 1969. "The one thing I've liked more than anything else," she says, "and that has kept my faith and my loyalty, is his fairness—with everybody, regardless of position, class, or whatever." Peggi Gresham, an associate warden at Angola, adds: "He's the kind of person who, if you disagree with him, you can let him know how you feel. That's not saying he'll agree with you. He may or may not. But he will listen. He's very open-minded." Phelps knows that an open mind is most unconventional among penal administrators and he takes a certain pride in having one. In early 1980, he flew to Angola for an editorial conference with two wardens and *The Angolite* editors to settle a dispute. In the middle of heated discussion between the parties, a smile spread across Phelps's face and he mused: "I was just wondering how I could ever describe this scene to any correctional administrator in the nation. They would never understand it, much less relate to it."

You get the feeling Phelps enjoys what he's doing, something he admits: "It's certainly the most challenging and exciting job I've ever had." And he still retains his sense of humor. Power and success have not changed him. He's still basically the same man who scrambled out of the plane on that cold December day in 1975 to assume the duties of acting warden at Angola. LaPuma observes, "He's still the same individual, only now there's a certain pride because of his accomplishments."

"We certainly have a sound foundation upon which to build," Phelps stated recently, pointing out that "the need to increase probation and parole is the ultimate key to the upgrading and success of the criminal-justice system." He is a staunch proponent of increased usage of probation and parole, seeing them as an alternative to imprisonment and long sentences. "If you have enough probation and parole officers, then you can make somebody do what you want them to do," he explains. "You can make him get a job, go to work, pay restitution, contribute to society, or whatever, and negate the need to send him to prison and, in the long run, prevent violence on the streets." And there is the financial aspect: The 1980 cost of parole supervision is $1.07 per day, while the cost of incarceration is now $22.66 per day and steadily rising. As the mood of the Louisiana public has grown hostile to offenders, Phelps has been unable to convince them of the need to expand probation and parole, but he says, "ultimately, they will change their minds 'cause the need for it will appear more attractive as the costs of incarceration rise." But Phelps can't wait for that to happen. The hostile public mood and the lock-'em-up-and-throw-away-the-key mentality that has gripped the state's criminal-justice system is creating a problem for corrections that will require remedy long before reason prevails. The present trend of imposing lengthier sentences is creating hopelessness among the pained and shackled souls locked within the system. As that feeling spreads, it is creating a dangerous potential, for hopeless men are desperate men, and desperate men are dangerous men—doubly so because, having nothing to hope for, they have nothing to lose. Phelps, cognizant of the monstrous potential looming on the horizon, is already searching for solutions.

"Dealing with the problem of long-term sentences will become a very high priority, not only here, but all over the country," he states. "We have to figure out ways of offering hope." Phelps is currently a member of an American Correctional Association committee studying ways to remedy the hopelessness that threatens to become the single biggest problem in America's penal institutions. But he isn't dependent upon the committee's findings; he's already hunting for ways to not only solve but prevent the problem in his own penal system. And it's that kind of independence that has made Phelps the most successful correctional administrator in Louisiana's history.

[June 1980]

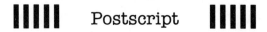

Postscript

Phelps's legacy would be a corrections system that respects and encourages freedom of expression, honest and meaningful communication between inmates and administrators, and inmate accessibility to official hierarchy. Louisiana inmates, consequently, have not felt the need to resort to desperate measures to communicate their concerns to administrators, thus avoiding the kind of major disturbances experienced in other penal systems.

The Angolite has since won some of the nation's most prestigious journalism awards and the editors have the privilege of leaving the prison to pursue investigations and stories. Angola now boasts the nation's only federally licensed, inmate-operated radio station, and an inmate-operated television station is currently being developed.

Phelps's corrections philosophy, which he always described as "just plain common sense," has had little, if any, application outside Louisiana.

CONVERSATIONS WITH THE DEAD

|||||

Wilbert Rideau

They've been here a long time, living yet not living, dead yet not dead. They eat, they breathe, they feel, and they suffer (or perhaps they're past that point). They've been here so long that they're like part of the woodwork. Wars have been fought, nations born, families lived and died, and man has even gone to the moon . . . but it all holds little, if any, meaning to them. They're men who exist without meaning or purpose. And they continue to plod—forever wanting and never having—through their sterile, empty existences, forever alone, for reasons that elude them, or for no reason at all. They're like so much human debris, shunted aside by the world—rejected, ignored, forgotten. The only acknowledgment of their existences is buried away in the form of a five-digit number in the bowels of a Baton Rouge computer with even less heart than a professional bureaucrat.

The dispossessed. The forgotten. Earl Goines was one of them. A first offender, he came to Angola at the end of World War II for a crime of passion, at a time when this prison was ranked the nation's worst, a time of pain and human misery that defies translation. He survived it all, all of the barbaric rigors of the world behind bars, only to be lowered into the cold ground at Point Look-Out, the prison cemetery, in 1978—still a prisoner and, once planted in prison soil, forever a prisoner. His funeral was like his life: cold, barren, lonely, and with neither tears nor regret. His death, like his existence, meant nothing to anyone—except perhaps to me, standing at the foot of his grave, stunned at the cruel obscenity of the life and death of him, awed by the absurdity of it all. Thirty years of pain and suffering, almost a lifetime of frustrating struggle—for what? To be thrown into the ground by strangers, rejected, unmourned, forgotten, with as little feeling as the burial of a cow, to be forever here even in death? . . . No, I hadn't known him. I had just caught the funeral—more out of curiosity than anything else—the end of him. But I had to relate. I had to feel . . . because the haunting knowledge that I might well be looking at my own end, hovering over me like a gigantic vulture, was chilling my bones more than the wintry air knifing my body.

Questions raced through my mind. If what I was observing was to be the ultimate objective of Goines's confinement, why didn't they kill him, in the beginning? Certainly that would have been more merciful than the nameless terror of life imprisonment imposed upon him through some mistaken notion of Christian charity, reducing his existence to a macabre joke. . . . And, too, why did he continue to live? But I already knew the answer. Louisiana's standard of justice had always been punishment tempered with mercy and a "second chance" for the rehabilitated, the deserving. Within that context, every lifer had a reasonable expectation of being freed. Few served more than ten and a half years; many, less. Having spent half my thirty-six-year life here, I still searched for the elusive key that would rescue me from becoming, like Goines, that rare lifer who ended up serving his entire life sentence. Hope—inspired by a system that encouraged it, in a time that permitted it. And, as the years pass, you soon reach a point where you've invested so many years and so much effort in the chance of getting out that, no matter how futile the situation looks, it's too late to quit the gamble, to throw it all away—a point where you've just got to ride it on out, no matter what it leads to.

Time flowed, but the nagging memory of Goines's funeral and what it represented wouldn't wash away. Were there more Goineses in the system, prisoners who remained prisoners because they had been forgotten, or because of imprisonment's adverse effect upon them, or because they had been sort of lost in the increased complexity of the criminal-justice bureaucracy? Goines's existence implied the possibility of more. We decided to check. The staff of the Prison Records Office, despite the office's library of inmate files, had no idea which prisoners might fall into the category we were seeking, and we had to enlist the aid of the Identification Department. And it was there, in those old files, that possibilities began to crop up. Taking several names selected from the files at random, we set out to talk with them . . . and hit the jackpot.

"We jest lak cows put up in a pen and jest forgot about," the old man told us, sitting in his shanty in the center of the horse lot behind Camp A. I sat beside him, a bit stiff, cradling the camera between my legs and wondering at the nature of the fumes assaulting my nostrils, a smell that revived long-dead memories of coal-oil lamps and wood stoves from a distant world of cornbread, cotton, wooden farmhouses, buggies and wagons, chinaberry trees and slingshots—a world I once ran through, barefooted and carefree.

It was dark inside the shack, despite the naked light bulb struggling valiantly to penetrate the gloom. An electric fan at the foot of the bed blew hard, cooling the inside. Long-browned sheets served in lieu of wallpaper, with old rice sacks covering the inside of the torn screen door. The wooden floor was patched in spots with pieces of tin. Bridles hung over three rain suits on the wall behind the inmate who had accompanied me, and clothes were strung along the length of the back wall. The rhythm and blues blaring from the portable radio on a shelf above the bed sounded strange to me, out of place. The shack leaked when it rained, "but Ah'm gonna fix dat up," he told us. "Gotta take a lotta dis down and reline it, git ready foah da wintah. 'Coarse Ah ain't none too worried 'bout no cold. Dat than' thar'—he gestured toward a makeshift wood stove made from a fifty-gallon drum—"keep it pretty warm in heah. Can't put moah den a few sticks of wood in it tho'. Any moah den dat, and it git so hot, it make you git outta heah." He gave a nervous laugh. A horse whinnied a short distance away.

The tin shanty, painted blue, was built for the old man by a friend about fifteen years ago and blended perfectly with the dilapidated wooden buildings of the horse lot, a scene reminiscent of a 1930s dirt farm. This is where the old man has his being, a place that permits him to get away from the prison-camp existence. It's his own little world. Few people come here, and the old man likes it that way. "Ah pretty much stick to mahse'f," he says. "Doan lak dat new breed o' prisoners and all da' tantalizing goin' on." So he stays in the camp at night as

Cocky Moore outside his tin shanty home at Angola in 1978 (Courtesy The Angolite)

required of every prisoner, but "when Ah check out in da moanin', dat wrap it till night." He can go almost anywhere he wants to around the camp. He's been out with horses day and night at times. He's trusted. "Dey know Ah ain't goin' nowhar. Ah ain't goan run."

"Why?" asked Billy, who had accompanied me. "Are you too old to run?"

"No. Ah'm not too old to run. It jest doan do a man no good ta run. He jest hurtin' hisse'f."

The old man is Frank Moore, Number 35510, better known as Cocky, the man with the dubious distinction of having the oldest active prison number in Louisiana. He's been a prisoner here longer than anyone else: thirty-three years. *Almost as long as I've been on the face of this earth.* The thought races through my mind like a bolt of electricity. Cocky first came to Angola back in 1939 to serve a three-to-nine-year sentence for a manslaughter beef, the result of a night of hard drinking and arguing that culminated in a barroom fight and a dead man. Angola was a harsh place then, but fortunately you didn't spend much time in it. He got out, only to return again in 1945 for murder and parole violation. Given the violence of his youth, his lengthy imprisonment would strike many as understandable, fair. But he was now a broken, harmless old man locked in a system that had released many repeat offenders. The nature of one's offense and criminal history had rarely been an obstacle to release consideration in the past. So, what was it that kept him here, making him an exception? He was reluctant to discuss the crime that brought him back to Angola; we didn't press the matter, instead asking about his past life. "Ah was pretty rough back dere in dem time." He nodded, staring downward impassively, as if there yet not there. "Usta lak to gamble, chase dem women and da bottle. . . . Dey got me now, though," he says, gesturing to his left arm, which hangs lifelessly at his side. "Bursitis," he explains. "Ah can't use it no moah. It happen three years ago Christmas moanin'. Ah went out ta feed da horses, and it jest fell dead on me."

He had just awakened and was feeding his horses when we intruded upon his world. "I heard you talking to the horses when we were coming up—trying to get them to eat," Billy said. "After all this time, you must know those horses pretty good, huh?"

The old man laughed, nodding. "Yeah, dat sho' nuff what Ah was doin'. Ah talks to dem and dey understand what Ah'm sayin'. Been tendin' dese horses since 'forty-five. Ah know all of 'em, all of dey li'l ways, and everything 'bout dem." The animals are his friends, probably the only living entities he feels any real relationship with. The horses, that is, and Runt, the little Chihuahua pup that follows Cocky everywhere he goes and shares the shanty with him. He has no friends or family on the outside and hasn't had a single visit during his thirty-three years here. There's never been a wife in his life. No kids. Nothing. He's a man alone in the world. But he's pretty well taken care of. Prison personnel mostly give him whatever he wants. "Most of dese youngsters heah," he says of the personnel, "Ah raised dem. When Ah need some cigarettes or something, Ah jest go 'round and ax jest 'bout any of 'em ta git me some, and dey do it. No problem."

He rarely rides the horses anymore. And, despite the fishing pole propped in the corner, he no longer walks down to the lake to fish. "Usta lak it but Ah guess Ah done got lazy."

"From the looks of things, you're pretty well fixed up here, Cocky," Billy says. "Do you want to be free or would you prefer staying here like this?"

"Ah want mah freedom." He shrugs. "But you know how dat goes."

He is totally illiterate, has no lawyer nor anyone else to help him

*Frank "Cocky" Moore
at the time of his arrest
in 1945 (Courtesy The
Angolite)*

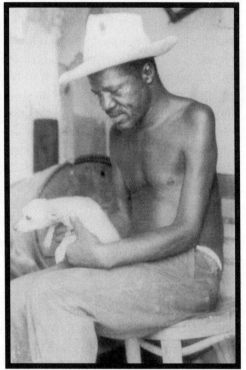

*Cocky Moore in 1978 (Courtesy The
Angolite)*

get out. He expresses the belief that he'd get out if he had people on the outside helping him. "But da way dey doin', dey jest done forgot 'bout me." He hasn't applied for clemency in "been 'bout five–six years." Why? "Well, Ah been holdin' up ta try ta git me a lawyer to take me up on da Pardon Board, but Ah ain't been able to git one." He pauses, then continues: "Lawyers want dey money, but dey got ta understand dat Ah can't pay him till Ah git out."

"Think they'll let you out, Cocky?" Billy asks.

"Ah hope dey do."

"But if they don't—say—they told you they weren't ever going to let you out, what would you do?"

"Ah'll jest have to stay heah, Ah guess."

"Do you think you deserve to be free, Cocky?"

He laughs. "Ah tell you—if air a man deserves his freedom, Ah do."

"You feel that, after thirty-three years, you've served your time, eh?"

"Done served mah time, an' some others' too."

We cut the interview short. I had to get away. Sitting in that little shanty—the old man's world—stirred the painfully chained need for some normalcy in my life: the need to ride a bike, take a swim, watch children playing; the need to hold a woman, to talk to normal people, to walk in the night with the wind in my face. . . . I felt smothered, as if the clammy hand of Death had reached from the grave and touched my soul. Never had the sense of Death been so real to me, so frightening. I had waded through an ocean of unrelenting struggles, danger, and unfathomable pain, and there had been many times I stared Death in the eye, even turned my back on it, but it had never, in all of its repulsive monstrousness, been this frightening. It was the same creeping feeling I had experienced at the foot of Earl Goines's grave, yet more real. Watching the old man, I knew I was looking at the face of a far more obscene and ominous kind of death than the physical—a living death. The face of tomorrow? My insides shuddered, my teeth clenched, as a quiet desperation began stealing through my veins. *No . . . not like this . . . never . . .*

"Cocky? No, I don't know anybody up there by that name," Louisiana Corrections Secretary C. Paul Phelps said over the phone. "What's his real name? . . . Frank Moore?" He paused. "No, I can't say that I do." After being told about Cocky and the peculiar situation he and others like him shared, Phelps responded: "Are they forgotten? If they have no family, it's conceivable they're forgotten."

It's more than conceivable. When we asked Associate Warden Peggi Gresham, who had been assisting us in our search for possible forgottens, to check the records of our test list of prisoners to determine the last time they had had clemency hearings, she informed us that the Prison Records Office discontinued keeping track of clemency efforts and results with the formation of the new Board of Pardons in 1975. "The Pardon Board keeps their own records of clemency applications and results," she said. But the Pardon Board keeps records only of those prisoners who file for clemency, not of the prisoners who don't. "So, they wouldn't have a record on Cocky," I said. "Probably not," Gresham agreed. Which meant that, in the bureaucratic shuffle, he was literally lost: the agency and people who determine whether he is ever to be released or not are unaware of his existence or his confinement. And he'll remain lost until someone files a clemency action for him and the petition brings him to their attention, or until he dies.

Jack Turner has been here twenty-two years. He's serving a life sentence for aggravated rape. He's a first offender and a shy, timid man, his body stooped from bad health. "Gotta lotta trouble with mah stomach," the Texas native told me. Back in 1963 he suffered some type of stomach rupture, which took about a year and a half to heal. "Had gangrene get in it," he says. "Had ta cut me open and dey laced it back up lak bootlace." He pulls his shirt open, showing me the gross disfigurement of his stomach. Camp H's Major Pittman, who had sent Turner to the main prison to see me, told me earlier: "He's been near death two-three times since I've been here. Thought he had cancer once. He's a first-class welder—though, with his condition, he could be on 'no duty.' He works all the time—and he doesn't have to. But I let him go on and work, long as he wants to, since it gives him something to do."

Turner has no lawyer and no help from anyone on getting out, though he feels that he could get out if he had some type of assistance. He says that he hasn't had a clemency hearing in about five or six years, and expressed little knowledge of the formation of a new pardon board.

"Do you really want to get out, or would you prefer just staying here?" I ask. "Would it be better for you, considering your health and all, to stay?"

"No, it's not better staying here." He wants to get out. Asked if he thinks he could make it in the streets, he answers without reservations: "I can make it out there."

"Where would you go, Jack? I mean—you have to have a place to live."

"I guess I could go to any of mah daughters or a brother," he replies. But he concedes that he hasn't talked to any of them yet about it. Prison records reveal that he hasn't had a visit since 1973.

Told that there was a strong possibility that the people who make decisions might be totally unaware of his existence, he shakes his head sadly: "Dey should go through the files to see if there's been any action and why. . . . You know—at least make an effort . . . let a man know dey tried, dey know he's there, and dey're not forgetting him. It makes a man feel better to know he not just stuck in some corner and forgot about."

A few states have some type of mechanism built into their penal system that requires authorities to check on each and every prisoner after a set number of years to see what, if any, action has been taken in his case—in short, some device to prevent a prisoner's being more or less forgotten, or lost within the system, his existence buried beneath the bureaucracy. But Louisiana, like a number of other states, lacks any kind of checking mechanism.

"There is no requirement in this state to check on such prisoners," Phelps said, "and the lack of a requirement has to do with the whole philosophy of pardon in this state. It's a privilege, not a right. And, if you want it, you apply at your own initiative for clemency."

The only door to freedom in Louisiana for persons sentenced to life in prison or to terms so long the prisoner can't possibly live to complete them is the clemency process. But the process is a hit-or-miss thing, usually dependent upon the individual's personal ability to utilize the resources available to him while in prison.

Enduring the physical and psychological rigors of the world behind bars has always been a grueling experience, an unrelenting struggle to survive the forces of danger, despair, and insanity. Now, in order to emerge an improved individual from it all one must transcend the entire prison experience, a feat requiring the determination of a fanatic, the adeptness of a master politician, and the tough fighting ability of a seasoned mercenary. The only immediate reward is the privilege to continue fighting, to continue to cling to dreams so distant as to make a person wonder at times if he's not insane. That's the reality, and to hell with what the classroom-bred, degree-toting, grant-hustling "experts" say from their well-funded, air-conditioned offices far removed from the grubby realities of the prisoner's lives. For most, the prison experience is a one-way ride on a psychological roller coaster—downhill. And the easiest thing to do, in a world where almost everything is an assault against you, is to permit yourself to be defeated by the overwhelming indifference and sense of hopelessness that steals into your daily existence, slowly, almost unnoticeably sapping your drive, your dreams, your ambition, evoking cries from the soul to surrender, to give up the ghost, to just drift along with the tide of time and human affairs, to not care. Only the hungriest can escape the chains of deterioration and apathy. Additionally, a continuous river of pardon denials kills initiative, leaving behind an individual who no longer has any faith in the system or incentive to utilize its avenues to freedom. This condition may be aggravated by his having been locked up so long that he has neither friends nor family and his sense of "belonging" is destroyed. The less-educated are worse off, particularly those who can neither read nor write and are at a complete loss when facing the whole criminal-justice apparatus. When you talk about a prisoner being lost or forgotten within the system, you're almost always talking about someone with a marked inability to pursue the avenues provided by the system. The inability could be natural or prison-induced; the person could be a functionally illiterate and/or mentally retarded individual—any or all of which every prison in the nation has its share of.

"The Department of Corrections has no obligation to pursue action for these men," Phelps stated. "We only take them to administer the sentence meted them. We have in the past—and we will continue to do so in the future—arranged medical furloughs for certain prisoners and put them in nursing homes, but it's not our responsibility to do anything more than administer the sentence the court meted." Asked about the fairness of a system that permits persons to remain prisoners because of their inability to pursue the remedies available to them, Phelps said: "That's not my business to judge whether it's fair or not. Tell me—what's the difference between one prisoner immediately confessing to a crime and another who keeps his mouth shut, hires a good lawyer, and gets off the charge? It's not a question of fairness. You've got people who can make maximum use of the resources available to them and you have those who can't. And, that's not confined to a prison situation. You have the same situation outside prison." And he insisted, in reference to forgotten prisoners and those with a marked inability to pursue relief: "Corrections has no responsibility to hunt them down and ask them if they want to go home. The Pardon Board has the power to do that, or anything else they want to do with them—and at their own initiative."

But while Phelps has certain reservations about prisoners whose inabilities prevent them from pursuing relief on their own, he stated that he wouldn't be opposed to some type of checking mechanism, making it compulsory for authorities to check on prisoners after a certain number of years to prevent their being buried in the criminal-justice bureaucracy.

Such a mechanism could perhaps assist people like sixty-four-year-old Edward L. Lassiter, better known as "Two-Life," about whom we could find out very little. When the warden's office looked for Lassiter's file, at our request, it discovered the file gone. Warden Peggi Gresham acknowledged that Lassiter's file had been checked out to the attorney general's office. We learned that Lassiter came to prison in 1957 on two counts of murder. In 1971, he reportedly received seven more years for an attempted murder charge, the details of which we know nothing about. One source informed us of the possible existence of a statement by psychiatrists stating that Lassiter once suffered from some type of psychosis that rendered him unable to distinguish between right and wrong. The existence of such a document might present legal questions about his conviction and/or confinement, but we were unable to talk to Lassiter, who was confined at Camp J for disciplinary reasons. Lassiter cannot read or write, has never had a visit during his entire period of confinement, and has absolutely no one in the world to assist him. Given his lack of ability and his isolation, he would have a more than usually difficult time dealing with the bureaucratic apparatus in the pursuit of any type of relief.

How many prisoners among the four thousand here at Angola possess some type of psychological, educational, or functional handicap that reduces their ability to pursue relief via the system, we have no way of knowing. We merely took several and checked them out. But "there could be more—very easily," one knowledgeable officer said. "Offhand, we don't know."

During the 1950s Governor Earl Long created a "Forgotten Man Committee" to ferret out the prisoners who remained prisoners because of personal inabilities and the lack of friends and relatives and who had been literally forgotten by the rest of the world. The committee found and subsequently freed 107 such prisoners. That was over twenty years ago, a different point in time and public feeling, a time less insensitive and punitive than today. There is no longer such a committee, and nothing comparable to it has come along to make another survey of the prison population. Now it's every man for himself and God for us all . . . and luck.

*   *   *

Luck is what rescued Earl Billiot. He came to Angola with a life sentence for aggravated rape back in 1953, which he says he's innocent of. "There was no trial or anything. It was a cop-out. My lawyer pled me guilty and they sent me here." In 1958, during an argument over the World Series, another prisoner tried to kill him. "I didn't have a weapon, but we fought all down the cellblock hall and I managed to take the knife and jooged him twice." Billiot was given an additional twenty-one year sentence for that. A functional illiterate, he gets no help from anyone. "I don't really know nobody no more. All I got is my sister and she sixty-some years old, and she don't know what to do," he says. But he was lucky. A couple of years ago he happened to meet Pardon Board member Edwin Scott here at the prison. "I owe a whole lot to Mr. Scott," Billiot says. "He took a real interest in me and my situation and tried to do what he could for me." The result: Governor Edwards commuted Billiot's sentence to a point which will permit him to be discharged in 1983, and the Pardon Board is reportedly recommending a further reduction in his sentence.

That was luck, but sometimes prayers work, too.

"I prayed for help and he came. My prayer was heard," Joseph Williams said, telling me how Lake Charles attorney Jack Rogers accepted his case free of charge last year. Williams has been here since 1951 on a murder charge, which "I don't remember," he says. "All I know was that I was sent here in 'fifty-one and shipped right away to Jackson [the state mental hospital]. I didn't know I was in penitentiary till my people come visit me there and ask me what I was doing in Jackson." He emphasizes to me that he's innocent, that he did not commit any kind of crime and that he's willing to take lie-detector tests, truth serum, or anything else that I might be able to get the Pardon Board to give him. Both Williams's parents have died during his confinement. "I'm mostly on my own. I only got one sister. She ain't got no education. She don't know what to do—she just like me." Williams says that he's never had a clemency hearing from the new Pardon Board. He wrote Rogers, asking his fee. "But he knew I didn't have no money when he talked to me, but he said that, as long as I'd been locked up and with the kind of prison record I have, I should've been out. He took my case and said he was gonna try to get me out." At the age of fifty-two, Williams appears to be in good shape, despite having suffered a mild heart attack about a year ago.

＊　　＊　　＊

But unless some lawyer or influential governmental official happens to find out about a case, as Rogers did with Williams and Scott with Billiot, and takes a personal interest, chances are that these prisoners, with little or no education, little ability to utilize the system's available resources, and no one in the world to assist them, will stay here, living here and, like Goines and others, dying here.

The way of the prisoner with reduced ability to deal with the criminal-justice system is fast becoming more difficult. The system is becoming bigger and far more complicated. For instance, in the past, lifers knew that they would receive release consideration almost automatically after serving ten and a half years, the sole criterion being "good behavior." However, many lifers have been trapped by changes in the release criteria, regardless of whether they meet the old criterion or not. They are learning quickly, like James Poindexter: "They said if you kept a good record and go up, the people'll try to hep you," the old man said. "Well, ain't nobody got a better record den me." He's seventy years old and has been here since 1954. He got a clemency hearing last year and received a recommendation that his sentence be reduced to eighty years. "What kin Ah do wit eighty years?" Poindexter asks. "Had Ah known Ah'd been heah dis long, Ah'd been run off. But Ah can't do it now. Mah leg too messed up to run or do anything." His expectations, based on the old law under which he was sentenced years ago, have been reduced to a study in frustration. New criteria have since been developed and are now being applied to him. In addition to a prisoner's prison conduct, there is: 1. the length of time served on his sentence; 2. his past criminal record; 3. whether law enforcement personnel favor or oppose his release; and (as if that weren't enough) 4. the nature of the original offense and the seldom-acknowledged, unofficial "Politics of the case." Wading through that obstacle course will require assistance from others. But Poindexter has no lawyer nor anyone else to help him. "If Ah woulda had some help before, Ah'd got out long ago." He admits that he's kind of given up hope. But—"Ah don't blame nobody else for mah troubles. If Ah'da thought first, Ah wouldn't be here. If Ah git something, Ah appreciate it. If they don't let me out, Ah'll just die here."

Poindexter doesn't know it yet, but when you've been locked up too long yet another barrier is placed before you, couched in a question thrown out by Phelps: "The question is—can they handle freedom?" Gresham also asks a question that others will ask, regardless of whether someone like Poindexter meets the formal criteria or not: "If they have nobody in the world to help them and they're old men, unable to care for themselves, wouldn't it be better to just leave them here? Throwing them out would perhaps be more cruel." Both points are well taken, but neither should be a consideration in an inmate's imprisonment or release. Besides, it's kind of late in the game to begin worrying about cruelty after you've taken a man in his youth, stripped his entire existence of all meaning and purpose and converted his life into a nightmare, until he's too old to do anything more than wait to die. The sole factors considered in an inmate's release or continued confinement should be: 1. Has he served a sufficient amount of time to satisfy his sentence? and 2. Does he constitute a danger to society if released? But that's trying to be fair, and fairness has nothing to do with the system.

The problem of prisoners becoming lost within the criminal-justice bureaucracy because of their own inability to pursue the available remedies represents only the tip of the iceberg. The question of equal treatment and justice aside, Peggi Gresham's question zeroes in on the most ominous aspect of the trend toward lengthier sentences, which society and its lawmakers have not yet faced. Louisiana's adoption of lengthier sentences on almost an assembly line basis means that prisoners are not released until they're old, broken, crippled by age and disease, perhaps senile, used to institutional life and incapable of taking on the burden of caring for themselves upon release. They are rendered friendless, without family, and utterly alone in the world, with no one to help them at all. Questions abound: What do you do with them? Keep them, turning prisons into nursing homes? Do you spend money confining and caring for them until they've been rendered incapable of any social contribution, then turn them loose for society's social-welfare agencies to care for until death? Can society afford an entire class of almost helpless and nonproductive people?

"What was that figure on the total number of lifetimers here, Rideau?" Warden Frank Blackburn asked over his shoulder, driving to the Camp A horse lot to see Cocky.

"Seven hundred fifteen total in the state," I said, "with six hundred forty actually here in Angola."

"You add about fifteen hundred more to that number—all those serving twenty-five years and up—and you get an idea of the size of the group he's talking about," Phelps told the woman reporter seated in the front of the car beside Blackburn.

"There's little difference between a guy serving a life sentence and one serving ninety-nine years," I remarked. "He's got to serve about fifty years before he can get out. Chances are he's not gonna live that long."

"We're entering a period in corrections where we're going to see more and more of what Rideau's talking about," Phelps said.

"How?" the woman asked, turning to look at Phelps. "Why?"

"Simple," he replied. "The longer a man stays in prison, the less likely he'll have any friends, relatives, or people on the outside to help him."

"And the way the system works," I interjected, "you've got to have help to get out of prison in the first place. You can't do it alone."

And, with prisons soon becoming human factories, converting those sent to it into almost helpless, nonproductive people, releasing them only when they're crippled by age and disease, unable to care for themselves, the need to have people to help them once they are freed becomes even more critical. But since, in all likelihood, there won't be anyone, the burden will fall upon society.

"But this is not a problem peculiar to this state," Phelps said. "This is a national problem."

He's right.

As a result of a spiraling crime rate, the violence of revolutionary groups, the senseless violence of the young, and the growing perception that prisons do not rehabilitate, the mood of the American public has turned ugly and vindictive. And, with the winds of vengeance raging, more and more lawmakers and prosecutors have been resorting to life imprisonment of offenders as a more effective means of stilling public fear and the ensuing political pressures. And offenders are arriving at prison gates across the nation in rapidly increasing numbers. During the fiscal year 1967–68, Florida's penal system received 62 new life commitments. By 1976, they were rolling in at the rate of 300 a year. New York's total lifer population had already increased 44 percent during the three-year period preceding December 31, 1974. But the number of persons receiving life sentences during the first seven months of the calendar year jumped from 173 in 1974 to 520 in 1975! In Louisiana, the penal system has been registering a 100 percent increase in new life commitments every three years for the past decade, and the rate is expected to continue to increase even more dramatically.

In no country in the world are so many people being buried alive as they are now in the United States. The most notable "buried prisoner" was the famed Birdman of Alcatraz, who spent fifty-four years behind bars before finally being permitted, as an old man, to emerge from his tomb to die in a federal hospital. Others, like George Jackson, of Soledad fame, never emerge, their lives spent trying to surmount, penetrate, or destroy the walls that keep them entombed, though managing only to discolor those walls with the red stain of their life's blood—until it's washed into a prison gutter with a water hose.

"The only thing is that here in Louisiana," Phelps told me, "we're dealing with the state's inability to differentiate . . . between people, between who's dangerous and needs to be locked up and who's not dangerous and doesn't need to be locked up. . . . No one has come face-to-face with the fact about how much it's going to cost. The first one to do so is [State] Senator Edward Barham, who has become increasingly concerned about the tremendous financial impact that all of this is going to ultimately have."

Financially long-term imprisonment will prove costly—and, ultimately, more than society can afford. Take, for example, the prisoners now in Angola serving life sentences. There are 640 of them and they make up 16 percent of the total Angola prisoner population. Louisiana taxpayers had to shell out $1.7 million to keep them there during the 1974–75 fiscal year. In 1978 it will cost approximately $4.5 million. State law requires many prisoners to serve at least twenty years in prison before the Pardon Board will consider reducing their sentences. Now, if it were possible to both hold lifers at the present population of 640 and keep the cost of maintaining these prisoners at its present figure for the next twenty years, the state would spend a total of $100 million. But that's impossible. And one must remember that this figure is directed only at the maintenance of Angola's *life* commitments, 16 percent of the total prisoner population. We haven't even begun to estimate the cost of the remaining 84 percent, many of whom will be here for twenty years or more because of the present trend toward fixed sentences carrying stipulations of "no parole," "no suspension of sentence," "no eligibility for any type of consideration for X number of years." The ultimate costs of imprisoning these inmates for the next twenty years will be astronomical. Then there will be the costs society will bear after these men are released, perhaps almost helpless and made nonproductive by the ill effects of lengthy imprisonment. They will very likely be a burden to social-services agencies until their deaths.

The situation is getting worse, not better. According to U.S. Justice Department figures, Louisiana is experiencing the biggest increase in number of prisoners of any state in the Union. While nationwide growth from December 1975 to December 1976 was 12 percent (13 percent for the South), Louisiana's prison population leaped a whopping 31 percent during the same period. The Department of Corrections budget is increasing at a rate unmatched by any other department in the state. It has already spent over $100 million on prison construction and renovations from 1975 to 1978, and Corrections Secretary Phelps states that a new prison will be needed every year just to keep up with the burgeoning inmate population.

While many of the men being sent to prison need to be locked up to protect society, a huge number are being confined needlessly and could be released tomorrow without posing any danger to society. Studies show that murderers, the most feared of all offenders, ironically show the lowest recidivism rate of any offenders. In 1968, P. G. McGrath, a criminal-justice researcher, reported the results of his study of 293 murderers who were released from Broadmoor, in England. Not one killed again.

A comprehensive study by the U.S. National Council on Crime and Delinquency reveals that 98.23 percent of willful homicide offenders were successful on parole during the critical transitional first year following their release. From the sample of 6,908 persons, convicted of willful homicide, who were paroled from prisons during the period 1965 to 1969, 6,786 had no new major conviction or allegations of offenses resulting in their return to prison; whereas over five times the number (on a percentage basis) of the other 72,192 parolees surveyed during this same period were returned. Another study in Michigan showed that none of the 268 first-degree murderers paroled in Michigan between 1959 and 1972 have been returned for *any* type of felony (0 percent recidivism), and since 1938 *no one* convicted of first-degree murder and then paroled has ever repeated the offense. The well-documented report "Order out of Chaos," which investigated parole reform in California, went so far as to recommend that many of the state's 1,100 murder and manslaughter prisoners should be classified as "nonviolent" since there was little likelihood that they would ever again resort to violence. These reports are not presented to suggest that murderers should be exempt from imprisonment because of their low recidivism rate. Society has a legitimate right to vengeance, and murder is the most grievous of offenses. These figures do illustrate the lack of logic and practicality in the increasing trend to keep murderers, as a class, locked up as long as possible, a practice that adds up to a tremendous waste of human life and money.

Pardon boards and governors are becoming increasingly reluctant to commute sentences, for fear of political repercussions. Legislatures are enacting laws increasing the amount of time prisoners must serve before being eligible for any type of release consideration. And nowhere is the situation worse than in Louisiana, where the legislature has—for lifers alone—increased the amount of time for eligibility from ten and a half years to twenty years in 1973, and in 1975 to forty years! And the emphasis is upon the potentially violent offender. Unfortunately, the public and its lawmakers are assuming that most rather than a few offenders are potentially dangerous, an assumption frequently encouraged by the mass media, with their inclination to sensationalize bizarre, atypical murders or rapes for the sake of increasing audience, sales, and profit. This negative information is seldom balanced in the press by positive reports. But because some ex-convicts repeatedly murder, rape, and commit other forms of violence, corrections and clemency authorities are being pressured to predict who will become violent upon release. And since no one (not even psychiatrists) can accurately predict this, authorities are playing it safe. Rather than risk an occasional misjudgment, they now prefer to overpredict violence, assuming that, since some convicts are dangerous, the one under release consideration will be. As a result, for every one who might commit violence, many potentially harmless individuals remain in prison. Of course, if the authorities misjudge too often and release prisoners who do become violent, with the media ready to sensationalize their cases, the officials will soon lose their positions. Instead, the prisoner population grows as authorities keep even the harmless in to prevent that random person from committing violence. As a result, much of the power to decide who is released has been surrendered to police and prosecutorial authorities at the local level.

This situation demonstrates, better than anything else, the inequities, the politics, the prejudices, and the contradictory aims of the criminal-justice system, the confusion within and around it. For the most part, long-term prisoners are hostages of fear and politics, their fate determined by the vagaries of the political mood.

The criminal-justice business is a growth industry, burgeoning at a rate that makes other companies green with envy. According to the Law Enforcement Assistance Administration, the record for annual tax dollars spent to repress crime and criminals stands at $19.7 billion, spent in 1976. From 1971 through 1976, crime-control spending increased nationally by over 87 percent. Federal expenses more than doubled, state costs went up over 94 percent, and an increase of over 86 percent was experienced on the local level. The total number of employees in the system had increased to 1,079,892 by October 1976. Corrections Secretary Phelps has expressed the belief that, as the cost continues to mount, economic factors will eventually effect a reversal in the lock-'em-up-and-throw-away-the-key trend, the burden on taxpayers forcing leaders to seek alternatives to present practices. That makes sense, particularly in light of the tax revolt sweeping the nation. The growing criminal-justice expenditures represent a financial drain on the nation's economy, since billions of dollars are being pumped into an operation that is nonproductive by nature, contributing little to the overall economy. But change won't come easy. Attempts at making the U.S. postal system more efficient provide an example of what an entrenched multibillion-dollar bureaucracy is capable of when it decides to resist change. The same principle will hold true for the criminal-justice business: The bigger it gets, the more powerful it will become, and the more resistant it will prove to change because of the vested interests involved.

In 1975, Angola, the nation's biggest penitentiary, was also its bloodiest. In 1978, Angola is one of the more peaceful—hard, to be sure, but peaceful. But that may change. Angola is rapidly being converted into a human graveyard by the steady entry of prisoners toting sentences so long that the inmate can't see or hope for anything other than a mound at Point Look-Out (prison cemetery)—or, if he's lucky, a rocking chair in the corner of some nursing home. And profound questions follow at these prisoners' heels. How many long-term commitments can a penal system realistically withstand? What is the saturation point? And what will be the effect of all these living dead upon the system?

"Man, that's scary—winding up like that," Billy remarked as we walked alongside the road on our way back to the main prison after visiting Cocky. "See, if that's an example of the compassion and Christian charity society wants to give me—baby, they can keep it. I'd much rather have the firing squad on a cold morning than face what that old man has—you can believe that." His voice had a touch of awe. "He's dead, and don't even know it."

I was still shaking off the depression that had touched me in the shack behind us, wondering idly about the psychology of those willing to live under any conditions just for the privilege of breathing, regarding the fact that they merely exist as a blessing, despite the manner of that existence. For a fleeting moment, I tried stepping into Cocky's mind, trying to imagine how he must feel and view things. I couldn't. I simply could not relate to spending all of my life suffering for the sheer sake of suffering, despite the half a lifetime I've already spent here. Where was the redeeming value in fighting to exist so that one could exist only to suffer? If one's only mercy in this madness was to be death, why should one wait through a lifetime of pain before knowing the peace of the grave? Why perpetuate a struggle for mere existence when existence will only be for existence' sake? Problem was that Cocky wouldn't think like that. He wouldn't question. He existed, I was sure, without thought or purpose. And that was the difference, would always be the difference between us, a difference as thin as a razor's edge yet as wide as the ocean.

We moved farther off the road as a car sped by. "That's one situation where a man is blessed by his ignorance," Billy said, adding: "Which is why he can live like that. Neither one of us could. We've got a problem called awareness. He may not know what's happening to him, but you'd better believe we know what's happening to us." He paused for a long moment, finally adding, "And we suffer more as a result."

We walked wordlessly, occupied with our thoughts. Cars passed by every now and then. We reached the trusty yard, but continued to follow the road, studying the long-worn dormitories, which would soon undergo renovation, as those on the other end of the yard now were. A line of new guard towers, still unoccupied, ran the length of the grounds, ending at a point where construction workers were busily erecting a new building to house bachelor employees. A lone inmate stood at the weight pile, pumping iron.

"I'll tell you, Wilbert," Billy said, "if there could've been some way for me to know from the start that I would've had to go through all that I did these thirteen years I've been here—yeah, I'da made them take me out in the beginning."

"Me, too—but it's too late now. We've got our dreams, and we've invested too much in them to quit the struggle now. There's no alternative. We've got to just keep on going like we're doing." I laughed. "Dreams . . . Ya know, I've been living off that all my life. A man's gotta live off something, and I ain't never had anything else . . . But after all I've been through, I'm determined to find me a little bit of beauty, warmth, and happiness, man, before I kick out—and I'm not talking about a wagonload of it, like most people want. All I want is a little, just enough to let me know that there's more to life than just pain and human misery, 'cause there's just got to be more. I don't want all of the pain and the effort to have been for nothing. In fact, if it turns out that way, I think the Lord is gonna have one rebellious son of abitch on his hands on Judgment Day."

"Yeah." We walked quietly, finally turning onto the main prison parking lot. The chief of security, passing by in his pickup, waved. Billy spoke, his voice heavy with feeling: "Man, we've gotta get outta this place."

Yeah, and soon. The shack in the horse lot with the old man and the puppy standing in front of it flashed across the screen of my mind and I felt my insides go suddenly weak, the wings of desperation beating urgently at my back. On the horizon, the sun's rays were softening, a softening that did not touch me, for there was the haunting knowledge that yesterday was lost to me forever, today was insufferable, and tomorrow loomed only as a question mark.

"You know," Billy said, "I'm convinced that Gary Gilmore was trying to tell us something."

Yep.

[October 1978]

‖‖‖ Postscript ‖‖‖

Frank "Cocky" Moore became a cause célèbre when his plight was widely publicized in the Louisiana news media. The warden's office was inundated with calls and mail offering him assistance, employment, visits, and even a few marriage proposals. Two attorneys, Vernon Claville and Michael Walker, along with the Lakeside Baptist Church, all of Shreveport, began an active fight for his freedom. In January 1980, Governor Edwin Edwards commuted Cocky's sentence to fifty-five years, and he was released. A long-lost cousin, who had become a successful New Orleans businessman, took him in. Several months later, Cocky and his cousin had become great friends and were spending much of their time together engaging in their favorite pastime, fishing.

Edward Lassiter and Earl Billiot were also freed. Within six months, Billiot committed another sex offense and was returned to prison, where he remains. James Poindexter's sentence was commuted to sixty years by Governor Edwards, and he was released a few days later after serving thirty-one years behind bars. On July 17, 1979, Edwards commuted the sentence of Joseph Williams, but his intended release, queered by confusion created by conflicting state laws, caused him to remain imprisoned for several more years. Jack Turner also remained imprisoned until he was paroled in 1989 to a nursing home in St. Francisville after spending thirty-three years in prison.

"Conversations with the Dead" won the 1979 American Bar Association's Silver Gavel Award. It was the first time in the ABA's hundred-year history that it honored a prisoner publication.

THE SEXUAL JUNGLE

|||||

Wilbert Rideau

Leaving the bullpen, he strolled toward the cell area. Stepping into the darkened cell, he was swept into a whirlwind of violent movement that flung him hard against the wall, knocking the wind from him. A rough, callused hand encircled his throat, the fingers digging painfully into his neck, cutting off the scream rushing to his lips. "Holler, whore, and you die," a hoarse voice warned, the threat emphasized by the knife point at his throat. He nodded weakly as a rag was stuffed in his mouth. The hand left his neck. Thoughts of death moved sluggishly through his terror-stricken mind as his legs, weak with fear, threatened to give out from under him. An anguished prayer formed in his heart, and his facial muscles twitched uncontrollably. He was thrown on the floor, his pants pulled off him. As a hand profanely squeezed his buttocks, he felt a flush of embarrassment and anger, more because of his basic weakness—which prevented his doing anything to stop what was happening—than because of what was actually going on. His throat grunted painful noises, an awful pleading whine that went ignored as he felt his buttocks spread roughly apart. A searing pain raced through his body as the hardness of one of his attackers tore roughly into his rectum. "Shake back, bitch!" a voice urged. "Give him a wiggle!" His rapist expressed delight as his body flinched and quivered from the burning cigarettes being applied to his side by other inmates gleefully watching. A sense of helplessness overwhelmed him and he began to cry, and even after the last penis was pulled out of his abused and bleeding body, he still cried, overwhelmed by the knowledge that it was not over, that this was only the beginning of a nightmare that would only end with violence, death, or release from prison.

Rape . . . for women, one of the most terrifying words in the English language. It haunts their footsteps like a vengeful ghost and creeps into their dreams like a silent thief in the night, stealing their peace and security, gripping their souls with icy fingers of fear. Rape and fear of becoming a victim of sexual violence are a part of every woman's consciousness—but, while many women live in fear of rape, so must the typical man walking into the average jail or prison in the nation, where rape and other sexual violence are as much a part of the mens' pained existence as the walls holding them prisoner.

Penal administrators rarely talk about the sexual violence that plagues their institutions, turning prisons and jails into jungles. Prisoners are too involved to ever want to do anything more than forget it once they regain their freedom. On the rare occasions when the subject is discussed, it is euphemistically referred to as "the homosexual problem," as if it's a matter of individual sexual preference or perversion, something done only by homosexual "perverts," sickos slobbering at the mouth for an attractive young boy. And it's often the butt of jokes. But rape and other sexual violence in prison has little to do with "heterosexuality" or "homosexuality" and is generally not the work of sex-crazed perverts. And, despite the humorous references to it, rape is a deadly serious affair in the pained world behind bars, almost always a matter of power and control—and often, of life and death.

Man's greatest pain, whether in life or in prison, is the sense of personal insignificance, of being helpless and of no real value as a person, an individual—a man. Imprisoned and left without any voice in or control over the things that affect him, his personal desires and feelings regarded with gracious indifference, and treated at best like a child and at worst like an animal by those having control of his life, a prisoner leads a life of acute deprivation and insignificance. The psychological pain involved in such an existence creates an urgent and terrible need for reinforcement of his sense of manhood and personal worth. Unfortunately, prison deprives those locked within of the normal avenues of pursuing gratification of their needs and leaves them no instruments but sex, violence, and conquest to validate their sense of manhood and individual worth. And they do, channeling all of their frustrated drives into the pursuit of power, finding gratification in the conquest and defeat, the domination and subjugation of each other. Thus, the world of the prisoner is ruled by force, violence, and passions. Since the prison population consists of men whose sexuality, sense of masculinity, and sexual frame of reference are structured around women, weaker inmates are made to assume the role of "women," serving the strong, reinforcing their sense of manhood and personal importance, and providing them the gratification of their needs that would, in the normal world, be provided by women. Within that peculiar societal context, an exaggerated emphasis is placed on the status of "man," and the pursuit of power assumes overriding importance because power translates into security, prestige, physical and emotional gratification, wealth—survival.

Rape in prison is rarely a sexual act, but one of violence, politics, and an acting out of power roles. "Most of your homosexual rape is a macho thing," says Colonel Walter Pence, the chief of security at the Louisiana State Penitentiary at Angola. "It's basically one guy saying to another: 'I'm a better man than you and I'm gonna turn you out to prove it.' I've investigated about a hundred cases personally, and I've not seen one that's just an act of passion. It's definitely a macho/power thing among the inmates. And it's the basically insecure prisoners who do it."

The act of rape in the ultramasculine world of prison constitutes the ultimate humiliation visited upon a male, the forcing of him to assume the role of a woman. It is not sexual and not really regarded as "rape" in the same sense that society regards the term. In fact, it isn't even referred to as "rape." In the Louisiana penal system, both prisoners and personnel generally refer to the act as "turning out," a nonsexual description that reveals the nonsexual ritualistic nature of what is really an act of conquest and emasculation, stripping the male victim of his status as a "man." The act redefines him as a "female" in this perverse subculture, and he must assume that role as the "property" of his conqueror or whoever claimed him and arranged his emasculation. He becomes a slave in the fullest sense of the term.

"Sex and power go hand in hand in prison," C. Paul Phelps, secretary of the Louisiana Department of Corrections, explains. "Deprived of the normal avenues, there are very few ways in prison for a man to show how powerful he is—and the best way to do so is for one to have a slave, another who is in total submission to him."

The pursuit of power via sexual violence and the enslavement of weaker prisoners is not peculiar to the Louisiana penal system. It is an integral feature of imprisonment throughout the United States, in both jails and prisons, and even in juvenile institutions—yes, the children do it, too. Dr. Anthony M. Scacco, Jr., a criminologist formerly with Connecticut's Department of Corrections, publishing the results of a study in his book *Rape in Prison*, reported that rape and other sexual violence were rampant in juvenile and young-adult institutions in Connecticut. Staff at Michigan's Wayne County Jail once candidly admitted that "guards are unable to prevent cases of robbery, assault, and homosexual rape among inmates." An exhaustive 1968 study of the Philadelphia prison system by the police department and the district attorney's office concluded that sexual violence, in the word of Chief Assistant District Attorney Alan Davis, was "epidemic." In 1968, Illinois' Cook County Jail officials reported mass rapes to be "routine occurrences at Cook County Jail."

And while few prisoner-victims ever want to talk about their experiences, every now and then one will. In 1977, during hearings in federal District Court in Cincinnati, an inmate from Ohio's Lucasville State Prison told Judge Timothy Hogan that he had been raped shortly after his arrival there. "The guys that raped me put a straight razor to my throat and held me down," he testified, adding that he had to become a "wife" to one prisoner in order to protect himself from random sexual attacks by others. "I had no choice, so I got a man," the inmate said. "I didn't want to be killed." He testified that he had been sold for sexual purposes by one prisoner to another. "I was sold four times to different guys," once for $400, he told the court.

Dr. Frank L. Rundle served as chief psychiatrist of the 2,200-man California Training Facility at Soledad, and also as director of psychiatry of Prison Health Services for all of the correctional institutions, both juvenile and adult, in New York City. His observations have led him to conclude that rape and other sexual violence are universal in the nation's prisons. "I think that that same picture is true of any prison," he states. "It's not just Angola or San Quentin or Soledad. It is a feature of prison life everywhere.

"This whole macho/power, master/slave thing certainly does go on, and it goes on in several different categories," Dr. Rundle explains. "There certainly are weak men who become forced into the position of being a slave or the 'whore' and accept it unwillingly—but accept it. They have no alternative—they're either going to be hurt or killed if they don't. On the other hand, there are a lot of younger, weaker guys who are unwilling to get into the struggle of establishing themselves as strong macho men and who will seek out a strong man to protect them—and in that case become a voluntary sort of slave, knowing that that is the only way they're going to survive. The alternative would be to be forced into it by someone else that they don't really want, or become sort of gang property . . . and that's much less acceptable to a lot of them." And Dr. Rundle points out that "generally, those who are turned out and made into slaves remain slaves and never can get out of that."

James Dunn was one of the exceptions: He freed himself from his enslaved state, but at a terrible price. Dunn first came to Angola in March 1960 at the tender age of nineteen, toting a three-year sentence for burglary. A month after his arrival, he received a call to go to the library, where an inmate "shoved me into a dark room where his partner was waiting. They beat me up and raped me. That was to claim me," Dunn explains. "When they finished, they told me that I was for them, then went out and told everyone else that they had claimed me." He recalls his reaction as being "one of fear, of wanting to survive. Once it happened, that was it—unless you killed one of them, and I was short [i.e., had a short sentence] and wanted to go home. So I decided I'd try to make the best of it." He cites an influencing factor in his decision: "During my first week here, I saw fourteen guys rape one youngster 'cause he refused to submit. They snatched him up, took him into the TV room and, man, they did everything to him—I mean, *everything,* and they wouldn't even use no grease. When they finished with him, he had to be taken to the hospital where they had to sew him back up; then they had to take him to the nuthouse at Jackson 'cause he cracked up." Shaking his head at the memory, Dunn says: "Man, I didn't want none of that kind of action, and my only protection was in sticking with my old man, the guy who raped me."

Few female rape victims in society must repay their rapist for the violence he inflicted upon them by devoting their existence to servicing his every need for years after—but rape victims in the world of prison must. And Dunn, like others, became his rapist's "old lady," his "wife." And, as the man's wife, Dunn did "whatever the hell he wanted me to do." The alternative, Dunn points out, was: "Back then, they'd throw acid in a kid's face, beat 'em up, and everything else you can think of." But Dunn was fortunate, in that all his owner required of him was to be a good housewife. And Dunn was. He'd wash and take care of his old man's clothing, make the beds, prepare meals, bust pimples on his face and give him massages, and generally do all of the menial things that needed doing. Like all other wives

James Dunn (Courtesy The Angolite)

around the world, he'd also take care of his man's sexual needs, with the only difference being that Dunn could never say no. His old man had a dope habit and once, not having enough money to get a fix, he sold Dunn for two bags of heroin and the settlement of a hundred-dollar debt. As a slave, Dunn had a market value at the time of $150. "Two weeks later," Dunn recounts, "he bought me back because he was loving me." Two months after that, Dunn was paroled.

At the age of twenty-one Dunn returned to Angola with a five-year sentence for parole violation and burglary. His former owner was still here, and "he let me know in no uncertain terms that things hadn't changed, that I still belonged to him, that I was still his old lady," Dunn says. "And he had a clique to back him up if I had any questions about it. Back then, cliques were running everything and that was how you survived."

Dunn did not rebel. He was eligible for parole again in two years and he didn't want to do anything that would mess up his chances of making it. But he had changed somewhat. While he accepted the role of slave again, he was already thinking of ways to free himself of that state. "I waited on the parole, playing it cool, so that I wouldn't jeopardize it," he recalls. "But I made up my mind that if I missed the parole, I'd do something to stop this and become a man again, the kind of man I could respect. . . . I was being used. I was a slave. There was nothing I could do on my own. I had to have permission from my old man for everything I wanted to do, even to just step out of the dormitory, to go anywhere or do anything. Hell, my life wasn't mine—it was his, and I just lived for his pleasure. I didn't want to live like that. I was tired of it."

The Parole Board denied Dunn's request for parole. "And I decided that I wasn't going to live that kind of life no longer," he says. "And when my old man went home, I had made up my mind that I wasn't gonna be for nobody else." He knew freeing himself wouldn't be easy and that he could be killed. "You know how it was back then, the attitude and all—'Once a whore, always a whore,'" he explains. "Everything and everybody in here worked to keep you a whore once you became one—even the prison. If a whore went to the authorities, all they'd do is tell you that since you already a whore, they couldn't do nothing for you, and for you to go on back to the dorm and settle down and be a good old lady. Hell, they'd even call the whore's old man up and tell him to take you back down and keep you quiet. Now, if you wasn't a whore and you went to them, that was different— they'd take some action. But if you was already a whore, their attitude was more or less that you just go on and be one, and the most you'd get out of complaining is some marriage counseling, with them talking to you and your old man to iron out your difficulties. As for the courts, they didn't give a damn about prisoners back then and they wouldn't interfere in what happened up here. So, when I decided to quit being a whore, I knew that I would be bucking everything— prisoners, personnel, the whole damn system."

Dunn told his old man how he felt and expressed the desire to be a man again. When his old man was freed from prison, instead of selling Dunn or transferring his ownership of him to a friend, he left him on his own, probably because he cared for Dunn. Now that he had no old man, other inmates moved in on Dunn in attempts to claim him as their property. It wasn't difficult for him to find the determination to stick to his resolution to be a man. "After literally being screwed in and screwed over, misused and treated like an animal for so long, I had learned how to hate," Dunn explains. So he fought. There were between fifteen and twenty fights during the next two months. But the strain and pressure he had to live under soon wore his nerves to a frazzle. "I was tired of this dumb shit. They wouldn't let me be a man, and I was tired of having to fight off everybody." His last fight was with Coy Bell, an inmate serving time for kidnapping and rape. "He threatened me," Dunn says. "I did the only thing I could do. I killed him." That cost Dunn an eighteen-month stay in a cell, but the killing made a difference. "Nobody tried to claim me anymore," he recounts. "I was finally free—but it cost like hell." That killing added a life sentence to his original time, and, after seventeen years here, Dunn is still paying the price of his freedom from sexual enslavement.

For the next four years, his life was relatively peaceful, and he was his own man. But this peaceful state of affairs only lasted until 1968, when Dunn had to fight once more to reaffirm his manhood. He stabbed another inmate, an act that added six more years to his sentence and got him a thirteen-month stay in solitary confinement, a period that proved beneficial to him. "Man, I got to thinking that this was all so futile," he recalls. "I wanted to get out of prison, but I was just getting deeper and deeper into it. And it was there that I decided that, no matter what happened, I would do everything in my power to try to prevent what happened to me from happening to other kids." That became Dunn's personal mission in life, one he's pursued since. Upon his return to the Big Yard, Dunn went to work, waiting for the weekly new arrivals to the prison and pulling the youngsters over to the side to educate them about the various games of con and violence that other inmates would play on them in attempts to turn them out. If they needed money or items from the store, Dunn would personally take them to the canteen and buy whatever they needed, to prevent them from borrowing things from guys who would later insist upon collecting the debt by turning them out. Over the years Dunn has led many young kids through the thicket of games and intrigues inmates use to snare the unlearned and unwary in a web of violence and slavery. Working to help and protect the young and the weak has been his constant theme. When Dunn learned that the Lafayette Juvenile & Young Adult Program, which houses local juvenile offenders, was in need of money, he conducted Green Stamps fund drives. With a group of other inmates he created the L.J.Y.A. Club of Angola, which operates a pizza concession at the prison, with all proceeds going to help support the juvenile home. When prison authorities approved him for outside travel a couple of years ago, Dunn took his tragic tale to Louisiana schoolkids as part of an Angola Jaycees juvenile crime–prevention program, telling them about his experiences as a slave and the violence he had been involved in, and pleading with them to obey the law and stay out of prison.

It is a truism that men will attempt to function as "normally" as possible given the situation they are forced to contend with. A world of deprivation is marked by the pursuit of substitutes—the law of supply and demand prevails. So, while homosexual rape in prison is initially a macho/power thing, slaves are created because a need exists for slaves—to serve as women—substitutes, for the expression and reinforcement of one's masculinity, for a sexual outlet, for income and/or service, for the sense of self-worth and importance, and so on. Slaves are "property" and, as such, are gambled for, sold, traded, and auctioned off like common cattle. What results is a widespread system of slavery and exploitation created and maintained by fear and violence, a system that involves all either by choice or by force, a system that also serves as the foundation for the maintenance of the peculiar macho/homosexual culture that exists in the nation's jails and prisons.

The deprivation of basic human needs and the effort to find substitute gratification are the forces that shape the world of prison, its culture, its values, and the roles of those trapped within it. Sharp class lines divide the prisoners who are "men" ("studs," "wolves," "jocks," and so forth) and those who are slaves ("whores," "turnouts," "galboys," "prisoners," "kids," "bitches," "punks," "old ladies"). An inmate is always identified by his place on the continuum of passive and dominant, weak and strong, with the weak and passive viewed and related to as "female." As those investigating sexual violence in the Philadelphia prison system observed, the "stud" in a homosexual relationship "does not consider himself to be a homosexual, or even to have engaged in homosexual acts." The prison sexual terms "pitching" and "catching" exemplifies how the definitions are based on aggressive and passive sexual roles. An elaborate subcultural code exists with respect to the treatment and behavior of the enslaved. As Dr. Rundle points out: "There are rules which every inmate is expected to follow in dealing with a man's boy or whore—that they're off limits and they know if [they go] past those limits, they're in trouble from the old man . . . even to the point of risk of death. On the other hand, all those who are identified as whores or punks are required to show respect to all those identified as old men or studs. I think that's part of the prison culture everywhere."

While the first sexual act performed on the prisoner, the rape, was essentially nonsexual, aimed at redefining his role, the ensuing sexual activity he will be made to engage in as a "female" while in prison will be sexual in nature as well as in form. Jails and prisons are crammed full of men at the peak of their sexual potential, and they need sexual outlets. But since the majority of the prisoners don't own slaves, their need for a sexual outlet creates a large market for potential profit. In an economic sense, a slave is capital stock, property that can be made to produce income, and prison pimps don't hesitate to put their whores to work hustling for profit. How many tricks a whore will turn depends upon how much administrative heat there is. If there's none, he handles as many as possible. As for physical limitations, one Angola "homosexual" explained: "Well, a man who has forced another into this life—do you really believe that he cares? The boy handles as much as he can, all day, every day, until he gets hemorrhoids, and then his old man might feel something for him and give him a break." But most of the turn-outs don't hustle because their relationship with their old man is mostly a "man-wife" thing, in which case all they have to worry about is satisfying their old man.

"—and don't come back in my face, bitch, unless you got the money!" a lean, sturdy young black was telling another prisoner at the railing of The Walk as I passed the Bandroom on the Big Yard. "Do you understand me, whore?" he asked the other prisoner, who nodded his head nervously and left quickly. "Having trouble with one of your whores, Silky?" I asked smoothly with a smile. "Man, you know how them bitches is," he answered, looking bored. "Ah tell the bitch to make me twenty dollars, and the bitch come back with fifteen. So Ah had to send her back out—got to make her know Ah mean business." It was 1974, and Angola was wide open; it was a time of cliques, violence, and lawlessness, and everything was possible, including owning as many boys as you were strong enough to claim and hold. Silky had two and he kept them hustling. They produced around $600 per month for him. After extracting what was needed to provide for their personal needs, Silky loaned out the remainder to other inmates at high interest rates, or invested in illegal or black-market enterprises that would turn a quick profit. Each month he was able to send $400 to $500 out of the prison to meet the expenses involved in his effort to secure his freedom. Ruining the lives of the two youngsters by making them prostitutes was immaterial. "Ah wish Ah didn't have to do this," he once explained to me, "but Ah ain't got no choice. I'm fighting for my freedom and Ah can't support myself and pay my lawyer on the two cents an hour the state gives me. So it's either Ah stay here with them, or Ah use them to get myself out of here." He did, and he got out of prison.

In some prisons, "prostitution of an organized sort does go on," Rundle points out. "There are young guys who are taken over by mobs, by the prison version of the Mafia, and who become the whore for this group of pimps, who set up their schedule every day and night. They tell him you go to this cell, and after that to *that* cell—they take either the money or the cigarettes or whatever the medium of exchange is." While organized, clique-controlled prostitution no longer exists in Angola, it is definitely a feature of life at California's Soledad Prison, according to Dr. Rundle. "A young kid who was in for the first time had been forced into it and was really upset about it and came to see me because of it. But he couldn't say anything about it to the administration because if he did, he's ratting, and he's setting himself up to be either killed or hurt badly or having to accept protective custody for the rest of his prison stay, and he was unwilling to do that."

One of the perverse mores of the world of prison is that the victims of sexual violence are rarely regarded as "victims." A key element of the prisoners' belief system is that a "man" cannot be forced to do anything that he does not want to do—a "real man" cannot be exploited. Those unable to meet the stringent demands of that standard are regarded as not being "men," as being weak and unworthy of respect from those who *are* "men." Their weakness both invites and justifies exploitation. Many prisoners, upon learning that someone has been turned out, commonly state of the victim: "That's his issue—if he didn't want it, he wouldn't have let the dude do it to him." The attitude reflected in that comment isn't that much different from that of the inmate's rapist, who often feels that he was not only "justified" in turning out the inmate but also had a "right" to do it because of the other's weakness. "He can't protect himself," one guy explained to me a couple of years ago, after having claimed and turned out an inmate. "Hell—I just proved that. He can't make it in here, and you know it. As his old man, I'll take care of him. He give me sex and I give him protection. That ain't no bad deal if you look at it right. Hell—it's more to his benefit than mine." Neither do the prisoners who patronize the services of galboys forced to prostitute themselves regard them as victims or see any wrong in having sex with them. "Ah ain't got him prostituting—his old man got him doing that," is the typical attitude. "Ah'm not making him a whore. He's already one. And Ah ain't misusing him in any kind of way. All Ah'm doing is buying what he's selling. And fair exchange ain't no robbery." The victimization and continuing exploitation of the inmate are regarded as part of the natural order of things.

And, with one of the major concerns of prisoners being sex, studs will "get down" with an available whore . . . during the day, at night, hidden behind doors or bushes or in the middle of a crowd of onlookers, in buildings or under them, anywhere circumstances will permit. The form of sex engaged in is dictated by opportunity, which in turn is determined by the degree of administrative "heat" or supervision. Where opportunity exists, anal intercourse will be the normal form of sexual expression. On the other hand, where tight security supervision is imposed on the inmates, prisoners will switch to fellatio. It does not require the removal of clothing, so it is quicker and easier to conceal from authorities. Administrative action does not halt sexual relations; it only effects a change in the form. The bitter reality for weak inmates is that what kind of sex they will have to perform for their exploiters—anal or oral—is, in the final analysis, determined by the jail or prison administrator's action or lack of it. "There is nothing that prison authorities can do to stop two consenting prisoners from entering into homosexual relationships," Phelps admits. It's a crazy world.

While the initial rape-emasculation might have been effected by physical force, the ensuing sexual acts are generally done with the galboy's "consent" and "cooperation." Given the combined factors of his personal weakness and the psychological pressure of the prison world, which dictates that once emasculated he must accept the role of a female, he generally resigns himself to his no-win situation and cooperates. Feeling that being a "good woman" is the path to good treatment and protection against abuse during his confinement, he pursues that goal, sometimes playing his female role as well as a real woman.

How extensive is homosexual activity in the nation's penal system? Rundle believes that it's almost universal. "That doesn't mean that everyone who is in prison is regularly into homosexual behavior," he states, "but almost everybody at least sometime." Colonel Pence estimates its extent at Angola: "Roughly, I'd say about seven out of ten inmates here either [are] now participating or have participated in homosexual activities at one time or another during their confinement." But Phelps points out that "they're not medically or clinically homosexual. Many resume normal heterosexual relationships when they're released from the institution." He adds: "Homosexual sex in prison is a natural phenomenon of all one-sexed institutions and environments."

Penal administrators generally claim that much of the violence between prisoners in their institutions results from the homosexual state of affairs, a claim that Rundle feels is somewhat exaggerated because it ignores the racial conflicts in many institutions. Phelps, on the other hand, admits that there is no way for him to know how much of the violence is attributed to the homosexual state of affairs, but "I do know that in the ten years preceding 1976, statistics show that the Louisiana State Penitentiary was the most violent prison in the nation."

It was. The fabric of life in Angola was woven by the thread of violence. The only law was that of the knife, and the only protection available to you was what you could acquire through sheer force of character and the ability to impose your will upon others. Slavery was widespread, and human life was the cheapest commodity on the market. It was a jungle that only the strong survived and ruled. The pursuit of survival fueled a heated arms race among the prisoners for the superior weapon: a sword over a knife, a broad ax over a sword, and a gun over everything. Individual disputes, gang wars, and factional feuding kept the blood flowing incessantly, leaving the concrete floors stained despite daily moppings. Locked in the violent fishbowl of that period, men fought, killed, and died with little thought. The knife claimed the lives of 40 prisoners between 1972 and 1975 and left 350 more seriously injured.

"The formation of inmate power groups or cliques is symptomatic of a high level of homosexual activity and enslavement," Phelps states, pointing out that "during the ten years preceding 1976, the inmate power structure at Angola was very, very powerful. And anytime that happens and a high level of homosexual rapes and enslavement is taking place, there has to be a tacit trade-off between the inmate power structure and the administration." Most of the trade-off, he says, generally takes place on the lower level of the administration. "When it gets down to the lower level, it's usually an agreement between the inmates and security officers, and the agreement doesn't have to be verbal. Much of the communication between inmates and between staff and inmates is on the nonverbal level. They have their own peculiar method of communicating what they want to say without really saying it, and each understands exactly what the other is saying. It's probably the most sophisticated nonverbal system of communication ever invented in the world."

He explains the typical minor trade-off: "Take the cellblocks, for example. You put two men in a cell together, then suddenly you're getting complaints—one of them can't get along with his cell partner. Then he tells you that there's another inmate farther on down the line who he *can* get along with, and would you put them in the same cell? We know what's happening there. But officers would prefer to have two people in a cell who get along rather than fight, spit, and yell at each other—so they put them together." The officers, playing dumb, grant the request, giving the two inmates the opportunity to engage in homosexual relations, in exchange for peace in the cellblock.

But the practice of "trade-offs," as Phelps calls them, is not peculiar to Angola. The generally unrecognized reality in the prison business is that smooth prison operations can only be achieved through the tacit consent of the prisoner population. While prison administrations possess the power of force, the prisoner population, on the other hand, possesses the power of rebellion. All penal institutions function through some form of accommodation or conscious or unconscious compromises between the keepers and the kept, to prevent or minimize conflicts and to ensure peace. Thus, the only differences among penal administrations and institutions lie in the degree of accommodation and in those peculiar factors in an institution that especially favor the accommodation process. Institutions burdened with a regimented chain of command and/or a sluggish bureaucracy, which prevents the needs of prisoners and personnel from being met quickly and effectively, automatically create a demand for short-cuts, thus fueling the accommodation process. Staffers at the bottom must meet the needs of their operations and those of the inmates and solve the problems that bureaucratic red tape doesn't, and they can do so only through trade-off. The process of accommodation flourishes in institutions plagued by insufficient personnel and supervision because, crippled by lack of manpower, staffers are forced to trade off with the inmates to a large degree in order to maintain control.

Accommodation manifests itself in a pattern of relations through which administrators and staffers maintain control and minimize their trouble through personal relationships and trade-offs with the prisoners they supervise. In the absence of meaningful incentives to make compliance desirable, and when there is little difference between reward and punishment, staffers are forced to sacrifice a degree of their authority through trade-off to secure compliance. Physical coercion and the threat of punishment are ineffective instruments to achieve long-term compliance because their power to intimidate is limited. The more they are used, the less intimidating they become, and once prisoners exist close to the tolerable limits of punishment and deprivation, their continued use will elicit rebellion. Within that context, staffers tend to choose accommodation over force. Recognizing their inability to achieve their ends through the enforcement of impersonal rules and the continued threat of force, they pursue their purposes through friendship, ignoring infractions that do not threaten the overall security of the institution, making deals, and doing favors—all consciously or unconsciously designed to bring both sides to a mutually tolerable, if not agreeable, working relationship.

While it is the accommodation process that determines what kind of sexual behavior will or will not be tolerated within an institution (with administrations generally drawing the line at actual rape), the almost natural inclination of the institutional security force is to be tolerant of any type of situation that divides the prisoners into predators and prey, with one group of prisoners oppressing another because

such a situation prevents the development of any unity among prisoners that could tear down the institution. A "homosexual" jungle–like
state of affairs is perfect for that purpose. It's another, perhaps the
most effective, means of control. Prison officials' readiness to utilize
any means to secure a division among inmates is confirmed by Rundle,
who points out that inmate gang divisions along racial lines are
encouraged in California prisons. "The whole system is set up in such
a way as to, if not overtly, at least covertly encourage racial war," he
says.

There is a certain amount of staff involvement in maintenance of
the "homosexual" status quo in penal institutions, via encourage-
ment, active involvement, tolerance, or silence. In his report on sexual
violence among the kids in Connecticut's juvenile institutions, Dr.
Scacco charged that "administration knows who the victims and
aggressors are, and in many instances, the guards are directly responsible for fostering sexual aggression within the institution." And
Davis's study of the Pennsylvania jail system revealed that many
security guards discouraged complaints of sexual assault, indicating
that they didn't want to be bothered or pressuring victims not to
complain by asking if they wanted their wives, parents, or friends
learning of their humiliation. An indictment of guard exploitation of
homosexual situations in institutions was leveled by Simon Dinitz,
Stuart J. Miller, and Clemens Bartollas, who, reporting the results of
their study of the situation to the First International Symposium on
Victimology at Hebrew University in Jerusalem, charged that "some
guards will barter their weaker and younger charges to favored inmates in return for inmate cooperation in keeping the prison under
control." The reality is that penal security forces operate much like
any police force in the world, pursuing control and peace in penal
institutions just as police pursue the maintenance of law and order in
any city; and one of the instruments traditionally employed has been
the utilization of prostitutes, gamblers, pushers, other minor criminals, and street characters as agents and informants, unofficially rewarding them by permitting them the freedom to practice their vice
in return for their cooperation. The matter of acquiring control and
access to information in prison "is a game played by both sides,"
Phelps acknowledges, pointing out that information is power in
prison. Penal security staffs will also, if not encourage, then definitely
tolerate a homosexual relationship by a potentially dangerous or

troublesome prisoner, theorizing that a prisoner who is getting some degree of emotional and sexual gratification from his prison "wife" is less likely to cause trouble than a prisoner who is not because he's comfortable and, once emotionally attached, he will not want to lose his "wife." On the other hand, the authorities often can threaten a partner in a homosexual relationship with the loss of his "wife" to elicit information and/or induce cooperation with the administration in pursuit of its ends.

Much of this tolerance and acceptance in penal institutions is a result of staffers' becoming conditioned to the prison's macho/homosexual culture. They eventually adopt the prison homosexual jargon and games and even some of its belief system, an effect evident in the banter that take place between bottom-line staffers, with jokes about turning each other out, and playful references to each other as "whores," "galboys," and "bitches," in very much the same manner as the inmates they work around daily (though this is not to imply that they practice what their language suggests, as inmates do). But the peculiar prison homosexual culture does have an effect. Rundle points out the preoccupation among staffers: "When I first went to Soledad, like for two weeks, *all* that the staff asked me questions about or talked to me about was homosexuality." While Phelps admits that he had no idea to what extent the continuous exposure to the prison's macho/homosexual culture affects the attitudes and behavior of Angola correctional employees, he does admit: "I know situations where staff got involved in overt homosexual relationships with 'boys' and even owned them."

In 1937, Haywood Patterson, chief defendant in the famous Scottsboro rape case, came face-to-face with that reality when he arrived at Alabama's Atmore State Prison and had to fight to prevent other inmates from making him into a "galboy." In his autobiography, *Scottsboro Boy*, published in 1950, Patterson said that homosexual rape was not only tolerated but actually encouraged by prison authorities, primarily because "it helped them control the men. Especially the tough ones they called devils. They believed that if a devil had a galboy he would be quiet. He would be a good worker and he wouldn't kill guards and prisoners and try to escape. He would be like a settled married man." Patterson stated that the most valued galboy was a young teenager. "A fifteen-year-old stood no chance at Atmore," he wrote. "I've seen young boys stand up and fight for hours for their rights. Some wouldn't give up." Patterson reported in his book that both prisoners and security guards would watch the assaults with impassive interest. "They knew a young woman was being born," he said. "Some just looked forward to using her a little later themselves." Once made into galboys, "some carried on like real prostitutes," he reported. "They sold themselves around on the weekends just like whore women of the streets. . . . Usually you could hunk up with a galboy for two or three dollars. Galboys got sold to different men. If a guy had a galboy but didn't get along with him any more, he could put him up for sale. He could sell him for twenty-five dollars. News of a sale went through the prison pretty fast and bids came in every time." He described the extent of sexual enslavement of Atmore prisoners: "I once heard Deputy Warden Lige Lambert tell some state patrolmen that fifty percent of the Negro prisoners in Atmore were galboys—and seventy percent of the white."

That was more than five decades ago, and there is no reason to believe that Louisiana's penal system was any different from Alabama's. Old-timers at Angola tell of how, not too long ago, staffers used to perform prison marriages in which the convict and his galboy-wife would leap over the broomstick together in a mock ceremony. That could not happen today in Angola, for any evidence of sexual violence elicits swift administrative reprisal and prosecution.

Ironically, most of the sexual violence occurring not only in Louisiana but across the nation takes place in the parish or county jails, which act as a sieve filtering the strong from the weak and producing the sexual slaves long before they reach the penitentiaries. A number of factors contribute to this situation. The major one is that the typical jail is grossly understaffed and constructed so that adequate policing of inmate activity within it is extremely difficult, if not impossible. Given that situation, jailers can only maintain some degree of control and order by unofficially designating a strong inmate or group of inmates to keep control and peace in exchange for favors and the privilege to practice their own vices (usually homosexuality and profitable rackets). But it's a forced bargain for the jailers; regardless of their efforts the strongest inmate or gang will, via the process of natural selection, do it anyway.

With the exception of the few prisoners serving short sentences, the jail population generally consists of people who are simply waiting, some for months, others even years—the majority go to court; the others waiting out an appeal or transfer to penitentiary. Their existence is dominated by prolonged idleness and profound boredom, accompanied by an urgent need to find something to do. The stronger quickly discover that the weaker prisoners are good objects for games of violence and abuse. The true and imagined tales about prison instill fear, and those convicts on their way to prison believe that they must secure reputations as tough macho men. They hope their reputations will precede them and intimidate convicts who might have designs upon them. It's a futile effort, but some pursue it anyway. Prisoners with minor charges, who are waiting to go to court, and weak and old men are the most vulnerable for exploitation.

The jungle in jail is vicious. In his book *Rape in Prison,* Dr. Anthony Scacco, Jr., wrote the following account:

Many cases could be cited of actual rape of an individual in jail, but one in particular is chosen to let the reader hear the events from an ordinary citizen. He is married with a family, no previous criminal record, and a former Georgia legislator and businessman who found himself the victim of a jail situation. William Laite was indicted and convicted in Texas of perjury relating to a contract he had with the Federal Administration Housing Authority. He was sentenced to the Terrant County Jail in Fort Worth, Texas. The moment he entered the tank or day room, he was approached by five men. The first comment from one of them was, "I wonder if he has any guts. We'll find out tonight, won't we? Reckon what her name is; she looks ready for about six or eight inches. You figure she will make us fight for it, or is she going to give up to us nice and sweet like a good little girl? Naw, we'll have to work her over first, but hell, that's half the fun, isn't it?" "I couldn't move," said Laite. "I was terrified. This couldn't be real. This couldn't be happening to me." Laite was saved from sexual assault when a seventeen-year-old youth was admitted to the day room as he was about to become the victim of the five men in the tank. The men saw the boy and turned on him, knocked him out, and then, "they were on him at once like jackals, ripping the coveralls off his limp body. Then as I watched in frozen fascination and horror, they sexually assaulted him, savagely and brutally like starving animals after a raw piece of meat. Then I knew what they meant about giving me six or eight inches."

The attack did not end there, according to Laite, for while the boy was still unconscious, the attackers jabbed his arms, neck and body with the burning tips of erasers, so that the boy's body twitched making it more sexually exciting for the aggressors. Then one of the attackers, "in a final sadistic gesture . . . shoved his fingers deep into the boy's rectum and ripped out a mass of bloody hemorrhoids." Laite was shocked by the unconcern shown by the guards. He stated that the "guards were protected from the violent prisoners, but I, an inmate myself, was not. The guards never made an attempt to discipline the prisoners. In fact I suspected that they might pass the time of day watching the fights and sexual activities from some secluded location."

Laite's experience is not the exception, selected because of its horror and ability to shock and offend. The Louisiana State Penitentiary and other prisons around the nation are crammed full of men who can attest that this kind of occurrence is fairly common. (Brutal and senseless incidents are rare, however, in penitentiaries with established cultures and inmate power structures influencing inmate behavior.) Davis and his team of investigators concluded that more than two thousand sexual assaults had occurred in the Philadelphia jail system during the two-year period they investigated, many of the rapes matching the horror of the Laite experience in the Fort Worth jail. According to Davis, "virtually every slightly built young man committed by the courts is sexually approached within a day or two after his admission to prison. Many of these young men are repeatedly raped by gangs of inmates. Others, because of the threat of gang rape, seek protection by entering into a homosexual relationship with an individual tormentor. . . . Only the tougher and more hardened young men," Davis stated, "and those few so obviously frail that they are immediately locked up for their own protection, escape homosexual rape." The district attorney attributed the sexual violence to the violent subculture's definition of masculinity through conquest and subjugation.

Davis's study also revealed race as a factor in sexual violence in the Philadelphia jails. He found "a disproportionate number of Negro aggressors and white victims." Fifty-six percent of the rapes were black-on-white; only 29 percent were black-on-black and only 15 percent were white-on-white. This corresponds with Dr. Scacco's conclusion in his study of Connecticut's reformatories that the homosexual rapes occurring there were usually blacks raping white boys for power and revenge; Scacco found that blacks saw more social prestige in having sex with whites. Rundle confirms the racial factor: "It does happen that blacks often have a preference for white slaves, and that gets into the whole business of racial subjugation and revenge—the same way it does in society. There are a lot of blacks who prefer white women and it has to do sometimes with a conscious kind of revenge and a conscious status which it confers upon them in the eyes of other blacks. I don't think it works that way with whites for blacks. I think in that instance it would be more of an individual matter and preference." However, he points out that the racial factor "really depends on the atmosphere of the prison. For example, in Soledad, blacks and whites stayed strictly apart and there was a constant power struggle. If any white associated with or consorted with a black in any way, he was in trouble with the white group." Interracial rape under those circumstances, Rundle states, would "precipitate racial clashes."

Classroom-bred "experts" generally attribute homosexual activity in the world behind bars to what they call the failure of prison authorities to properly identify and segregate overt and latent homosexuals from the general population. That sounds practical. But, as Rundle points out: "One of the unavoidable facts is that, considering the organization of the inmate society, the hands of the administration are often tied." One of the strengths of the society and the exploiters is the refusal of the inmate-victim to admit that he was raped or is being used as a "female," for fear of his family and friends ultimately learning of his humiliation. Given that situation, who will distinguish who's a "girl" and who isn't in a world in which everyone looks the same? If the administration were to make an official determination of who is homosexual and who isn't, it would inevitably touch off a flood of lawsuits requiring the authorities to prove their allegations and demanding civil damages if they can't. However, the whole effort would prove fruitless. When people talk about homosexual activity in penal institutions, they automatically think of the obvious homosexuals, the gays, the "effeminate" homosexuals. If they were responsible for the horrendous situation in these institutions, the problem would be easier to deal with since they are often easily identifiable. But the reality is that the passive homosexuals are not responsible for the sexual violence. On the contrary, they are often also its victims, though generally treated better than non-gays by their exploiters. The truth of the matter is that sexual violence, the turning out of youngsters, and the enslavement and abuse of weaker prisoners is primarily the product of criminally corrupt "heterosexual" males, the "studs." Trying to identify them before they commit their first homosexual rape is almost impossible, much the same as trying to identify the potential rapist in a city before he assaults a woman. Given that reality, removing "girls" (usually "gays") from a prisoner population solves nothing. It automatically creates a demand for a new batch of "girls" to be found or made to replace those removed. As Angola warden Frank Blackburn points out, "The studs will just turn out some more"—the law of supply and demand.

That doesn't mean that the situation is hopeless. While little can be done to stop homosexuality, given the pragmatic approach to the psychological and sexual needs of heterosexuals confined in single-sex institutions for long periods of time, rapes can be reduced to a tolerable level. While they used to be a regular feature of life here at the Louisiana State Penitentiary, they are now a rare occurrence. Homosexuality still thrives, but the violence and forced slavery that used to accompany it have been removed. In 1976, Federal District Court judge E. Gordon West ordered a massive crackdown on overall violence at the prison, which paved the way for the allocation of money, manpower, and sophisticated electronic equipment to do the job. Since then, *any* kind of violence at all between inmates elicits swift administrative reprisal and certain prosecution. This, more than anything else, has made Angola safe for the average youngster coming into the prison today. No longer does he have to worry about being raped. Of course, if he lets himself be conned into giving up his status as a man, that's his business—the institution is only concerned about the possible use of violence.

Every prison in the nation has a section that it refers to as "protective custody." This is where authorities keep prisoners who request protection from the possibility of being killed or exploited by other prisoners. Generally, persons confined to protective custody are there at their own request. Usually this more restrictive situation eventually forces the weaker inmate to reach a point where he decides that he would rather permit himself to be sexually exploited and enjoy a certain amount of freedom than suffer the mental and physical anguish of solitary confinement. The punitive and painful nature of "protection" is one of the major factors in rape victims' decisions to accept the role of a "female" rather than report the victimization to the authorities and request protection. In many respects, the "protection" offered is seen as being worse than the exploitation by the inmates.

In the prison's pursuit of protecting weaker inmates from sexual exploitation, the authorities also arbitrarily lock some up who do not wish for this "protection": the gay prisoners, a small class of prisoners who are locked up simply because of what they are, homosexuals. For the most part, they are transvestites, the "queens" and "ladies" (as distinguished from turn-outs and galboys). Of the four thousand prisoners at Angola, "I'd roughly estimate that there are between sixty to eighty, but not over a hundred," Colonel Pence states. Unlike the turn-outs, the effeminate gays want the role of a female, as they regard that as their natural role. They don't want to be "protected" from the men. Despite what they want, the authorities lock up many of them.

Gary "Sheila" Keylon is a twenty-five-year-old gay from Oklahoma serving five years for receiving stolen property. He's been here two years. "I've been in lockdown ever since I been here. . . . When I came to Angola and arrived at AU [Admissions Unit], they looked at me and my record and just bluntly told me that I was a whore and that I go to Camp H lockdown, giving me no choice in the matter." Sheila asked to be permitted to live and work with the other prisoners, but the authorities refused. In an attempt to be transferred someplace else, he deliberately cursed the camp supervisor. He was immediately transferred—to Camp J, the prison's punishment unit. Brought before the Disciplinary Court, he explained that he had violated the rules in the hope of achieving any type of transfer that would remove him from his lockdown situation, that he didn't want to be locked up, and that he wanted to live and work with the rest of the prisoners. Sheila was lucky: Colonel Pence was acting as chairman of the court on that day and, instead of imposing a punishment, he tried to help Sheila by transferring him to the main prison's Cellblock B, where he could at least work in the field in the special work detail made up of "protection" cases. And that's where Sheila is now, a little freer but still segregated from the rest of the prisoner population.

"Security shouldn't put as many bonds on us as they do, because if we feel that we can't live on The Walk, we'd be the first ones to know it," Sheila says. "I'm not afraid to go anywhere in this penitentiary. Many of us are perfectly capable of taking care of ourselves, but they won't let us go down The Walk. They're more afraid than we are—and we're the ones involved. I don't need no protection. I want *out*, to get myself an old man of my choice and to live as normal an existence as is possible for me here."

Thirty-four-year-old Calvin "Carol" Clark from New Orleans also lives in Cellblock B and, like Sheila, does not want to be protected. "Hell, what are they supposed to be protecting me from—sex? I do it in here anyway. So I don't see why I can't do it in population. You see, you have to understand—I'm a homosexual and doing it is a

Calvin "Carol" Clark (Courtesy The Angolite)

natural thing with me." He points out that he's been "doing it" since the age of twelve. "I feel that if we need protection we can ask for it. We don't need it forced on us. Boy/gals are comfortable with this lockup situation 'cause they can lay up here and do their thing together—they relate to each other. I don't and can't relate to a turnout. I feel like I'm caught in a mental cobweb, having to live with them all the time. I don't want to be locked up like this. I've got time to serve and it's hard doing time like this. I even signed papers saying that I don't want protection, but they still locked me up. I want to go down The Walk, choose an old man, and do my time peacefully and constructively."

As Carol points out, doing time in protective custody is hard. "Protection cases" are always segregated from the rest of the prisoners, denied the kind of freedom and wide range of activities afforded ordinary inmates. They are also denied access to the prison's education and vocational programs and, so long as they are confined in protective custody, they carry the social stigma of being a "catchout," a "rat," a "coward." The regulations and restrictions governing their existence are the same as those governing the prisoners locked in Cellblock A, across the hall from them, for "punishment." "You're caught between two extremes," Sheila states. "Sure, you may be mistreated by some inmates in population, but then security turns right around and mistreats you in the name of protecting you from it." Then, too, the "girls" say that there is abuse among those confined in protective custody, with the gays sometimes being exploited and abused by the non-gays confined with them—a case of the stronger among them becoming the top dogs, the rulers in the house of the weak. (Following our interview, we received reports that Sheila received a black eye from a non-gay in protective custody for refusing to have sexual relations with him.)

"They keep saying that homosexuals start arguments and fights in this penitentiary no matter where they go," Sheila says, "when actually it's not the homosexuals at all—they're just the excuse used by the authorities for a lack of security."

Phelps points out that prison administrators are generally convinced that homosexuals and kids with violent backgrounds are more likely to cause trouble than anyone else. For example, Colonel Pence cites the problems at Camp D, which houses the more sexually attractive and younger inmates. "Now, here's a camp with about 530 prisoners," he points out, "and you have damn near as many discipli-nary actions and problems in that camp as you have in the entire main prison where you have in excess of eighteen hundred men. Of course, not all of the problems are sexual, but that serves to demonstrate that there are problems with whores." Colonel Pence adds: "Every time you put a whore in population, you're reestablishing the pecking order—which is a particularly dangerous thing to do in a prison. You got to worry about more than just their own protection. You've got to worry about all of the mess you're going to kick off among the other inmates by putting them in there."

Gwen White is a twenty-five-year-old Morgan City native serving time for prescription forgery. Openly gay ("I've never made it with a woman and have never had a desire to be with a woman"), he is also confined to B Block. He recognizes Pence's concern about putting gays in population because of the definite power and influence they can wield over other prisoners, the feminine charm and grace they can utilize as a weapon to pit prisoners against each other, to foment jealousies and rivalries. But, he points out, "it depends upon the individual—she can be a lady or a whore. She can conduct herself where she don't create chaos, confusion, or conflict, or she can con-stantly keep trouble stirred up." But Gwen feels that "most of your problems in this area comes from the prison turn-outs—they don't really know how to handle themselves as real homosexuals do. We've lived this life all our lives, not just our prison lives, and that gives us more experience at it. . . . I don't like playing the field," he points out. "I get me one man and stay married. If I see anything else developing with someone, I let them know quick that it can't go like that." Sheila points out that he's also not promiscuous: "When I'm with a man, I stay with that man." Colonel Pence, acknowledging that all of that may be true, stated that "there's always the possibility that no one will permit them to settle down." And that's where the problem enters the picture.

"I feel like I'm being punished simply because I'm a homosexual," Carol complains. "And I'm not the only one. The rest of the girls—the real ones—will tell you the same thing. We all feel as though they've singled us out and locked us up."

"We do the same thing with young people coming in with long sentences for acts of violence," Phelps states. "We lock them up until we, the administrators, are satisfied that he can do his time without bothering anyone. So homosexuals are not the only ones locked up."

"They're a source of violence and as long as that's the case, we have to separate them," Warden Blackburn says of the present practice of arbitrary lockup of gays upon arrival. "They should go to some type of lockdown until we can judge them." However, he does feel that they should be given a chance to work their way out of the cell and into the normal prison population like all other prisoners, on the basis of merit.

Mark Dwayne Smith ("Melody"), a twenty-one-year-old homosexual, worked his way out of his former lockdown status and into the prisoner population. Serving a life sentence for murder, he was initially confined to Camp H, where he participated in that camp's incentive program, then transferred to Camp D, and a few weeks ago to the main prison, where he now lives in a dormitory on the Big Yard. "I haven't had any problems since I've come here," he says. "Free

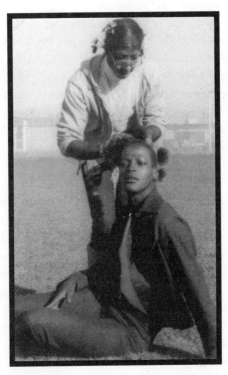

"Carol" doing "Gwen" White's hair
(*Courtesy* The Angolite)

folks [personnel] say that girls cause trouble—well, some do and some don't. It all depends upon how you carry yourself and what you do. If you're into criss-crossing [dangerous intrigues] and all that, eventually it'll come back on you. I don't engage in that kind of thing. The only trouble I'll get, if I get any, will come from the free folks," Melody states. "With me being the only out-front white gay on The Walk, any kind of trouble that might come up, I'll probably get the rap for, even if it has nothing to do with me. They have a lotta out-front black whores on The Walk and, while I've only been here three weeks, I don't see where they have any problems. But with me, free folks are always kind of watching me and all. I have to be extra careful." Toward that end, he points out, while he tricked at Camp D, he no longer does so. In addition to now having an old man, "I know that if I started doing that here in the main prison, pretty soon I would be gone, and I don't want to go back to no cell." He's perfectly content as a "housewife."

Gay prisoners are the only prisoners in Angola who are locked up because of what they are rather than what they do, and the practice of arbitrarily locking them up raises the question of discrimination. "Homosexuals are being discriminated against here because of the fact that they are homosexuals," Sheila states. "They should be allowed the same choices and privileges as other inmates—the freedom to make right decisions and to make bad ones, and even to fall on your face if that's the case. But classification [nonsecurity inmate affairs] officers, and especially security officers, tell us no to almost everything . . . because we're homosexuals. They aren't supposed to treat us this way—we have rights too."

Just what "rights" gays have as prisoners, other than the right to protection, is still unclear at this point. A couple of jailhouse lawyers, asked to research the matter for this article, reported back that they could find nothing on the books in the prison's law library pertaining to the treatment to be accorded gays in prison, other than that they have a right to protection from sexual abuse. "Apparently, it's still pretty much left up to the authorities," one of them said. While the United States Bureau of Prisons appears to have no firm policy on the treatment of gays in federal institutions, it does advocate that "the feminine appearing, sometimes 'pretty' prisoner, must never be classified as a suspected homosexual . . . nor be issued identification that

Mark "Melody" Smith in 1979 (Courtesy The Angolite)

differentiates him from other prisoners."* However, it urges personnel to be careful in selecting housing for him, for his own protection placing him in a single cell if possible.

Phelps points out that the federal court order by Judge West requires the segregation of overt, aggressive homosexuals from the rest of the prisoner population. But some jailhouse lawyers at Angola contend that the order does not apply to the "effeminate" gays, as they are "passive" homosexuals, not "aggressive." "They don't rape

*The Jail, Its Operation and Management, U.S. Bureau of Prisons and University of Wisconsin.

anyone," one pointed out. "If anything, they might get raped."

Phelps agrees with the gays in principle, stating that "nobody should be discriminated against just because of who and what they are. But if who or what they are presents a security or control problem, then it is our responsibility to see to it that they don't cause a security or control problem—and in that context, they are not being discriminated against. We're not dealing with classes of people. We deal with individuals, and they haven't proven discrimination as a class."

Still, the gays claim that they are discriminated against as a class of people merely because of what they are. "There is built-in discrimination against homosexuals," Gwen says. "That's part of the society within the prison. Most people, free people and inmates alike, think that we have some kind of mental problem because we're homosexuals. That traditional attitude has a lot of discrimination built into it." Gwen, who is a first offender and who intends to return to college to continue his education in medicine, was a registered nurse prior to coming to Angola. According to him, prison hospital administrator Diane Peabody and medical director Thomas Beamon refused to let him work in the prison hospital because of his being a homosexual. "I was denied a job assignment there," Gwen states, "simply because I am a homosexual. There are other homosexuals working over there, inmates and one free person I know for sure. But I am quite obviously a homosexual, and that's why they would not let me work there. That's part of the discrimination thing we constantly have to put up with."

"I'm a first offender with five years," Sheila adds, "not a violent person. I wrote the officials at the State Police Barracks,* told them I was a high school graduate with two years of training in air-conditioning and refrigeration. I've never heard from them, though they've responded to other inmates who wrote them. Instead of denying me, they just ignore me, which puts me in a situation where I can't do nothing. I can't even appeal because they have not actually denied me." Sheila doesn't really think that they would seriously consider him, "simply because I'm a homosexual. They'll let your old man go to the Police Barracks, but not you, because you're homosexual.

*the least restrictive facility in the Louisiana penal system

Hell—what he's doing to you doesn't make him that different. He's homosexual, too."

"Discrimination? . . . That's the system," Warden Blackburn acknowledged after being apprised of the gays' complaints. However, he states that he will look into the matter of their being given no choice, and their charges of being discriminated against, "and, hopefully, see what can be done to remedy the situation, to make it fairer for them." Colonel Pence is also studying the matter.

"Sexual deprivation is apparently a part of the system, an unwritten rule or part of the punishment," Phelps states. But it doesn't have to be.

"While it wouldn't end it, I feel that a lot of the homosexual activities could be reduced through a conjugal-visiting program tied into the disciplinary system or some type of honor system," Colonel Pence, the prison's chief of security, says, adding that it would have to be restricted to only medium- and minimum-security prisoners, not maximum-security inmates. "It would be controversial, but it wouldn't be the first controversial thing to come up in this business." He feels that most of the prison's security force would accept conjugal visiting if it's adopted as a policy. "There will always be some disagreement," he states, "but we will stand with policy and enforce it. Naturally, there would be problems, but I feel that the overall good would offset the problems."

Pence is not alone in his desire to see conjugal visiting in prison. Professor Columbus B. Hopper of the University of Mississippi spent ten years making a comprehensive study of the evolution and effects of the practice of conjugal visits at the Mississippi State Penitentiary at Parchman. He concluded that conjugal visiting is at least a partial solution to the sexual problems plaguing the nation's penal institutions. While admitting its inadequacies, he states in his book, *Sex in Prison*, that "conjugal visiting deserves serious consideration by those who wish to develop normal sexual adjustment among the inmates of American penal institutions." He concedes:

As its critics argue, conjugal visiting may have relatively little effect on the biological needs of prisoners. Under current visiting regulations in most prisons, the conjugal visit could not occur often enough to significantly reduce the sexual needs of those participating in such a program. What it would influence, however, is the image of a man. It would allow a man to keep his masculine image and reduce the need to establish it through homosexual conquests.

Unfortunately, too many people, including penal administrators, see conjugal visiting as strictly a physical thing. However, as Professor Hopper discovered, and the inmates in his study indicated: "Physical satisfaction is not the most important aspect of conjugal visits. The most important element is emotional satisfaction. Its influence on his self-esteem and emotional needs keeps a man who has conjugal visits from resorting to homosexuality." And emotions are also a factor in many prison homosexual relationships. Dr. Rundle points out that, despite the junglelike state of affairs, "a lot of inmates form very close emotional and affectional relationships which many times include the sexual. And that's purely voluntary—that doesn't get into this whole power and domination and [is] what we would consider a normal emotional relationship. And as far as I'm concerned, for that to happen in prison is healthy. It can in some way ameliorate the really desocializing process which goes on in a prison."

While Warden Blackburn states that he does not see conjugal visiting as *the* answer to sexual violence and homosexuality in prison, he would like to see it instituted, "but sort of at the end of the prison process—a family-type affair with emphasis more on family than just sex."

And, while both Angola's warden and chief of security would like to see some form of conjugal visiting instituted here at the prison, Colonel Pence doesn't really expect to see it happen anytime soon at Angola. "I wish it would," he says, but acknowledges that the political atmosphere in the state will prevent it, much as it has virtually killed the furlough program that the Louisiana Department of Corrections had promoted as a better solution than conjugal visits.

So, while politicians play politics, the "experts" theorize, and penal authorities censor *Penthouse* and *Hustler* to prevent a possible "obscene" influence upon the inmates, the nation's jails and prisons continue to be incubators of violence, abuse, murders, suicides, and warped psyches. The effect of it all upon prisoners has to be a contributing factor to the recidivism rate among ex-convicts and to the

institution's failure to rehabilitate them. How can rehabilitation suc-
ceed with one segment of an institution's prisoner population enslaved and the other in a constant struggle to escape deprivation,
abuse, and exploitation? A prisoner too often has a tough enough time
just keeping his head together, staying alive and safe.

The effect of it all upon the victims of sexual violence? "It's got to
be bad," Corrections Secretary Phelps states. "If you're a sexual slave
or in a homosexual relationship for an extended period of time, it will
have a great effect upon you. While most return to normal heterosexual relationships, there is the strong possibility that, having become
comfortable in a homosexual relationship, you'll choose to stay with
it, rejecting heterosexual relationships."

That's what happened to Melody. "I got turned out in St. John the
Baptist Parish Jail and discovered that I liked it," he admits. "So I just
stayed with it. . . . I enjoy it. The attention turns me on. When I was
young, I didn't get much attention. This way, I get plenty of attention
and I like it."

"It does happen that sometimes although the relationship may be
established against the will of another, it may become a relationship
which becomes positive, desirable, and the person who is forced will
then continue in it voluntarily," Dr. Rundle states. "But to say that
if that happens, the role is accepted as a natural role in life, has to be
taken in the context of the prison, where I would see it as a healthy
kind of compensatory or coping behavior. It could certainly mean, for
someone who had been in prison for a long time, that that would
become established as the kind of relationship most desirable and
would continue after release. For instance, I knew people in Soledad
who had gone into the Youth Authority Institutions when they were
twelve to thirteen or fourteen, stayed there till they were eighteen,
transferred to the Adult Authority, which meant going to adult
prison, and had been there for ten years, so maybe had never had any
kind of normal social, sexual relation with women, and who would
say, 'I don't know if I'm homosexual or not—never had the chance
to see what it would be like with a woman. All I know is that I've been
for fourteen years in prison and that I only know what it's like to be
with a man, both emotionally and sexually.' " Melody states that he
has never had a "normal social, sexual relationship with a woman"
and has only had one nervous sexual experience with a woman in his
life. He feels that the lack of a healthy relationship with a woman

"definitely had some bearing on my willingness to accept homosexuality."

Unlike Melody, however, most sexual slaves forced to play the role of a woman during their confinement do return to heterosexual relationships upon release. But the experience is not without its effect. Dr. Rundle states that "if this was all against his will, he has to deal with all the fear and anger and resentment and frustration that goes along with that. It would really mess up his head." And it does. To what extent, nobody knows.

The deprivation of basic human needs imposed upon prisoners, and the violence resulting from that deprivation, have created a horrible situation in the nations' jails and prisons, one that adds an extra dimension to the punishment of an offender, one that it can be reasonably assumed no sentencing judge intended. It would be easy to blame the whole affair on the prisoners, to use the violent situation as proof that they're criminals or animals and justification for the present penal practices. But their behavior merely reflects their desperation; they are locked in a cruel and abnormal situation, exercising the only avenues left them to cling to the very normal need to feel strong, masculine, and worthwhile, to keep in touch with the "real" world by creating an artificial one patterned after the one they left behind. The violence, the murders, the suicides, and the human debris left in the wake of their effort, are the cost.

> "The degree of civilization in a society can be judged by entering its prisons."
>
> DOSTOYEVSKI
> *THE HOUSE OF THE DEAD*

[December 1979]

▐▌▐▌▐ Postscript ▐▌▐▌▐

James Dunn's sentence was commuted to forty years by Governor Edwin Edwards on February 2, 1987, and he was released later that summer, after twenty-two years in prison. Gary "Sheila" Keylon and Gwen White were released after completing their prison terms. Calvin "Carol" Clark is still confined. In October 1982, Mark "Melody" Smith and another inmate swam across the Mississippi River in an escape. Smith made it to San Jose, California, where he was captured three months later; he was returned to Angola, where he remains confined. His accomplice wasn't so fortunate; he drowned in the Mississippi during the escape.

"The Sexual Jungle" won the 1980 George Polk Award and was cited as the most definitive work on the subject. It also reaped a 1980 National Magazine Award nomination for *The Angolite*.

The advent of AIDS has affected the state of homosexual affairs at Angola, but not dramatically so. The overwhelming majority of the 5,200 inmates here are serving sentences that consign them to die in prison, a situation marked with a fatalism that undermines the terror of AIDS.

THE ESCAPE OF NIGGER JOE

|||||

Wilbert Rideau

It was a sultry June day in 1976. Some of the prisoners at Camp H had made a brew of "mushroom tea" to help them escape the pain of their existence and wasted pasts. Joe Williams drank a couple of cups of it with them—"Man, I started seeing beautiful things," he recalls. Later, he went to supper but found that he couldn't eat. Rather than forget, the tea made him remember. He sat at the table brooding. He had been harrassed by certain camp officers because of a dispute with them. And the threats they had made against him, combined with the weight of his twenty-five years in prison was simply too much. "I sat there thinking about all of this—everything," he explains, "and that's when I decided I had to leave here."

He left the dining hall, walked into the camp's maintenance shop, and told twenty-three-year-old Daniel Ordner: "I'm going down the river—right now." Ordner was serving a nine-year sentence for theft and simple burglary. "Danny said, 'I'm going with you,' " Williams says, adding: "The people had been messing with him, too."

Williams had been a trusty for the past seventeen years, leaving the camp often to go fishing at Sugar Lake, a mile and a half away. So no one thought anything of it when he and Ordner strolled out of the camp about five that afternoon. "We even told a couple of officers who we passed by that we were going down the river," Williams says. "They thought we were joking." But Ordner and Williams weren't the first prisoners to joke about going down the river and, given the trust the guards had in Williams, they had no reason to think the two were serious.

An inmate friend of Williams kept a little homemade pirogue at the lake, which he used to fish in. Williams and Ordner took the pirogue across the lake, then carried it the additional mile and a half to the Mississippi River. Dusk was setting in when they put the boat in the water.

Ross Maggio was warden of Angola then. "As I remember, they traveled by night down the river and along the edges during the day," he recalls. "Moving at night the way they did, they were lucky they didn't drown. There was one place we found where they had turned over in the river and had pulled themselves up on a sandbar."

No one expected the chase to be an easy one. "Joe was known as a woodsman," Maggio explains; so he was not the typical escapee. He knew how to survive in the woods, the swamps, and off the land. The prison chase crew knew that they had their work cut out for them. And they were right. The chase lasted several days, and the chase crew covered a large area of the rugged terrain around Angola under a harsh June sun.

One night about three in the morning, Maggio and his chase crew had finally called it a day and were preparing to bed down on the levee for the night. Bobby Oliveaux, one of the crew, stood looking idly out across the river. A tugboat flashed a beam of light across the water. The light hit an empty boat floating in the river. Oliveaux called out and they pulled it in. It was the pirogue.

By the next day, the chase had extended to just a few miles outside of Baton Rouge—almost sixty miles from the state penitentiary. Security Major Bert Dixon, an old chase hand, was standing on the west bank of the Mississippi River that morning, just a few miles outside of the city, looking across the river, when he spotted the fugitives on the east bank, "playing in the water, celebrating," Maggio recalls. "They thought they had beat us. We called for a boat and it came up and took after them. They took off running, with the boat crew hot on their tails shooting at them. They ran into the woods, bullets whipping at 'em."

Maggio didn't wait for the boat. He and then–Deputy Warden Michael Beaubouef jumped into Maggio's truck and sped to the Mississippi River Bridge in the city, "which was the only place for us to cross the river and get on the other side where they were." Crossing the bridge, they sped down Scenic Highway and back down into Devil's Swamp right outside the city, where they were joined by Security Major W. J. Norwood. Beaubouef took off on foot in one direction and Maggio and Norwood headed in the opposite. A few minutes later, Maggio and Norwood ran into Williams and Ordner, who were squatting in the bushes. They stepped out, surrendering. "And I'll never forget what Joe told me when he stepped from those bushes," Maggio says today. "You not gonna believe this—Joe told me that he wanted to take his pills 'cause he thought he was about to have a heart attack. . . . I told him, 'Heart attack, hell! You been running four goddamn days and now you want to have a heart attack on me?' "

Williams had run long and hard, but it didn't cost him the heart attack he feared. But in time, his escape was to prove costly for him and one of the most costly in Angola's history.

Lafourche Parish is one of the largest and oldest parishes in the state of Louisiana. And, like many other places, it has its own distinctive feature. From the French word meaning "fork," the parish is named for Bayou Lafourche, a fork of the Mississippi River, which runs the length of it. It boasts of having the longest "line village" in the world—sixty-five miles of farm and homes fronting the bayou.

The original inhabitants of the land were the Washa, Chawasha, and Chitimacha Indian tribes. Intermarriage between Indians and the French produced a mixed breed. Williams is one of them. Born Joseph Drubie Williams on October 2, 1926, in Madisonville, Louisiana, he was raised in Golden Meadows, where "the people mostly lived off the land," he recalls. "We was seven brothers, four sisters. We all had to work to survive—never went to school." He was lucky—he went to the local two-room school for two years. But, like that of many other kids in America during those days, his good fortune was short-lived. When he was in the second grade, his mother became ill, and he had to quit school to help his fisherman father earn a living. By the age of twelve, he was going out on fishing boats in the Gulf of Mexico. But fishing didn't earn enough money; when Joseph was fifteen, he lied about his age and got a job as a roustabout in the oil fields. His employers soon found out "I was too young and I went back to fishing."

He recalls that between 1940 and 1951, "the people who had

money and everything—the whites—were trying to run us trappers and fishermen out. They used to put chains and locks running across canals to stop our boats. I dunno why they did what they did—maybe for selfishness, greed, or jealousy," Joe says. "Our people used to be able to live off the land and water, off anything—we could survive when they couldn't, and they hated us for it." It's doubtful if the reasons were that simplistic. But there was strife . . . and racial problems. "We had a rough time because we was a mixed breed, Indian and French, and white people didn't care no more for us than they did for blacks. They used to treat us the same way they did the blacks."

It was a racial confrontation outside of a Golden Meadow night-club that sent Williams to prison. "A white dude called me a nigger bastard," he recounts. "He had a beer bottle and tried to hit me with it, but I got my knife out first and stabbed him seven times." That got him a five-year sentence for aggravated battery, and on March 28, 1946, at the age of nineteen, he walked through the gates of Angola for the first time. "When I come here in 'forty-six, my people left Golden Meadow and moved to New Orleans on account of the harassment they was getting from the white people."

He was paroled out of Angola in 1949 and joined his family in New Orleans, where he met a young Spanish-Indian girl; they set up house-keeping in a small rented apartment. Williams remembers it as a warm, loving, and beautiful period in his life—the only one: "It was hard—we was just making ends meet." Off and on, he worked on an oyster boat and did odd jobs. "I liked to dance, but she didn't dance," he recounts wistfully. "She liked the movies, so we'd go to the movie, to the beach, the park, fishing—the things that we could afford or was free. . . . It was hard, but it was a beautiful life. It was love there." They had two children and she was pregnant with their third when he was arrested and accused of murdering a Golden Meadow woman during a burglary. Convicted six months later, he was returned to prison as a parole violator, with an additional life sentence.

Williams arrived at Angola on May 7, 1951, during a time of scandal and controversy. Three months earlier, thirty-seven Camp E and Camp H prisoners had slashed their Achilles tendons to protest brutality and the barbaric conditions of their imprisonment. The mass self-mutilation catapulted Angola into the national spotlight, provoking investigations into the operations of the prison and the manner of

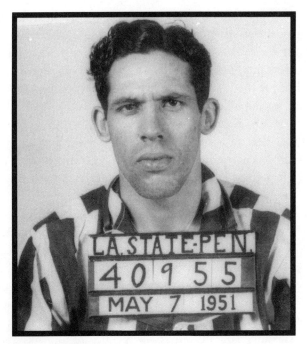

Joseph "Nigger Joe" Williams in 1951 (Courtesy The Angolite)

treatment accorded the prisoners. Bossing the convict-guards who rode herd over the prisoners were "redneck farmers and French-speaking Cajuns." Inmates lived in "camps," each under the dictatorial control of a captain who administered punishment as he saw fit. Testimony before a state investigating committee depicted the prison as a "sewer of degradation." Whippings and beatings were described as common. Vice and homosexuality were open and almost universal.

A few days after his arrival, Williams was transferred to the East Louisiana State Hospital at Jackson because "I was full of drugs, half crazy from being beaten and badly treated from when I was in jail in Lafourche." A month later he was returned to Angola, where he joined the rest of the prisoners in the cane field. About a year later, he was made a convict-guard, a position of trust and privilege and one that rescued him from the backbreaking labor in the field. Two months later, he quit. He was punished with eight days in the infamous Red Hat (solitary punishment cell), then sent back to the field. He cut cane for four years before being switched to the cotton field;

picking cotton was a little easier. Altogether, Williams spent ten years working in the field. And, like most prisoners, he acquired a nick-name—"Nigger Joe." Grinning sheepishly, he explains: "I got that a long time ago 'cause when I'd be out in the sun, I'd get so dark till they started calling me Niggah Joe . . . plus, they said that when I'd get mad, I'd act like a niggah."

It was a hard and violent time, and Williams saw his share of danger, fights, strikes, violence, and death—but he survived. He was a fighter, but "he was a good prisoner," says Deputy Warden R. Hilton Butler, who arrived at Angola a year after Williams.

Henry A. Kellogg is a Shreveport businessman. His son came to Angola with a five-year sentence for simple burglary. That was in 1973, a particularly violent time when rape and murder were part of the fabric of life in prison. "He [Kellogg's son] was only seventeen," Kellogg told The Angolite. "Joe helped him, kept him out of trouble and protected him from being turned into one of those punks. He had compassion for our son, and we really appreciate it." But it wasn't until the son was paroled in 1975 that Kellogg and his wife, Patricia, learned that Williams had protected their son from sexual violence. "That's when we took an interest in Joe, and started writing him regularly, and sending him little things at Christmas," Patricia Kel-logg says.

Williams wanted his freedom, but he had a problem. He was basically a man alone in the world. His relatives and former friends had gone on with their own lives. Both his parents had died during his confinement and he had only one sister left trying to help him, "but she ain't got no education," Williams told The Angolite. "She don't know what to do. She just like me." When the pain of his imprisoned existence got the best of him, he and Daniel Ordner simply escaped. Once they were apprehended, the prison's disciplinary board took twenty-five days of earned goodtime* away from each of them, then took them to court in St. Francisville, where they were both convicted of simple escape and sentenced to an additional two years. Williams also lost his trusty status and was made to spend a year in the cellblock because of the escape. He also had an application for clem-ency pending before the Louisiana Board of Pardons when he escaped. Because of the escape, he was denied. (Ironically, Ordner was granted

*sentence reduction awarded for good behavior

parole a year later by the Louisiana Board of Paroles—in spite of the escape.)

In 1977, Williams had been locked up twenty-six years. He sent off a letter to Lake Charles attorney Jack Rogers, asking his fee. "But he knew I didn't have no money when he talked to me," he said. "But he said that, as long as I'd been locked up and with the kind of prison record I have, I should've been out. He took my case for free and said he was gonna try to get me out." Rogers filed an application for clemency for Williams with the Board of Pardons.

For the first time, Williams called upon the Kelloggs for help—but not for himself. He sent them copies of the story *The Angolite* had just printed about Cocky Moore, the old black man who had been locked up longer than anyone else. "[He asked] if we could help find a place for him to stay and all," Patricia Kellogg recounts. "He wasn't even thinking of helping himself. He was trying to get help for Frank Moore."

"First our son, then this old man—that told us a whole lot about the kind of man he was," Henry Kellogg says, "a man who thought of other people before he thinks of himself. A man who could do that has to be a good man, a man with compassion for others." "So, later on, we asked him: 'What about you, Joe?' " Patricia Kellogg explains. "What can we do to help you get out of there?" And that's when he told us he was going up before the Pardon Board, and we told him that we would appear before the board for him and try to help him." They contacted Jack Rogers and became actively involved in the effort to get Williams out. They appeared before the Pardon Board, informing it that they would provide both employment and housing and any other assistance Williams might need if the board released him.

The Pardon Board also wanted to help Williams, and recommended a commutation of his combined sentences to fifty years. Shreveport evangelist Jerry Golden, a friend of the Kelloggs, threw his support to Williams and appealed to the governor on his behalf. On July 17, 1979, then-Governor Edwin Edwards signed the commutation, reducing Williams's sentence. "When Governor Edwards signed the pardon to have his sentence commuted to fifty years," Henry Kellogg says, "he signed it thinking that Joe had been in there almost thirty years and with his accumulated goodtime credit, he was releasing him with a fifty-year commutation."

"When the Pardon Board reduced his sentence," Rogers told *The*

Angolite, "I thought that there wouldn't be much question to his being released. That was the general feeling of those who were there at the board hearing."

"But then, we waited and waited, and he didn't get out," Patricia Kellogg says. "We didn't know what had happened—why he hadn't been released yet. We called the prison and it was then that we found out about him losing his goodtime."

Paul Seawell, prison records custodian, explained to *The Angolite:* "We ran across this escape charge and the law applicable to it, which says that, if convicted of escape, you lose all goodtime earned prior to the escape." Because of that clause, which applied to Williams's conviction for his 1976 escape, he had lost the extraordinary amount of twenty-eight years of goodtime. In the face of that loss, his release date was set at June 23, 1987—seven more years for him to serve before he satisfied the now-reduced-to-fifty-year sentence.

"Man, I had some real heat on this thing," Seawell recalls. "We got quite a few inquiries about why he wasn't out. Believe me, we didn't want to see him stuck here in prison with all of that time. None of us did. We tried our damnedest to find something in the law that would be beneficial to him—but there wasn't anything. We've got to go by the law in computing his time, and when he escapes . . . You know, I don't know why they even put that little clause in the law when they drafted it. Before then, the warden was able to restore goodtime if it was lost, but not after they drafted that law."

The reduction of Williams's sentence to fifty years would have meant his immediate release had it not been for that clause in the escape law. But knowledge of the clause came *after* the actions of the Pardon Board and the governor.

"The governor thought he was releasing Joe," Patricia Kellogg says. "We were at the pardon hearing and kept up with everything going on. Look, nobody knew about the escape thing. We were at the Pardon Board hearing, and they didn't know about it. Nobody brought it up. It was just overlooked by everybody." The Kelloggs contacted lawyers and friends in search of assistance. They appealed to Golden to talk to the governor again, who reportedly informed him that, if they could get a second commutation recommendation processed and back before him, he would sign it. "He had thought that, with Joe's goodtime, he was releasing him when he signed the papers," Patricia Kellogg told *The Angolite,* "but he added that he didn't think there would be time before he went out of office."

Had a mistake been made in not taking into account the clause in the escape law that demands forfeiture of all goodtime? Had the Pardon Board intended to release Williams when it recommended his sentence be reduced to fifty years? "Honestly," Margaret Bolton, vice chair of the Louisiana Board of Pardons, told *The Angolite*, "I can't truthfully tell you exactly what our intentions were. But, to the best of my recollection, and if I had to venture a guess at it, I would say that our intentions were probably to provide him immediate parole eligibility rather than discharge—in light of the fact that his escape was on the file and we would have known about it."

The possibility that the Pardon Board and the governor had, as the Kelloggs claim, intended to release Williams is strong. Seawell states that, prior to the board's action on Williams, he received a call from someone on the Pardon Board (he doesn't remember who) asking for computation information. "They didn't ask me specifically about Williams's case," he told *The Angolite*. "They asked me how many years would a man have to do on fifty years if he was sentenced before 1972, and I gave them the amount of time that the inmate would have to serve—which, on fifty years, is twenty-four years, eight months, and twenty-two days." Seawell says that he didn't know that the original query from the board was about Williams until Mel Pierce, a classification officer at Department of Corrections headquarters, called to convey information concerning some commutations that had just been received by his office. "One of the commutations Mel gave me was for Williams and, in view of how long he had been here and his time being cut to fifty years, there was a good chance that he would be overdue for release. But I had his record in front of me and I saw where Williams had received a conviction and sentence on simple escape. And I was hoping that it was an *attempted* escape, so that he wouldn't lose all his goodtime." But further checking proved that Williams had been convicted of simple escape. "It was then that I realized what had happened," Seawell explains. "When the Pardon Board called me, asking for information, they had asked just about the life sentence. They didn't ask for any other information . . . just how much time was needed to discharge a fifty-year sentence."

Seawell states that, when Williams wasn't released, the Pardon Board called his office to find out why. While he doesn't recall who he talked to, he distinctly remembers the conversation because he estimates he spent about a half hour explaining the situation. "They talked to me about Joseph D. Williams and they said that they thought the fifty-year commutation would have cut him loose," he told *The Angolite,* "and I told them it would, under normal circumstances, but not in this case because of the escape."

On December 10, 1979, Seawell made a personal trip to meet with Williams in the main prison's "A" Building to explain to the old man why he wouldn't be getting out of prison.

The application to Williams of the clause in the escape law demanding forfeiture of all goodtime has provoked profound questions about its constitutionality. Seawell, who must enforce the law in his computation of the sentences of inmates, is one of the first to express his dissatisfaction with it, and particularly with its application to Williams.

"I personally don't like to see a man lose that much goodtime as a result of an escape. I feel we should be able to discipline an inmate without penalizing him so severely," he told *The Angolite.* "This man had been here—let's say twenty-eight years. Now, he had earned twenty-eight years' goodtime. He escaped. The law provides for an additional two years' penalty for escape, which it gave Williams. That should have been sufficient. . . . You have a situation in which his punishment for escape is even longer than the amount of time he's already served on the original charge of murder. That's too harsh. . . ."

"I probably know Joe Williams better than anybody you could talk to about him," Deputy Warden Butler stated. Butler has worked in prison security for twenty-eight years and went on almost every chase during that period. He knows about convicts and escapes and doesn't see Williams's 1976 escape as a reason to keep him in prison. "I don't think he had any real intention of running, 'cause he had many chances to leave," Butler explains. "If he really had wanted to escape, he could have left here anytime he wanted, with a twenty-four-hour head start—but he didn't. Hell, he went unsupervised. We trusted him. He'd go as much as twenty-four hours without an officer ever seeing him. . . . I think he just got drunk and run off. If he hadn't fooled with that alcohol, I don't think he would have run." The amount of significance that Butler attaches to the escape is demonstrated by the fact that he restored Williams's former trusty status after the escape and wrote a letter to the Pardon Board requesting that the board grant Williams clemency. "He's done a lot of time, and I've known him for many years," Butler says. "And I feel that, especially after doing that much time, he deserves another chance in the free world."

Butler doesn't like the application of the escape law's goodtime-forfeiture clause to Williams. "I don't think it's right," he declares flatly. "They took too much of his goodtime. The two years they gave him for escaping was enough. There should be a limit on how much goodtime you can lose. I mean—where an ordinary escapee loses only two years or so, Joe Williams lost what—almost thirty? That's wrong."

A jailhouse lawyer–substitute, David Nelson (since released from prison), filed a petition in the Nineteenth Judicial District Court challenging the constitutionality of the application of the escape law's goodtime-forfeiture clause to Williams. Kathleen Stewart Richey, an attorney with the Baton Rouge Public Defender's Office, is handling the case. In her presentation of the issue, Richey is zeroing in on the question of whether or not the state has the right to sentence someone for simple escape and simultaneously deprive him of all earned goodtime. She argues that to do so violates the double jeopardy prohibition of the Constitution. A second argument is that the clause's application to Williams, in particular, violates the "cruel and unusual punishment" prohibition of the Constitution, in that the goodtime Williams lost far exceeds the maximum penalty provided for the charge of simple escape itself. Unlike the federal constitution, Louisiana's constitution also prohibits "excessive" punishment.

Argues Richey, "It seems to me that twenty-eight years, eight days is an awful lot of earned goodtime to lose because of simple escape. The problem is that the law doesn't make distinctions—a prisoner who has served only one year loses only that if he escapes, whereas the man who has served thirty years loses thirty if he escapes. The statute applies equally and it has harsh applications. In this case, the application seems rather harsh."

Seawell agrees. Like Butler, he believes "there should be a limit on how much goodtime, as well as commutation, a man can lose." He's pleased that the Williams case is before the courts. "It's only been contested once, in 1979, but the inmate didn't question the constitutionality of the statute itself," he says. "It's too vague as it's written, and there's the matter of application—in which it is extremely harsh but only for a few selected individuals, like in the Williams case.

Nigger Joe in 1980 (Courtesy The Angolite)

There's definitely the need for a limit and clarification of the law."

The State Attorney General's Office, in its response to litigation filed on Williams's behalf, is arguing that the application of the good-time-forfeiture clause to Williams is not unconstitutional and has asked the court to dismiss his claim. The staff attorney handling the Williams case declined to discuss it with *The Angolite*. Action on the case has been delayed by the commissioner, pending the outcome of another case on the same issue awaiting a ruling by the State Supreme Court.

While the escape law's goodtime-forfeiture clause prevented Williams from being immediately discharged, the commutation of his sentence to fifty years did make him eligible for parole consideration.

And, in the face of the snafu over Williams's goodtime, Jack Rogers asked the Parole Board to grant him a parole. Following a hearing on the request, the Parole Board refused. "It was a surprise to me that they didn't parole him," Rogers told *The Angolite*. In fact, it was a surprise to everyone. Rogers added: "I don't think that anyone really had any thought that the Parole Board wouldn't release him."

But the board didn't. The official reasons given for the denial of parole:

1. nature of original offense (which is why Williams is in prison)
2. prior felony conviction (which he served time for in 1946)
3. parole violation (which is why he was sent to prison in 1951)
4. escape (which few prison officials attach any significance to)
5. law-enforcement and judicial opposition (which is twenty-nine years old, political, and beyond Williams's ability to do anything about)

"They didn't deny me," Williams declares. "They *judged* me. They denied me because I'm an innocent man in prison and they know it."

Innocence. That's something Williams has maintained since he came to prison. He's been saying it for the past twenty-nine years. No prisoner in Louisiana has remained so steadfast, for so long, in a claim of innocence as he. When *The Angolite* talked to him in 1976 during our investigation of the plight of long-termers, he emphasized that he was innocent and implored us to try to interest the Pardon Board or some state official to give him lie-detector tests, truth serum or anything else that would allow him a chance to prove to someone that he's telling the truth. But once you're in prison, no one hears the cries, no one is interested. Too many have cried wolf in the past. The general feeling among the public is that you must have done something wrong, otherwise the police wouldn't have brought you to court. And once you're in prison, people doubly disbelieve that you could have passed through the police, the lawyers, the courts, and a trial, and yet be innocent.

But Williams never had a trial. And those few who have bothered to look into his case have serious reservations about his guilt and the rightness of his conviction. Richey had not yet been born when the crime occurred. "In this minute entry I have set forth all of the evidence the state had against Williams," she told *The Angolite*, "it would not have been enough to convict him."

Williams was indicted for the October 23, 1950, murder of a Mrs. Louis Pitre of Golden Meadow. A description of the crime and the reasons for Williams's conviction are on file in an entry of court minutes, dated May 9, 1951, and signed by the district attorney and the sentencing judge. According to the entry, the victim was a widow. Her unmarried son, Louis, lived with her in her small home beside Bayou Lafourche about five hundred feet below the corporate limits of Golden Meadow. He was a fisherman, and absent from the residence on the day and night the crime was committed. The victim was last seen alive at seven P.M. on the night of her death; she had been visiting a close neighbor, and at about that time she entered her home. Her body was found the next morning by one of her daughters in the front room of the house. She had been choked to death, and her feet were tied together. Her home had been ransacked and authorities took that to indicate that robbery was the motive for the murder. The coroner placed her death at a short time before midnight.

According to the court document, Williams was reportedly seen "by a disinterested and reliable witness, walking rapidly away from the direction of the residence" at eleven o'clock on the night of the murder. When seen, he was sixteen feet from the front step of the house. At five o'clock the following morning, he was reported to have been seen again, by another reliable witness, at a point less than 150 feet from the front gate of the yard "and standing on the side of the public highway along Bayou Lafourche, in a fashion indicating to witnesses that he was waiting for an opportunity to secure a ride either by truck or automobile, to some point away from the scene of the crime." While Williams was in jail, the document continues, he made "a number of incriminating admissions [to the parish sheriff] of facts respecting which he could have known nothing unless he had been recently in the residence of the victim." On May 5, 1951, the entry states, Williams pleaded guilty in open court and was sentenced to life imprisonment.

There appears to have been little real evidence that Williams actually committed the murder. Testimony during the Pardon Board hearing revealed that the victim was a relative of Williams and that people regularly went in and out of her home at all times of the day and night, so that anyone could have gone into the house and killed her without attracting much attention.

"I told the law that I was innocent and that I knew nothing of the crime," Williams says. "But they said that they didn't want my statement. They wanted me to sign the statement they had. They beat and threatened me—every day. They used to come at night most of the time. They beat me with a rubber hose, their nightsticks, and did different things to me." Williams states that he refused to give in to the brutal interrogations and continued to claim his innocence, that he signed nothing.

Sam Monk Zeldon was retained to defend him. "My parole officer told my people I needed a good criminal lawyer and that he was a good one," Williams recalls. "He came three times, trying to get me to talk to him. I told him that I was in New Orleans with my wife and baby when this happened. I told him I didn't know nothing about the crime. Later, when he told me he was a personal friend of the chief of police, I didn't want to talk to him no more."

The grand jury indicted Williams on the basis of the sheriff's claim that Williams had made incriminating statements during interrogation. On March 9, 1951, Zeldon filed a motion asking the court to make the sheriff produce the "incriminating statements" allegedly made to him by Williams. Whether they were produced or not, *The Angolite* cannot determine. But Williams claims that he was pressured to change his plea to guilty. On May 5, 1951, he asked the court to do so. "I did that only in the hope of staying alive so that one day I could prove my innocence," he told *The Angolite*. A couple of days later, Williams was transferred to Angola. While *The Angolite* could not locate any correctional officer who knew about what condition Williams was in when he arrived at the prison, prison records show that Angola authorities found it necessary to transfer him soon after to the East Louisiana State Hospital for some type of treatment. Williams says it was because "I was full of drugs, half crazy from being beaten and badly treated from when I was in jail." He remained in the hospital a month.

"Since we got involved in trying to get Joe out, we've done a lot of checking," Henry Kellogg says. "And I can tell you this—and even lawyers have told me—that, if Joe would have went to court today with the evidence they said they had against him, they'd throw the case out of court. . . . I don't say that Joe did it or not—but he's paid for it. I don't believe in holding a man down all his life because he may have made a mistake."

If it weren't for the oversight of the escape law's goodtime-forfeiture clause, Williams would be free today. But even more than the questions of fairness and justice that the application of the law to Williams provokes, there is the haunting wail of his declared innocence over twenty-nine years of pain and suffering, the plea of one who has never complained against even the hardest conditions of prison but has never ceased to cry his innocence. He has served more time than anyone in the state's entire prison system today . . . and still he cries.

"I've looked into it and read everything there was on it," Rogers says. "The case they had against him was circumstantial. It was merely a matter of who you believed. He said that he didn't do it, but they had others who said he did and placed him in the vicinity."

"If they ever give me a day in court with a good attorney, I'm going to prove to the public that I'm not no vile man, that I did not commit the crime—and all I ask is to be given this chance," Williams says. "It's not like it used to be. People in the courts now will listen."

[August 1980]

 Postscript

After serving thirty-five years, Joseph Williams walked out of prison the day after Governor Edwin Edwards signed a second clemency, to time served, on May 14, 1986.

That same year, the Louisiana legislature amended state law to limit the forfeiture of accrued goodtime for prisoners who committed "simple" escape to "not less than one month nor more than two years," but leaving the forfeiture of *all* accrued goodtime only for those who commit "aggravated" escape.

Williams's court case became moot when his second clemency was granted by Governor Edwards.

THE DYNAMICS OF PAROLE

||||

Wilbert Rideau

 ## Myths, Politics, Realities

The early-morning countryside whips past as the petite blonde gazes out the window of the car. Her thoughts are elsewhere. Like her companions, she's traveled this route so regularly that she's come to know the sights and smells along the highway, the wording of the road signs, and even the traffic patterns of different areas. She is the chairwoman of the Louisiana Board of Paroles.

Pamela Harris and her fellow board members are en route to one of the state prison facilities to conduct parole hearings. With a sky-rocketing prison population, the Parole Board members find themselves spending more time traveling around the state to conduct hearings than they spend in their Baton Rouge offices. And, as the car speeds toward its destination, Harris perhaps feels more like a truck-driver married to the highway than a chic state official. "The chairmanship of the Parole Board is a very over-glamorized job, not at all what it's generally thought to be," the thirty-four-year-old Mississippi native told *The Angolite*.

A prison official is there to greet their arrival at the institution. Somewhere, a group of prisoners awaits the start of the proceedings.

Aside from a trial or a court hearing, this is the only time during their incarceration that the criminal-justice system affords prisoners the opportunity to address a decision-making body with the power to free them or continue their confinement. Some use the waiting time to visit with lawyers, friends, or relatives who will appear before the board with them.

The prisoners know that most, if not all, will be denied freedom, and will have to wait another six to nine months before being able to apply for reconsideration. Some wait anxiously, hope winging in their hearts; others expect only that they can take advantage of being off work for a day. All are generally neat in pressed prison uniforms and shined shoes as they mentally go over the questions they feel board members might ask them.

"I know they're attempting to put their best foot forward and I appreciate the fact that they do," board member Albert Alexander told *The Angolite*. "Although they may sometimes be considered as trying to con the members, I believe this is a point in their favor in one sense." Philosophically, Alexander regards himself as a conservative, but his belief system extends hope and compassion to others. "People make mistakes," he explains, "and a lot of people are due forgiveness for those mistakes. I don't hold a personal grudge against anyone. Parole is a second chance—if the person deserves it."

He likes the job, but it has its drawbacks. "You see some people that you put a lot of confidence in and they disappoint you," he states. "I have a lot of faith in people and I guess I just brush it aside and go on, but it's disappointing, especially when you give a young person, who's already on thin ice to begin with, a real opportunity to correct his life and he promises you faithfully that he will, and then immediately starts doing wrong again." But the outcome of one doesn't affect Alexander's judgment of others. As he points out, each individual is different.

The Parole Board consists of five members, all of whom are appointed by the governor and serve at his discretion. Since there are no special qualifications required by law, the membership of the board generally reflects the politics of the state and the philosophy of the governor. As a result, today's board is all-Republican and very conservative.

The proceedings begin and the inmates are ushered in, one at a time, to face the board members, all seated behind a rectangular table.

Questions are asked and the inmate and his supporters are given the opportunity to speak on his behalf. Law enforcement representatives also appear, usually to oppose the inmate's request for parole. The average hearing takes about thirty minutes, but there is no official time limitation and the board will generally accord a case whatever amount of time it deems necessary, sometimes even continuing a case to secure additional information. Far more information is available to today's Parole Board to aid it in making a decision than ever before—police reports, the results of tests, prison progress reports, court records, unofficial information gathered by prison security and police intelligence, medical records, and so on. The board sometimes orders psychological tests and evaluations of parole applicants and assigns parole agents to investigate and secure any additional information it might desire.

Seeing and talking to the applicant is felt to be essential to the decision-making process. "We definitely should look at him," Alexander told *The Angolite*. "I would be opposed to just studying his file and not looking at the individual, because his appearance, behavior, and reactions before the board tells us a lot too."

But there is no formula that will enable the board to positively detect whether the inmate appearing before it is a good guy or a bad one. "Burglars have the highest recidivism rate, and forgers are high up there," Harris states. "Murderers have the lowest. . . ." But those studies deal with classes, not the individual who is standing before the board.

"I look at his record," Harris says. "I look at his behavior in the institution. If he's taken part in clubs and activities, that's fine. That's no major hurdle for me, though. It's like—people say, well, he should have completed his education or gotten a G.E.D. Not everybody is meant to have a G.E.D., not everybody benefits by it so much. I think everybody needs to learn to read and write, but the fact that a guy got his G.E.D.—that doesn't make him look any better to me. That's to his benefit while he's serving time, to make it as easy as possible and to pursue something he wants to do."

But even the prisoner's file is considered with a grain of salt. "I've seen men come before the Parole Board who, for one year prior to coming before the board, will discontinue any disruptive behavior," Harris explains, "and if they are turned down, they go right back to that disruptive behavior.

"I look at what their plans for the future are going to be," she adds. "I look at what sort of support they have in the community or the family, if they've got children to support, if they have a wife who is emotionally supportive. I look at everything. I wouldn't turn a man down because he has no one, but I look at all the factors. In my mind, I run through kind of a little point system."

The board members all do basically the same thing. "Regardless of how the member next to me looks at [each case], I look at it on its own merits," Alexander explains. "I check his institutional behavior, his progress in the institution. If he has made no effort since he has been in there, if he hasn't accomplished very much—he's better locked up than he is outside if he's not trying to better himself."

In the final analysis, it's a very arbitrary decision, based on the subjective feelings of each individual board member, and the majority vote wins. Harris doesn't like the arbitrariness of it and would like to see the present method changed. "The federal people work on a point system and what that does is it sets up certain criteria that you look at and you add points for certain crimes, for behavior in the penitentiary—that sort of thing," she explains. "One of my goals with this board, in the future, is to get us to a point of understanding where we can review a file and sit back and say, All right, the nature of the crime—you can go from zero to five points. If it's a violent crime, rape of a child, he gets five points. Prison behavior—and I'm not talking about your face cloth being on the end of your bed—I'm talking about homosexual acts or, you know, if I see fights, I want to know the reason why. If someone's trying to turn you out, I'd expect you to fight. But, if what you're doing is displaying just violent behavior for the sake of being a violent person, you ought to get five points on that. See? If you've shown a pattern of violent behavior since you've been incarcerated, you ought to get five points on that, and so on."

The Parole Board of today must function in a hostile political atmosphere, given the present crime hysteria and law-and-order politics. Because parole has never been properly explained to the general public, they have never understood it and, over the years, have come to view it as "coddling of the criminal," something they don't want. This foundation of public ignorance has made Parole Board decisions extremely vulnerable to unscrupulous law enforcement officials and grandstanding politicians hunting for political mileage or a thirty-second TV spot on the evening news. As a result, some parole decisions are particularly courageous.

The board doesn't forget victims. Wherever possible and reasonable, they insist on restitution to the victim as a condition of parole. Harris reports that, during 1980, $110,000 was collected from parolees for their victims.

The decisions the board is called upon to make aren't easy ones. Sybil Fullerton served as Parole Board chairwoman for sixteen years before retiring in 1979. "The last decision was just as hard to make as the first," she observed. "You can't win. You have trouble from this side or another every time you parole an inmate. But you have to keep an open mind. Every case is an individual case."

Once the board gets past the initial difficulty of deciding who will be released on parole, the most important aspect of parole then comes into play: supervision.

The task of supervising the parolee falls to the Department of Corrections' Probation and Parole Division, headed by William Dunn. It has a staff of 297 agents, working out of sixteen district offices around the state. In addition to parolees, they are also responsible for the supervision of all persons placed on probation by courts around the state. Since the supervision of parolees and probationers is not handled separately, and the two are essentially the same, all of the agents function as both probation and parole agents. At the end of March 1981, the 297 agents were keeping track of 17,733 people—about 16,000 probationers and only 1,629 parolees. Without this parole supervision, it would cost the state almost $1 billion to house prisoners in penal institutions, and an additional $300,000 a day to maintain them there.

Paul Piercey is a probation-parole agent working out of the Baton Rouge office. A former insurance investigator, he's been with the Department of Corrections for the past eleven years. "Basically, we try to get a probationer or parolee to just do the things that an average citizen would do," he explained. "When you boil it all down, that's what it amounts to. We try to get them to work, to hold down a job, support their families, to stay out of trouble, to not violate the law, and generally meet the conditions of their parole or probation." If, at any point, the offender proves uncooperative or violates the conditions of his parole or probation, his freedom is terminated and he is sent to prison to serve out the remainder of his sentence. It is this threat and his fear of it, officials point out, that gives the offender incentive to discipline himself and stay out of trouble.

"Each case is different," Piercey says. "I've seen cases where a guy goes into prison and the shock of it scares him so badly, he comes out and never acts up again—I mean, he won't even spit on the sidewalk. He is straight. On the other hand, others go up to prison and because of their individual personalities, come out a little worse and, yeah, they require a little more supervision, but, again, it's a matter of individuals."

Probation-parole agents function as a combination social worker, police officer, and counselor, helping a parolee with his problems on one hand while policing him on the other. There is always a personal risk factor with the job. The agents are authorized to carry guns but, unlike cops, they generally don't do so unless they feel a necessity for it. "Of course . . . you really never know exactly when it's going to be necessary," Piercey points out. "Some little guy that you think will never give you any trouble at all might be the one to lower the boom on you one day." So "when we go to make an arrest, we'll wear one."

Probation-parole agents must have college degrees, but their starting pay is less than that of state police officers, who are only required to be high school graduates. The state trooper is provided with a gun, ammunition, a vehicle, and a clothing allowance, while a probation-parole agent must furnish his own. It's a neglected profession. "We've always realized that," Piercey told *The Angolite,* pointing out that "when I first started, we were at the tail end of everything. As far as funding went, we were at the very bottom of the ladder. . . . Our turnover rate was just atrocious—seventy-five percent of [the staff] had just left. We were always hiring and rehiring." That situation has only begun to stabilize over the past several years because of retirement benefits and a gradual increase in pay. But Piercey still points to inadequate salaries as the biggest obstacle facing the probation-parole operation: "You just can't attract too many good, qualified people without adequate salaries."

The agents' work loads are intimidating. "The caseload right now is 101 cases per field agent," Charlie Adams, a staff specialist with the division, told *The Angolite.* "The ideal caseload is fifty per agent."

If law enforcement forms the front of the criminal-justice system, then the parole-probation agents act as the system's backbone. "We do very important work for the courts," Piercey explains. "Every time somebody commits a felony in this state, we nearly every time do a presentence investigation. It's a background check on the offender and it helps the judge determine what sentence to give them." The agents also do clemency investigations for the Board of Pardons, as well as pre-parole investigations for the Parole Board—"a whole slew of different types of investigations that takes up as much as half of an agent's time."

A common belief among convicts is that the Parole Board is more likely to grant a parole if they're leaving the state rather than staying in. "That's a big grapevine rumor," board chairwoman Harris retorts. "The reality is that it doesn't make any difference." This is because of the Interstate Probation and Parole Compact, which governs all fifty states. "The compact was originally formed when John Dillinger and Pretty Boy Floyd, who were parolees, were going from one state to another committing crimes," explains compact president Victor Townsley. "Back then, you didn't have extradition and you didn't have the compact. A probationer or parolee was pretty well free to do what he wanted to if he went to another state. And, of course, there were 'sundown paroles,' where some people just wanted to get rid of a guy, so they'd just turn him loose in another state, putting him on parole and telling him not to come back. Well, it was as a result of all these abuses that, in 1934, the Uniform Crime Control Act was passed, permitting the states to go into a compact or compacts."

The Interstate Probation and Parole Compact was one of the agreements deriving from that authority; it enabled states to transfer offenders to other states and ensure that supervision of them would be maintained. "Once you go under the compact," Townsley told *The Angolite,* "there's no such thing as extradition." If the parolee violates the conditions of his parole in another state, he can be returned to Louisiana immediately without going through extradition proceedings.

The compact is basically a legal agreement between the states to supervise each other's parolees and probationers. The compact has also made parole and probation conditions and supervision more uniform among the states. The Parole Board or a judge can send an offender to another state and the receiving state will assume supervision of the individual. Because of the reciprocal nature of the compact, Louisiana supervises a number of parolees and probationers from other states. And, according to Townsley, an increasing number of offenders in other states are asking to be placed on probation or parole in Louisiana. "Jobs are good here," he explains. "Jobs are better here than in most states, especially the type of job that you can get if you have been in trouble—you know, like in the oil field, offshore, and so on." As a result, he states, "we supervise more people from other states than other states supervise for us . . . and we've got a helluva lot of parolees and probationers down here that we don't even know about who ran off from other states. They're picking them up daily—they're on the run, and the oil industry is a good place to work, and they don't ask too many questions."

Despite the problems of inadequate pay and staffing, Townsley points to Louisiana's probation-parole operation with pride, calling it the most professional in the nation. "You can take all the states, any state, and compare their operation with ours, from top to bottom," he says, "and I guarantee you won't find a state that's set up as good as we are."

But parole officials are not without complaints, and the biggest one has to do with the public's confused conception of parole, which is perpetuated by the news media's own lack of understanding of what parole is.

Parole is the conditional release of a prisoner, under supervision, at some point after he has served one-third of his sentence in prison. This is the only form of release that the Parole Board is responsible for. However, parole is commonly confused with:

1. Probation, which is the suspension of the enforcement of a sentence imposed by a court upon a person convicted of a crime, with conditions laid down by the court that must be met within a specified period of time. In Louisiana, only judges possess the power to place someone on probation.
2. Pardons and commutations of sentences, which are acts of executive clemency and can only be granted by the governor, upon the recommendation of the Board of Pardons.
3. Goodtime release, which is a statutory reduction of a prisoner's sentence in return for good behavior, something that is determined solely by the legislature and earned by the prisoner.

Unfortunately for parole and the entire system facilitating it, the general public has never been able to distinguish it from the other forms of release and usually calls all of them parole. This confusion about parole has plagued it throughout its history, resulting in a public image that has little in common with the reality.

In his book, *Conscience and Convenience,* a penetrating analysis of the criminal-justice system of the past eighty years, Columbia University professor David J. Rothman points out that parole has always been the "most unpopular of all reform measures. Parole became the whipping boy for the failures of law enforcement agencies to control or reduce crime. Whenever fears of a 'crime wave' swept through the country, or whenever a particularly senseless or tragic crime occurred, parole has invariably born the brunt of attack."

Parole, being the last link in the criminal-justice chain, has traditionally paid for all the inadequacies of the system. To understand why parole has survived all these years of criticism, one must look at whom it served. Originally, the strongest supporters of parole were prison wardens. Before 1925, wardens routinely sat on parole boards, and by the mid-1920s they had helped establish a parole bureaucracy. Rothman writes that:

> wardens found themselves locked into the system once it was in operation. They were compelled to favor its perpetuation for the critical reason that any talk of diminution in the availability of parole (let alone its outright abolition) provoked substantial inmate hostility—and wardens did not enjoy suppressing riots. Under indeterminate sentences, any effort to restrict parole had to mean significant increases in time served. Almost invariably, then, wardens were eager to see more and more paroles granted to keep peace among the inmates.

The running feud one warden maintained with the Washington State Parole Board illustrates that kind of reasoning. His position was that when a convict puts in a lot of time and is denied any chance of making parole, resentment occurs—and enough pent-up resentment leads to serious trouble for the prison. The warden went so far as to take issue with the Parole Board's policy of refusing to grant paroles to third offenders. He was not alone in his thinking. Most wardens traditionally recommended parole because it maintained discipline. Rothman states that "wardens were parole's warmest friends. They supported the system and were eager to keep the numbers granted parole as high as possible—always excepting that difficult case which had to be made into an object lesson."

Decision makers in the justice system have long recognized that parole serves as a safety valve for overcrowded prison conditions. Such conditions not only pose a serious problem of control for the wardens, they also force legislatures to appropriate more funds to construct new prisons to accommodate the overcrowding. That solution has never been popular with the taxpayers; therefore, legislators also liked to see paroles handed out. The legislators, while sometimes stung by scandalous investigative news reports about parole or the failure of a parolee, were still not prepared to spend fifty-plus million in tax dollars for a new prison, because that meant increasing taxes.

The benefits of parole did not go untapped by judges, either. While they lost some of their control over sentences to parole boards, they made up for it by increasing the minimum sentence-service requirement on indeterminate sentences. Parole permitted judges to have their cake and eat it too, because they were able to satisfy society's demand for long sentences while knowing full well that the inmates would not serve them. If inmates were forced to do so, prison populations would burst the seams of the nation's prisons.

Of all the links in the criminal-justice chain, district attorneys have traditionally favored parole more than any other. Rothman explains why:

> Their instincts for law and order tempted them to join in the chorus condemning the release procedures, but no matter how keenly they may have wished to endorse a get-tough-with-the-criminal position, to lengthen sentences and to curtail parole, their self-interest precluded it. The district attorneys, as we have noted, wanted to facilitate plea bargaining; and reducing parole board prerogatives or allowing judges to set minimums that were just short of the maximums would complicate the process. So too, longer sentences might discourage those charged with crimes from striking a bargain; if the difference in time to be served between robbery, first-degree, and robbery, second degree, was not substantial, or if the penalty remained severe, they might choose a jury trial over the plea bargaining alternative. Parole offered the prosecutors another critical advantage [:] . . . [a] parolee apprehended for a new crime or suspected of one

could be revoked [returned to the penitentiary] without going through [the formality of a trial]. . . . And, to the district attorneys, who always had one eye trained on the court docket, this was no small advantage.

The nation's departure from determinate to indeterminate sentencing didn't help the parole system at all, because people compared the maximum sentence with the actual time served. The general public felt that offenders, by being given a parole, were cheating the maximum—but they never troubled to look at how much time the offender might have served under the previous determinate sentences. Actually, parole increases the supervision of the offender after his release. Rothman quotes one crime commission, which pointed out: "Parole is not leniency. On the contrary, parole really increases the State's period of control. It adds to the period of imprisonment a further period of months or even years of supervision." Rothman adds that "the introduction of the indeterminate sentence and parole encouraged and promoted an increase in time served. . . . It is clear that the maximums established under indeterminate sentences were generally longer than the fixed time that judges dispensed under determinate sentences."

Thus, in conclusion, it can be said that parole has been good to the criminal-justice system because it has faithfully served the legitimate interests of wardens, judges, legislators, and district attorneys.

Conversely, however, release decisions by parole boards have come under concentrated political attack by legislators, criminal justice system officials, and the public, with cries for either the elimination of parole or the restriction of the discretionary powers of the Parole Board. During this period there has been a national trend toward restricting parole and replacing it with mandatory sentences.

Two divergent and contradictory forces prompted this movement. One was the public's alarm over the continued rise in crime and violence and the criticism that parole release undercuts the deterrent effectiveness of criminal law, depriving sentencing of certainty and thereby contributing to recidivism and high crime rates. The other force evolved from discontent with the arbitrary and inequitable way in which parole is issued, the wide disparities in prison terms, and the unfair treatment accorded the many prisoners whose requests for parole are denied as arbitrarily as others' are granted. Thus, the assault on parole has come from the combined efforts of law-and-order advocates and reformists—two usually opposing forces.

But, as Michael Kannansohn of the National Council on Crime and Delinquency pointed out in December of 1979, following his annual survey of parole-related legislation for the Justice Department, the momentum of this trend has slowed considerably. State legislators around the nation have come to recognize the substantial economic implications and the inevitable corrections problems inherent in lengthening sentences and ending any mechanisms to shorten prison terms in the future. As prison populations skyrocket and penal institutions continue to explode in violence, the voice of reason has apparently begun to reassert itself, and more and more legislators and state officials are beginning to recognize the reality, that parole is not a coddling of the criminal but a realistic, economical, and effective way of maintaining control over an offender.

‖‖‖ The Face of Parole ‖‖‖

The United States locks up a greater proportion of its population than any other country in the world except the [former] Soviet Union and South Africa. According to *Corrections* magazine, the U.S. prison population has risen 42 percent since January 1, 1975, when the number incarcerated was 225,528. On January 1, 1981, federal and state correctional facilities held 320,583 adult prisoners, an increase of 13,376 inmates since January 1, 1980. Most states report overcrowding in their facilities, with many prisoners held in local jails awaiting vacancies in the state penal system.

A prison's population level is governed by the number of court commitments and the average length of incarceration of its inmates. The length of incarceration is determined by a number of factors. The first is the maximum amount of time that a prisoner can be kept in prison as determined by law, the judge, or the paroling authority. Other factors are the various kinds of discretionary release—parole, executive clemency, or a court order modifying or setting aside a sentence. A prisoner may escape his confinement, or death can terminate it. Goodtime can reduce the maximum and, in some states, may shorten the time until parole eligibility or the date of parole release. The parole violation rate, the parole usage rate, and prison time served are controlled by the paroling authority, and the impact of the discretionary control of paroling authorities on prison population is considerable.

From a management perspective, discretionary parole has traditionally been viewed as a safety valve: Reducing prison sentences and increasing the number of inmates paroled have been two means of reducing and controlling prison population growth. The state of Georgia recently employed this method to deal with overcrowding in its penal facilities. On March 16, 1981, the state released 1,100 prisoners who were within six months of their official release dates. News reports quoted Parole Board chairman James T. Morris as stating that while his board was "very, very reluctant to engage in this kind of release program . . . the state has a problem, and we are the only authorized agency that has the legal authority to address it." His board is expected to release as many as 150 inmates a month for the rest of the year.

A new form of parole release is on the increase nationwide, and California has adopted it for all prisoners leaving its institutions. It is mandatory parole release, by which prisoners are denied the conventional, discretionary parole but required to accept parole conditions and sanctions when released early as a result of goodtime deductions. Traditionally, prisoners obtaining early release through goodtime reduction of their sentences were simply discharged from prison at the gate and allowed to go their merry way. However, concern over recidivism has caused more and more states to pass legislation mandating some type of supervisory control for a specified period after their release from prison.

Nationwide the majority of prisoners are released on parole. According to the U.S. Bureau of Justice Statistics, an estimated 155,000 people were on parole in the United States at the end of 1974. By the end of 1979, there were 196,500 adults on parole, and an additional 25,000 who were "mandatory releases"—that is, prisoners released to parole supervision as a result of goodtime or other statutory sentence-reduction measures.

Change in the use of parole from 1965 through 1978 was not uniform across the nation. According to the National Council on Crime and Delinquency, the greatest increase in the parole rate over that fourteen-year period occurred in the South. A substantial increase also appeared in the North Central states, while parole use remained comparatively stable in the Northeast and the West. The regions showing the least change in the relative frequency of parole started from much higher base rates—in 1965, the West's rate was close to 80 percent and the Northeast's rate was close to 75 percent. The South's high increase in parole started from a 1965 base rate just half as high, about 40 percent.

Contrary to the popular conception of parole that is created by sensational headlines about a parolee committing a crime, by the rhetoric of politicians, and by the Hollywood-manufactured image of people on parole, it is one of the most successful features of the nation's criminal-justice system. To be sure, some parolees fail and commit crimes, which is the side of parole that the public hears about. The side they don't hear about is that of the majority of parolees, who go on to become law-abiding and productive citizens. In 1981, the U.S. Department of Justice announced that a three-year study of the experience of the 64,000 people paroled during 1974 and 1975 found that only 25 percent had their paroles revoked. It also pointed out that many of those had been revoked for technical reasons—violating the conditions of their paroles—rather than for having actually committed crimes. It stated that "the traditional view that three-fourths of persons paroled are classifiable as successes is further reinforced by this latest study."

While parole usage has increased nationwide over the years, rising even faster than the prison population, the parole use rate in Louisiana actually declined. In 1960, Louisiana had 1,655 persons on parole. In 1980, there were 1,633 parolees—22 fewer, and this decrease came during a twenty-year period when the state's prison population rose 250 percent, from 3,633 in 1960 to almost 9,000 by the end of 1980! Probation, on the other hand, which is controlled by the courts, skyrocketed from 1,706 persons on probation in 1960 to 13,996 in 1980, an increase of 720 percent!

Of twenty-eight states studied by *The Angolite* to compare just how extensively they use parole, New Jersey was found to have 69 percent of the convicted felons in its custody on parole. Florida and Kentucky tied for second place, with both states having 68 percent of their charges on parole. The state of Louisiana ranked twenty-seventh in parole use, with only 15 percent of its adult correctional population on parole. Only Nebraska was lower, with 14 percent.

The states with the highest parole use rate were those with indeterminate sentencing. Their average was 41.5 percent. Louisiana and eight other states use determinate sentencing. The average parole use rate for this group was 31 percent. When compared specifically with this group of nine, Louisiana's parole use rate was the lowest.

(A comparison of Louisiana's parole use rate of 1960 with that of 1979 also shows a sharp decline. Of the 1,679 prisoners released from Department of Corrections custody in 1960, 904 [54 percent] exited via parole. By 1979, only 417 [22 percent] of the prisoners exiting the system during the year did so via parole.)

The poorest parole performance occurred in the Nebraska system, with that state having found it necessary to revoke the paroles of 47 percent of its parole population. Nebraska, however, has the twenty-seventh-smallest parole population of the twenty-eight states studied. Nebraska's high revocation rate was followed by Illinois, which revoked 39 percent of its paroles, and California, which revoked 31 percent. Of the states studied, twenty-three had a parole success rate of 82 percent or better for 1980.

Louisiana has one of the seven parole boards restricted to handling only paroles. The remainder of the twenty-eight boards studied have additional responsibilities, with eighteen of them also handling various forms of sentence reductions, commutations, and executive clemency and pardons.

Fifty percent of the states studied had no law requiring specific background qualifications for parole board members. Louisiana was one of those states. Of the states studied, twenty-two possess a full-time parole board. With twelve members, New York has the largest board, followed by Illinois, with ten, and California, with nine.

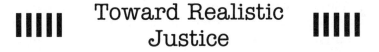

Toward Realistic Justice

Of conditions in all the penal systems in the United States, "the situation in Louisiana is perhaps the most grave," *Corrections* magazine stated in its April 1981 edition.

> The number of prisoners backed up in local jails nearly tripled there last year, to 1,267, accounting for a large part of the 1980 increase of 16 percent in the state's prisoners. The state opened two new prisons in the last year and a half, but these were immediately filled. A 1975 federal court order set a ceiling on the number of inmates that could be held at the Angola penitentiary, throwing the problems of increasing prison commitments back on local authorities, who must hold the sentenced inmates until there is space for them in state prisons. Last year, 21 prisoners died in Louisiana jails, mostly from suicides and fires. Sporadic riots have broken out.

The article pointed out that thirty of the state's sixty-four parish jails are currently being sued for overcrowding.

Louisiana's prison population has risen 81 percent in the past six years. The year 1975 began with 4,759 prisoners in the custody of the Department of Corrections. By January 1, 1981, that figure had jumped to 8,586, with 1,267 of that number being housed in parish jails because of lack of room in state penal facilities.

In every other state in the Union, the parole mechanism is the major instrument controlling the prison population level, but, while the prison population ballooned and the issuance of probations skyrocketed during the past twenty years, there has been a sharp decline in parole usage in Louisiana. Parole was employed with 31.1 percent of Louisiana's convicted felons in 1960. By 1980, that percentage had fallen to 15—a 51 percent decrease.

This decline can be attributed to a number of factors:

1. the increased usage of probation by the courts, which has reduced the number of persons going to prison who would ordinarily have been eligible for parole

2. the increasing number of offenses being made nonparolable by the legislature, so that one-third of the prison population is already excluded from parole eligibility
3. the ever increasing number of convicts being committed to prison with sentence stipulations prohibiting parole eligibility either for specified periods of time, or altogether
4. heightened public awareness and fear of crime in the streets that has increased interest in the workings of the criminal-justice system.

"People generally don't know what parole is all about," Parole Board chairwoman Pamela Harris states, pointing out that the public's ignorance is aggravated by the false public impression of parole created by the news media's inclination to misreport almost any probationer or ex-convict who commits a crime as being a "parolee." "Misreporting has more than anything else to do with a parole board being very conservative and treading lightly in paroling someone," Harris told *The Angolite.*

On the other hand, public officials playing the politics of crime are feeding a grossly distorted picture of criminal-justice operations to the public. The courts and the mechanisms of prisoner release are the most vulnerable operations. Numerous charges are hurled—some, distortions of truth; others, blatant lies. The most popular charge against the courts is that the judges are soft on criminals, that not enough punishment is being meted out by them. Yet the skyrocketing prison population indicates, if nothing else, that judges are sending people to prison at an unprecedented rate.

The most fashionable charge against parole is that it causes sentences to lose the deterrent effect they might otherwise have had. But what deterrence? According to FBI statistics, police departments as a whole only solve about 25 percent of all major crimes that are reported. Any Las Vegas bookmaker would snatch up a bet that offers him a three-to-one chance of winning; and when one considers the fact that the majority of crimes are never reported and that a much smaller percentage of those apprehended will ever be tried, convicted, and sent to prison, the odds of getting away with a crime are enhanced considerably. Given that context, it is reasonable to assume that the typical criminal does not expect to be apprehended to start with. If he did, he wouldn't commit the crime. So in talking about deterrence, one is necessarily talking about reaching and intimidating someone who does not believe he is going to be caught—and that belief alone destroys all possible deterrence. As Diana Gordon, executive vice president of the National Council on Crime and Delinquency, pointed out: "The misplaced faith in deterrence sometimes stems from a confusion between the effects of 'certainty' and the effects of 'severity' of punishment." Studies show that certainty has a deterrent effect, while severity does not. Punishment, no matter how severe, can only be imposed if the criminal is caught; as long as he believes that he will not be caught, there is no deterrence. Deterrence lies in swift and certain apprehension, not severity of punishment.

The reality is that Louisiana's parole operation is one of the best things the criminal-justice system has going for it, with a success rate that ranks among the highest in the nation. During 1980, only 1 percent of those on parole had to be returned to prison for violating the conditions of their parole, and the majority of those violations were technical ones, not new crimes. (In 1979, only 7.5 percent of paroles had to be revoked.) It should also be pointed out that parole revocation for a technical violation does not represent the failure of *parole*—failure of the parolee, yes, but the revocation still represents the success of the parole operation, because it has done precisely what it is supposed to do: get the problem parolee back in prison *before* he commits a crime. "And we're doing that with a degree of success that is nothing short of phenomenal. While law enforcement authorities must spend months and even years trying to convict a criminal and get him off the street, we have our revoked parolee back in prison in less than thirty days," Harris states.

Parole in Louisiana is an unexplored and underutilized resource, one with an immense potential that has gone largely unrealized. "There are many people who could successfully complete parole that aren't given the opportunity," Harris points out. "And every year, it seems like there are more and more crimes that become nonparolable," adds C. Paul Phelps, secretary of corrections.

Given enough parole officers to supervise them, Phelps estimates that "conservatively, a third" of all those locked up in state prisons would do well on parole. But, while she would also like to see increased usage of parole, Harris warns: "If we say that we are going to parole more people just to alleviate overcrowding, then parole is going to explode—it'll be done away with, and you're going to shut off that tunnel altogether. . . . You have to first sell parole as a workable alternative, because right now the general public doesn't think parole works. And why not? Because anytime someone out on goodtime or probation or any other reason botch[es] up, they're called a parolee."

Phelps agrees that parole has a poor public image that must be improved before parole can be expanded, but getting the public to regard parole as a viable alternative to imprisonment is going to be difficult. He explains: "In the United States, we have a mental mind-set that the only way you can punish somebody is to put them in prison. Well, for a significant number of the people that we have in prison, prison is bad, but it's not the worst thing that you can do to them. It's a comfortable life. You don't have to think, you don't have to make any decisions, we feed you reasonably well. And things have improved over 1973–'74–'75; the chances of you getting out alive are significantly better than they were then. But the worst thing that you could do to many of these people is to make them stay at home, make them get up in the morning, make them go to work, and make them come in in the evening, and not let them out on the street in the evening to have a good time. Just have them under house arrest, which is probably the most severe punishment you can do to somebody— make them do what they've never done before in their lives . . . and it's cheaper."

It is. It costs $1.42 a day to maintain a prisoner on parole, $518 a year, only a fraction of the cost of keeping him in prison. The parole officer's job is much the same as that of the prison guard: to see to it that the parolee works at a full-time job, supports his family, pays his taxes, and obeys all the terms of his parole (the violation of any one can send him back to prison). "It's almost like Big Brother," Phelps explains. "Given enough parole officers, you can make anybody safe, you can guarantee somebody to be safe. If the Parole Board tells the probation-parole department, 'Now, we're going to parole so and so, and I want to know that he gets up every morning and leaves the house at a quarter to six in order to get to his job. I want him back in his house at six o'clock. I want to know what he does with his money. I want to know what he's doing. I don't want him in bars, or I don't want him here or there.' . . . If the Parole Board had the authority, if we had the resources, we could make sure that that happened."

Harris, like Phelps, is aware of the untapped potential of parole and has been studying the system for the past year toward instituting improvements and changes. She feels that parole can be converted into the most cost-effective operation in the entire criminal-justice system by requiring the parolee to pay part or all of the cost of his own parole supervision. The governor supports Harris's idea and has submitted legislation requiring parolees to pay a portion of the supervision cost. The legislature is now considering it, and it appears that the bill will pass. As Harris points out, this is not a unique idea. In the states of Mississippi, Florida, Georgia, and Texas, probationers and parolees are required to pay at least a part of their supervision costs. She sees no reason why the same practice cannot be adopted in this state. With parolees bearing the costs of their own supervision, parole usage and the staff to supervise parolees could easily be expanded, and prisoners who present no danger to the public could be taken out of prisons and placed in jobs, supporting their families, making restitution to their victims, and paying taxes and contributing to the overall economy of the state. The fact that it would cost taxpayers nothing might make the idea of putting more people on parole somewhat more attractive. An additional benefit would be the automatic reduction of the prison population to manageable levels, eliminating the need for the state to commit so much money to the construction of nonproductive prisons.

Sentencing and penalties have much to do with parole, and Harris doesn't like the present setup, something she's made clear; she has called for the present sentencing laws to be trash-canned and for judges and prosecutors to get together and come up with something more realistic. "We have got to decide who we want to put in prison and be protected from," she says. "The check forger or the armed robber, the auto thief or the murderer or rapist? The answer is obvious—people want to be protected from the violent criminal more than the other." Harris points out that there are limits to financial resources and manpower, so the state must be realistic, reserving prisons for the really dangerous. Toward achieving this end, she believes, the state should review its entire sentencing and criminal penalty structure and come up with priorities—"who we're going to put in prison and who we're going to devise alternate methods for. We must rearrange our sentencing structure so that it is realistic, equitable, and effective, reserving prison for violent offenders and coming up with other means of dealing with [those who commit crimes against] property and with nondangerous offenders."

Harris also proposes mandatory sentencing, which she feels would end the gross disparities in sentencing that breed so much resentment among prisoners. "I hear judges say, 'But I look at this set of circumstances and I look at that, and, well, this guy was killed in a barroom fight—that's understandable.' " She feels that this kind of discretion leaves too much room for manipulation of the system. "If you murder somebody, a life is taken, you ought to know what to expect," she explains. "I shouldn't be able to expect that I can go blow away someone I dislike and play with the system enough that maybe I get five years—and I've seen it happen. I don't believe there's any such things as manslaughter, negligent homicide . . ." Harris's position is that a death is a death, a burglary is a burglary, and everyone should get the same penalty for the same crime, with the only difference coming as a result of offender status.

"I think if we're going to cut down on recidivism, we're going to have to have more people under supervision," she told *The Angolite*. She wants to see the present practice of unconditional goodtime discharges replaced with mandatory parole supervision, for a specified period of time, of all offenders leaving prison.

Phelps agrees. "I believe that nobody should be released from prison without some form of supervision, whether you call it parole or what-have-you," he told *The Angolite*. "There are too many people, and I've seen them, who have not made the investment in themselves—that is, they have not really convinced themselves that they are going to change, and there are too many people in our system who will bypass parole for a goodtime discharge, just so that they don't have to be hassled by the man. . . . I think it's absolutely insane to take somebody who has been in prison for a significant period of time, and he just walks out. There are just too many things that you have adjusted to in prison that you need to unadjust to. And if you don't have anything to worry about—I mean, if your mind is set straight, then you don't have anything to worry about—me, or a parole officer, or anybody. It may get a little irritating, but you don't have anything to worry about."

There is another problem area about which Harris has expressed concern, and that is the plight of the 914 people serving life sentences in Louisiana. Eight hundred seventy-five of them are at Angola, and their number is fast increasing. "The reality is that life imprisonment has never, and doesn't now, mean life imprisonment anywhere in the nation," she says. All but a small number of lifers ultimately get out of prison. Harris points out that every state has some sort of release criteria and mechanism for lifers, except Louisiana. The only release mechanism at the moment is via commutation of their sentences through the State Board of Pardons, which can release them at whim regardless of whether they've served one year or fifty. Harris considers it impractical, uneconomical, and counterproductive to invest a fortune in keeping someone in prison for his entire life rather than expect ultimately to release him and get some kind of return out of that investment.

"We must become realistic in our dealings with lifers," she says, pointing out that, as a class, they possess the lowest recidivism rate of the entire criminal spectrum. In "Understanding Parole: Politics, Myths & Realities," a booklet prepared for the Parole Board, Harris cites the numerous studies showing that murder is primarily a onetime offense, and that murderers are the best prisoners and the best parole risks, with the best success rate. She feels that lifers in Louisiana should be treated the way they are in other states and provided basic and consistent release criteria instead of the present hit-or-miss clemency process. She would like to see all releases of lifers placed under the control and authority of the Parole Board, which could apply a fixed criterion that would ensure that all lifers serve at least the minimum time required, releasing them only on parole. A recent nationwide survey by *Corrections Compendium** found that in the states studied the overall number of years a lifer served before being paroled was fourteen and a half. Harris states that Louisiana could adopt that number or require any other condition before parole consideration. At the moment, there is nothing.

In her booklet on parole, Harris states:

An important by-product of this [fixed parole-eligibility dates for lifers] would be the assistance it would lend to correctional authorities in the management of their institutions because lifers constitute the most influential class of prisoners in any prison. Because of the length of their imprisonment, influence automati-

*a national journal in Lincoln, Nebraska, for corrections professionals

cally accrues to them. It has been the lifers who have generally set the tone of the prison in Louisiana, helped manage Angola in the past, and kept the lid on potential trouble and violence. They've done this because there was always hope in the past, something that no longer exists since there is no longer any release criteria for them. And there must be hope in every prison, otherwise rebellion, violence and deaths are inevitable. Prisoners exist and struggle for the same reason that law-abiding citizens do—hope of something better or more in life, hope of tomorrow. Other prisoners throughout the system have traditionally looked to lifers as a barometer by which to tell them what they can expect. We must inject some hope into what is fast becoming a hopeless prison population. Perfectly sane and reasonable and peaceful men, whether in prison or in society, are made desperate when they find themselves without hope in their lives, and we must try to avoid the terrible consequences that follow that awakening. Based on what we know about prisoners and their recidivism rates, it makes more sense to inject that hope through lifers since they remain imprisoned the longest and generally turn out to be the safest.

There is a need for hope, says Phelps. "Talk to any correctional administrator in the United States that's been on the job very long or knows anything at all about prisons, and if you ask him what is necessary to run a safe, constitutional prison, hope is going to be the number one thing. Without hope, it's just a matter of sheer physical force."

If Louisiana were to upgrade, expand, and explore the full potential that exists in parole, it would free much of the state's resources to allocate where they would do the most good. But, as Harris points out, the Parole Board can't do the job alone. It requires the understanding and cooperation of other agencies and the general public. But that will never be achieved until an end is put to the myths and politics that besiege parole operations. The public must come to understand that, contrary to popular opinion, parolees do not commit crimes as often as thought, a fact reflected by the small number of parolees whose paroles are revoked. And since the majority are revoked for technical reasons, the reality is that few parolees go out and commit new offenses. It must also be understood that parole is not leniency— it is control and supervision of the parolee's behavior and life situation, based on his fear of being returned to prison if he violates a parole rule, not to mention commits another crime. Parole has been a neglected resource for too long, and there is immense potential in its expanded utilization toward realistic justice.

[June 1981]

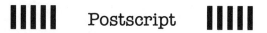

Postscript

Shortly after *The Angolite* published this article, the Louisiana legislature passed laws requiring parolees to pay a fee to help defray the costs of their supervision; the money funded, among other things, the hiring of additional probation-parole agents. Since then, these fees have amounted to millions of dollars annually.

When Democrat Edwin Edwards regained the governorship in 1984 after soundly defeating Republican Dave Treen, all of the Parole Board members were replaced. Both William Dunn, director of the Probation and Parole Division, and deputy director Victor Townsley retired in 1984. Probation-parole agent Paul Piercy retired in 1986.

In 1988, the funds collected from parolees were transferred to the state's General Fund by the administration of Governor Buddy Roemer. In its September/October 1989 issue, *The Angolite* reported the transfer of those funds, and the story was picked up by Baton Rouge's WBRZ-TV. State probation-parole chief Morris E. Easley, Jr., informed *The Angolite* that in fiscal year 1989–90 the monies generated from probation and parole supervisory fees were being returned to their original purpose, the funding of probation-parole operations.

On June 30, 1990, the state's Department of Public Safety and Corrections reported having 27,731 adults under probation supervision, 3,019 on parole, and an additional 8,220 mandatory goodtime releases under its supervision. Nationwide, the Bureau of Justice Statistics reported that there were 457,797 people on parole and 2,520,479 more on probation.

THE FISCAL CRUNCH

|||||

Wilbert Rideau

From 1979, when the Iranian Revolution sent shock waves through oil prices, until the early 1980s, Western industrialized countries experienced the worst recession in fifty years. More businesses failed during 1982 in the United States than in any other year since the Great Depression. This crisis, however, proved immensely profitable to oil-producing nations and oil-related businesses. Louisiana, rich in oil and gas resources, was one of the benefactors, riding the soaring oil prices to unprecedented wealth. Its huge petroleum industry made the state recession-proof, protecting it from the economic hardships ravaging the rest of the nation. While other states found themselves strapped for funds and fighting to stave off huge budget deficits, Louisiana was enjoying an embarrassment of riches. But while Arabian sheiks and princes funneled their petrodollars into banks and investments outside the oil industry, Louisiana spent its newfound wealth as if the heavens would forever rain oil instead of water. Such lavishness could not last.

The Public Affairs Research Council of Louisiana (PAR) warned in May of 1979: "The boom will not last." In its September 1980 analysis, *State Finance: Boom and Bust,* PAR warned: "The spending spree Louisiana went on this year must be stopped before the state reaches a financial crisis that will require higher taxes or meat-ax cuts in government programs." No one listened. In May 1981 PAR predicted: "While Louisiana is enjoying its bonanza, most other states are being forced to raise taxes and cut costs. Louisiana's envious position will be short-lived. Spending practices in state government are building up to a major financial problem which will likely become apparent in

1982–83 and become more critical for the remainder of the 1980 decade."

As the year 1982 progressed, Louisiana, one of the wealthiest states in the nation only two years before, found itself running out of money to meet state operating expenses. With the state relying upon its domestic oil and gas industry for 40 percent of its revenue, the flow of dollars into its tax coffers dropped dramatically. Continuing federal budget cuts only compounded the shortage of revenue. The lack of sufficient money soon impacted state governmental operations, forcing Governor Dave Treen to impose a hiring freeze on new state employees. But that wasn't enough. In the fall of 1982, the state's unemployment compensation system was bankrupted by paying out benefits to so many jobless Louisianians. The state was forced to borrow from $11 million to $12 million a week from the federal government to keep the system functioning. While other states resorted to deficit spending rather than reduce operating expenses, Louisiana's constitution prohibits deficit spending, a restriction that forced Treen to order a 4.4 percent across-the-board budget reduction among state agencies and departments. State agency heads scurried for ways to slash their expenditures to meet the governor's demand. After imposing those cuts, they were then informed that proposed budgets for the next fiscal year had to be cut by 15 percent.

Traditionally, when states experience fiscal problems, they cut prison expenditures first. After all, prisoners do not vote and are generally a despised class of humanity. The Louisiana of two decades ago was no exception. Faced with a deficit accruing from overspending in other areas, the legislature in 1962 cut the operating budget of the Louisiana State Penitentiary by one-third, forcing massive layoffs of prison employees and replacing them with convict-guards. "The number of escapes increased, violence among prisoners broke out more frequently, and convict-guards resumed their traditional vocation of brutalizing and killing fellow inmates," Louisiana State University professor Mark T. Carleton reported in his book, *Politics and Punishment.* In the ensuing years, Angola gradually skidded into a state of barbarity. (Federal courts have since prohibited the use of convict-guards and require prison authorities to provide basic services to the inmate population.)

"There's no question that we're going to have to find some means to economize and save money everywhere we can," Warden Ross

Maggio told *The Angolite*. "We've trimmed two million dollars off the current Angola budget." The proposed budget for the Louisiana State Penitentiary for the next fiscal year is $47,512,538. It's a standstill budget, and will in effect be smaller than the current one due to inflation and rising prices. "But at the same time, it's better than what some departments are experiencing," Maggio states. "They're going to get fifteen percent less than what they got this year, after the cuts. I know that's going to hurt a lot of people, but the Department of Corrections is taking some steps to do everything it can to streamline and economize—particularly at some of your medium-custody and newer institutions."

Where did the $2 million cut come from? "We've had to trim back on supplies and equipment expenditures," Maggio explained. "But that hasn't affected our being able to feed and furnish clothes and the basic necessities for the inmates."

"Food, clothing, and medical services were not affected by the budget cuts," reports Harvey Grimmer, the prison's business administrator. "One point two million of the two million dollars saved was in equipment and seven hundred fifty thousand was in supplies. The prison did not buy any furniture, typewriters, or office equipment this year, which was a big disappointment to many." To eliminate waste and reduce the use of supplies, Grimmer moved on the prison warehouse. He told *The Angolite*, "If you're going to reduce cost, you've got to get control of the flow of your supplies, the manner in which they're being issued. Once we did that, we were able to tighten down by closely monitoring every single request by the various departments, making sure that what they requested was absolutely necessary." Grimmer established a new system by which his office sets a weekly budget for each department in the prison, then monitors each to ensure that the money is being spent in the appropriate manner. "It's been a good education process and, I have to admit, all of the various administrators have been real cooperative in trying to help in this endeavor. They're getting more out of current equipment and they're stretching supplies farther."

Angola sprawls over 18,000 acres; the housing units for the 4,700 inmates are widely dispersed over its grounds. The prison is located in the remote wilderness of central Louisiana, sixty miles from Baton Rouge with its courts, hospitals, Department of Corrections headquarters, and numerous other places to which prisoners must be regularly transported. The distances involved, both within and out-side the prison, place a high premium upon transportation vehicles. Nine-passenger patrol wagons are the workhorses of the penitentiary, and a fleet of them meets most of the in-prison and out-of-prison transportation needs. Because of the heavy demands placed upon prison vehicles, new ones must be purchased each year. The prison needed thirty-three new vehicles this year, but Grimmer reports that only five were purchased. "This means stretching our current vehicles by using them more and driving them longer and farther," he ex-plained. "Of course, that increases your cost for repairs, but it will save money in the long run."

"What money we have had, and will have, I'm pushing over into the trip vehicles," Maggio added. "Those are things we must do. We don't have any choice about court orders, funeral trips, and hospital trips. Those are the three big things that keep these vehicles running up and down the highways of the state. I'm gonna take care of the vehicles in that area—nobody will miss a hospital trip, either to a free-world hospital or the prison hospital, because there is no vehicle. These are the things we must do—and we're going to be able to do it with the budget we have. Now, we will still try to save money in that area. I've already ordered some trucks and vehicles with diesel engines. Instead of seven or eight miles per gallon we're now getting out of the vehicles, we will probably get twenty miles per gallon and still have a vehicle heavy enough to carry ten or twelve men in it. That will cut the cost of our gasoline bill."

But there's a limit as to how much cutting can be done at the prison. "You don't have the flexibility to cut things here and still provide what the courts say are basic constitutional requirements in order for the state to run the prison," Maggio stated. Prison is a labor-intensive operation; of the current $45 million Angola budget, $33 million is for the salaries of the 1,616 employees, including secu-rity, medical, and administrative staff. In 1962 the state laid off the bulk of the prison security staff, replacing them with convict-guards. Maggio, who opposes a convict-guard system, points out that the 1962 action couldn't be repeated because the system has since been declared unconstitutional. "So how are you going to slash that now?" he states. "You can't do it. There are certain levels of basic services that the state is going to have to furnish to run what the federal courts have said is required to maintain a constitutional prison setting. So our situation is one of economizing—it's that simple."

An effort is being made to make the prison grow more of its own food. "It's more important to us to produce as much of our food as we can instead of emphasizing profit as we previously did. What we grow here, we're going to feed to the prisoners here first and if there is something left over, we will call DCI [Dixon Correctional Institute] or some other institution to see if they need some for their inmates. Now, if there is still something left over, then we'll start talking about making some money off it." To that end, Maggio is pushing to have the state build a new cannery at Angola. "We can grow enough vegetables to feed us the year around, but we have to have a way of preserving them."

The prison's food operation currently relies heavily upon commodities, food staples made available by the U.S. government. Without the federal commodities, Maggio acknowledges, the quality of food being served the inmate population would drop considerably. Another economic cushion is the prison's plasma program, which provides the inmates with a source of personal income. "Most prisons don't have a blood plasma program at all," Maggio said. "So our inmates probably have a higher level of purchasing power than most prisoners." That income enables Angola prisoners to spend about a million dollars a year in the prison commissary, primarily on personal items. The plasma program also enables the inmate population, through its Inmate Welfare Fund, to financially support the prison's recreation program and numerous other needs for which the state does not currently supply funding.

Maggio acknowledges that, even if the state's financial status doesn't get worse, "we may have to cut some more, but there is only so much you can cut. Let's face it—there is a limit, and once you reach it, you're courting problems if you lower the quality of certain things." He thinks Angola is close to that limit.

Grimmer feels the prison has already reached it. "Right now, the prison is operating on a bare-bones budget," he told *The Angolite*. "I don't see where we can really cut any more." But he anticipates that the prison will have to—"probably next year and maybe the year afterwards. Even if the legislature doesn't cut our budget, there will still be a certain reduction due to inflation. But there will be no deficit. I think we're going to have to make more cuts in the future—that may just be a reality we have to live with."

"There has to be a better way of supporting the prisons than what we're doing," Maggio told *The Angolite.* "In other words, the inmates are going to have to do more toward contributing to their upkeep, one way or the other. The state eventually, maybe five years from now, is going to have to look at what we can do to maximize the use of this inmate manpower . . . , because it is getting to be too much of a tax burden. I don't see anything wrong with an inmate paying some degree of the cost of his incarceration. He's sitting up here costing the state twenty-eight dollars a day. Well, he could pay part of it, maybe five dollars—you realize how much that would save?"

Maggio feels that the establishment of private, light industry in the penitentiary is a possible solution, one that would be beneficial to both the state and the prisoners. The prisoner would be paid a reasonable wage, but keep only two-thirds of his salary while the remaining third would go to the state as partial payment for his incarceration costs. However, Maggio acknowledges there are obstacles to implementing the idea. "If you decided to bring in a little light industry in here—let's say a shoe factory—you'd probably have about four hundred shoe manufacturers down there at the capitol raising hell, charging that we're going to put them out of business," he explained. "But I think, eventually, somebody is going to have to face up to the fact that we're not going to put them out of business, but we will lower the cost of keeping an inmate by a substantial amount. I think sooner or later someone is going to have to have the courage to come forward and say, 'Let's do it.' I think you could get an industry. You tell them, 'Here's some captive labor for you. You pay them three dollars a day and they are yours. How many you want? You want seventy-five? You want four hundred seventy-five? I'll have them over here. They're not going to join a union or anything else.' The companies would go for it. But you're going to be stepping on someone's toes somewhere who's not going to go for it. But sooner or later that's going to have to be overcome."

Maggio doesn't expect that placement of light industry to happen soon. "I think it will eventually happen, but the people paying the taxes are going to have to realize its need," he said. "The taxpayers have to realize that if you're going to keep people locked up, it's expensive. . . . They will realize that when they start feeling it in their pocketbooks." But he points out that the public mood isn't receptive to it at this point. "The public mood is getting tougher," he said. "They just passed the DWI laws and the sentences coming in this institution are longer and stiffer. There has to be a turnaround in the thinking outside. And I don't know when that's going to come."

The current public mood, ugly and vindictive, is precipitating a flow of prisoners into the state's penal system at an unprecedented rate. On July 1, 1982, there were 9,547 inmates in the system. That number is expected to increase to 12,500 by July 1, 1984, the Legislative Fiscal Office has reported to the Legislative Budget Committee. Corrections officials reported that an estimated 1,800 more state prisoners are currently backlogged in local jails. They estimate that the state can expect to build a new prison every twenty-one months with little hope of catching up.

Charles Davoli, assistant secretary of the Office of Adult Services, has pointed out that the average cost of building a cell is about $60,000. To keep someone in that cell for a year costs another $25,000. "One of the trends coming into play is the expectation that prisoners contribute more for their care and custody, in terms of a restitution," Davoli said, "whether that means working on a farm program, or whether that means expansion of the garment industry or an expansion of other prison enterprises." Davoli cited a recent study that shows that prisons are generally built with bond money—and pointed out that by the time New York taxpayers paid off its bond money and accumulated interest, they were forced to dish out almost $200,000 per bed on a maximum-security cellblock. "That's an exorbitant cost, both in terms of developing as well as operating it," he added. "So, I think one of the things you will see in the future is alternative punishments—a situation where the offender is paying restitution back to the community."

With the Department of Corrections gaining a net increase of approximately 850 prisoners each year and with fewer funds available for prison construction, corrections officials will be forced to educate the public about workable alternative punishments for certain nonviolent offenders. Still, Davoli cautions that "the attitude of the public is that they're not going to tolerate lawlessness."

Davoli is high on expanding the prison's vocational school. "I'd love to see the printing program here expanded and take over the printing for the state—I think we could save the state a helluva lot of money." He says that the vocational program could easily be turned into profitable prison industries by expanding all the current vo-tech programs. "But it would require some capital investment—and it would also require more productivity on the part of the inmates . . . and if we could get more productivity, then maybe there would be an increased willingness to put more incentives into the system."

When asked which comes first, productivity or incentive, Davoli responded: "I think that sooner or later the two will go together. What I'm saying is that you don't get something for nothing—and you've got a lot of inmates who basically want something for nothing."

Wanting something for nothing is not a trait peculiar to prisoners. Ralph Perlman, Louisiana budget director, was recently quoted in *The New York Times* as saying: "People here want all the services and don't want to pay for them . . . and the state doesn't have the money to pay for them." While he was referring to governmental services in general, his observation applies equally to public attitudes toward criminal justice. The public wants more and tougher punishment of offenders, wants to lock people up for longer periods of time—but doesn't want to pay for it.

Prior to coming to Louisiana, Davoli served as special assistant to the governor of Michigan; he was charged with responsibility for criminal-justice planning for the state. "We polled the public every year," he told *The Angolite*, "to determine whether they would support a tax increase to build additional prison beds to relieve the overcrowding. The polls came back negative—seventy-two percent of them said no. We didn't believe it, so we put it on the ballot. It got soundly defeated. And that's been the experience in almost every other state." Except in California, where, Davoli pointed out, voters recently approved a bond issue to build more prisons. "But in the majority of states," Davoli said, "they essentially said, 'Yeah, we want to lock them up, we want mandatory sentences—but we ain't going to pay for it.' And I can't explain that."

So, while prisoners ponder the future quality of prison life, and penal officials grapple for solutions, Louisiana continues on a course committed to increasing its prison populations—as if cost were not a factor. Federal judge Frank Polozola recently approved a $34 million plan, sponsored by the governor, which will allow the state to increase the number of prisoners from 9,500 to 12,000 by the end of the year. This will be accomplished by double-bunking at the Louisiana Correctional and Industrial School at De Quincy and The Work Training Facility–North (Camp Beauregard) at Pineville. Double-bunking will also be allowed on a one-year experimental basis at the new Washington Parish facility in Bogalusa. Additional prisoners will be accommodated through the erection of "prefabricated buildings" at the Hunt Correctional Center, the Wade Correctional Center, the Louisiana Correctional Institute for Women, and the Washington Parish facility. While double-bunking was specifically prohibited at the Louisiana State Penitentiary at Angola, its prisoner population will be increased from 4,500 to 5,200 through the current renovations and the opening of a new working cellblock.

Polozola's order was described by the Baton Rouge *Morning Advocate* as "an obvious compromise between what Polozola considered ideal and what the state sought in its effort to avoid further spending on prisons." Treen was quoted as saying that the judicially approved plan was "the result of our sitting down together and working out our differences. I appreciate and commend the judge for the time and effort expended toward the resolution of this long-standing problem."

Michael Sherman, coauthor of the book *Imprisonment in America,* in an article in *Corrections* magazine, said that increased prison population is caused by "broad and poorly understood trends in public opinion, and perceptions or misperceptions by judges and other responsible parties about what the public wants." Sherman added that the public fear of crime is being "exploited" by "people who should know better."

Davoli told *The Angolite* that the general public is losing its "patience in terms of tolerating crime and unlawfulness" and that "ballooning populations of prisons" are not going to soften that attitude. An example of Davoli's assertion was evidenced during budget hearings last year before the Arizona House of Representatives, when the state's corrections director, Ellis McDougall, told the lawmakers that there was a problem with the prison's air circulators which help the inmates survive the 120-degree summer heat. Representative Jane Hull said one way to solve overcrowding would be to turn the air circulators off and "suffocate them to death."

That sort of irresponsible attitude has been created by an orchestrated law-and-order campaign fed by an equally irresponsible press. It does absolutely nothing to educate the public about the gut issue of prison overcrowding: economics. And some penal officials are beginning to recognize that tragic mistake. "We're trying to explain the economics of overcrowding to the people of Alabama," John Hopper, Alabama's commissioner of corrections, told *Corrections* magazine. "The general population wants to get tough on crime, have longer sentences, and more strict parole guidelines. What they don't understand—perhaps we've been lax in informing them—is the cost."

[April 1983]

 Postscript

By 1991, the budget for the Louisiana State Penitentiary had increased to over $60 million. The Louisiana legislature is facing a revenue shortage of over $1 billion in its next fiscal year, which will require raising taxes, borrowing money, or cutting state services.

DYING IN PRISON

IIIII

Wilbert Rideau

It was a nice spring morning, with a soft breeze rustling the leaves of the tall trees. But its beauty was lost upon the handful of inmates who had just finished digging a deep rectangular hole that would be the final resting place of James Cripps, Number 76069. Laying their shovels aside, the gravediggers inspected their work. They had done a good job: The hole was deep and the sides were smooth and even. Tired and dirty, they loitered around the grave, chatting as they waited for the scheduled funeral to take place. It wasn't what they wanted to be doing, but was better than working in the field.

A few prison officials arrived soon, followed by the warden. Then a yellow school bus pulled up on the side of the road, directly across from the burial site. Some two dozen inmates, all trusties, filed out of the bus. Slowly they began to wander through the cemetery, exploring it with wide-eyed fascination and calling out to each other in awed voices as they recognized familiar names of former inmates on some of the tombstones. Point Look-Out was a place they had all heard about throughout their imprisonment, but one that most were seeing for the first time. In a significant departure from the typical prison funeral—normally attended only by the chaplain, the undertaker, one or two officials, and the gravediggers—the warden had granted the request of the prisoners, all friends of Cripps, to attend the funeral.

Murmuring voices signaled the arrival of a black hearse, which pulled up alongside the road in front of the grave and stopped. The driver conferred briefly with Warden Ross Maggio and Chaplain Gary Penton. Maggio turned to the waiting inmates: "Give me six of y'all to serve as pallbearers." Six inmates moved forward, took hold

*James Cripps's freshly dug grave at Point Lookout
Cemetery is examined by the inmate gravediggers.*
(*Courtesy* The Angolite)

of the coffin as it was slid out, and slowly walked the short distance
to the grave. The chaplain led the procession, with the warden bringing up the rear. Two inmates carried floral wreaths, purchased by
inmate organizations. The typical prison funeral has no wreaths, but
Cripps had been popular, well liked by his fellow inmates. The coffin
was placed on wood planks above the grave, and the pallbearers stood
on each side in strict formation.

It was a cheap beige coffin, made of some synthetic material that
looked almost like wood. Someone had written HEAD across one end
of it with a Mark-a-lot so people would know the difference.

Penton stepped to the head, bowed his head, and began the service by announcing to the gathering that Cripps's mother was an aging and seriously ill lady who wanted them to know that her son was not being buried in the prison cemetery because he was unloved but because she was financially unable to bring him home and have him buried near her. She would have liked to attend the funeral services, Penton told the gathering, but was too poor and ill to make the trip. She requested that the Twenty-third Psalm be read over her son.

Moreese "Pop" Bickham stepped beside the chaplain at the head of the grave. Normally a spry man who moves about pretty well despite his sixty-seven years, Bickham moved with a slowness that mirrored his depression. He had been a prisoner for the past twenty-six years and had been a close friend of Cripps. He first met Cripps on Death Row, where they had spent many years awaiting the execution that never came. When the U.S. Supreme Court spared the nation's condemned prisoners with its 1972 ruling that the death penalty as administered violated the Eighth Amendment, they joined the prisons' regular populations to serve life sentences.

"The Lord is my shepherd; I shall not want. He maketh me to lie

Chaplain Penton conducting Cripps's burial service (Courtesy The Angolite)

down . . ." Bickham faltered as he read the passage from the Bible. The words soon blurred from the tears that filled his eyes. He continued to recite from memory, fighting the anguish that stirred in his gut. He and Cripps had struggled many years for a freedom that neither had realized. They had been through a lot of good and bad experiences, had slept only a few beds away from each other, and now he had to read the psalm over his friend. It unleashed his own fears of death and of dying in prison.

". . . though I walk through the valley of the shadow of death, I will fear no evil . . ." With the psalm read, the chaplain asked another prisoner to lend a song to the occasion. Warren Lewis stepped forward and began "Here I Stand Before Your Throne." His strong voice filled the hushed stillness of the cemetery.

> I stand at your throne,
> O God, pleading my case.
> O Lord . . .

Following Lewis's solo, the other inmates were invited to step forth and say whatever they wished about the man they had known. Cripps was born and reared in rural Michigan—an only child. While living in New Orleans, he and a traveling companion murdered a man and, in 1968, he found himself under a death sentence. After his sentence was set aside, he was resentenced to life imprisonment in 1973. He adjusted well to the prison community, despite its then-violent nature—and, according to prison officials, he was never a disciplinary problem.

Like so many other lifers, Cripps tenaciously clung to the dream that he would one day regain his freedom, but, since he was poor and essentially alone in the world, it was a lonely struggle. With his mother living so far away, he rarely received visitors, except for a male religious advisor who occasionally came to see him. For a long time, he worked in the prison's Print Shop. A tireless worker who rarely complained, he was always cooperative and willing to do whatever he could to help others. A sports enthusiast, he rode the animals in the annual prison rodeo for several years. He also played softball and football, once even playing on an otherwise all-black softball team and earning the monicker "The White Shadow."

Several months before his death, Cripps was transferred to the main prison's maintenance crew, but something was physically wrong with him, though he didn't know what it was. He started losing weight rapidly and was finally admitted to the prison's infirmary in February. Over the next month, he was admitted several times to hospitals in Baton Rouge and New Orleans. He died in the New Orleans Charity Hospital, of heart disease. He was thirty-seven.

At the end of the service, the pallbearers lowered Cripps into the ground. The men picked up small clods of dirt and threw them atop the coffin in a ritualistic farewell gesture. As the mourners departed, the gravediggers immediately began shoveling dirt into the hole. The dry, hollow sound of the dirt hitting the cheap coffin unnerved Pop Bickham, and he looked back as he climbed into the bus.

Point Look-Out is the prison's burial ground, its pauper cemetery. Located a short distance from the prison's employee residential area, the cemetery is nestled against a forest of pine trees. A paved road runs in front of it, across from which is a dilapidated horse barn for employees. A deep gully runs behind it, separating it from a thick wooded area where some of the employees' hunting dogs are penned. It is a quiet and tranquil place, its silence interrupted from time to time only by the whishing of a passing vehicle. Clusters of sweet gum and oak trees dot the well-tended lawn. The graves are laid out in scattered clusters. Toward the front, seven rows of 296 white concrete tombstones stretch out across almost the entire width of the cemetery. On a few of the stones names, or names and numbers appear, but most carry only numbers. In the past few years the prison administration has tried to bury the dead in a uniform manner and has attached little white metal tags with the deceased's name and number to the headstones.

Point Look-Out is not a typical cemetery. No one goes there except to clean the grounds or to bury another prisoner. There are no visitors. Prisoners are not permitted to go. Employees generally have no reason to visit, and since those buried there are the dispossessed and unclaimed, there are no friends and relatives to come and lay flowers. Even if there were, Bickham points out, they would have to make special arrangements to enter the prison and visit the grave. If they're poor and lack transportation, the prison is too remote for regular visits.

"There's no way in the world that someone can catch a ride with somebody all the way to Angola, be dropped off at the cemetery, and then catch a ride all the way back to where they came from," Pop Bickham told *The Angolite*. "People can do that at cemeteries in the free world, but not way up here. You'd have to find someone coming to Angola in the first place just to catch a ride."

Bickham knows about such matters. He spent over two years working as an attendant at the cemetery. "As long as I worked there," he said, "not one person visited anybody in that cemetery. I'd rather have anything than to be confined, then die and have my body placed where it would be confined too—'cause don't nobody go to Point Look-Out. Once you're buried there, pretty soon nobody knows

Morese "Pop" Bickham in 1984. He has been a prisoner at Angola since 1958. (Courtesy The Angolite)

where you're buried at—and the whole world forgets you. There won't even be a stranger to come along and at least wonder about you."

Bickham is right about the world forgetting those buried there. Except for the most recent burials, prison officials can tell little to any inquirer about the dead at Point Look-Out. In fact, while there are 296 tombstones, Assistant Warden Peggi Gresham points out that "it seems inconceivable that, given the number of deaths which have occurred over the years here at Angola, there are not more people buried at Point Look-Out."

Prisoners were first sent to Angola in 1869, after the state leased all its convicts to Major Samuel Lawrence James to ease the financial burden of housing them. One of the first moves by James was to transfer state prisoners from the penitentiary, then located at Baton Rouge, to his Angola cotton plantation. James had huge ambitions about how best to utilize inmate labor to make money. For the next twenty-five years, he operated the most profitable and brutal enterprise in the history of the state, often violating state law and the terms of his contract. While lessees prior to the Civil War had used inmate labor in manufacturing operations within the prison facility, James knew there were enormous profits to be made taking inmates out of the prison. And while he started out with only a couple of hundred inmates, he used them on Mississippi River levees and railroad construction, as well as on other farms and plantations, utilizing brute force to maintain discipline and productivity. The result was a living nightmare for the convicts but an empire for James. In a matter of months during his first year, James made a half million dollars, a king's fortune in those days.

But by the 1880s the lease system began to receive public criticism, which grew louder as the major and his subcontractors continued to work, mutilate, and kill prisoners throughout Louisiana. In 1886 a newspaper in Clinton "described what was by then common knowledge" when it stated that the

men on the [James] works are brutally treated and everybody knows it. They are worked, mostly in the swamps and plantations, from daylight to dark. Corporeal [sic] punishment is inflicted on the slightest provocation. . . . Anyone who has travelled along the lines of railroads that run through Louisiana's swamps . . . in which the levees are built, has seen those poor devils almost to their waists, delving in the black and noxious mud. . . . Theirs is a grievous lot a thousand times more grievous than the law even contemplated they should endure in expiation of their sins.

C. Harrison Parker, editor of the New Orleans *Daily Picayune,* a leading critic of the horrors inflicted upon the prisoners by James, asserted that it would be more humane to execute anyone sentenced to more than six years in James's lease system, because the average convict didn't live that long anyway. In 1890 State Representative C. W. Seals, of Claiborne Parish, also condemned James and his brutal system, charging on the floor of the House that "the death rate is about four times as great in proportion to the number of convicts as the death rate in any other penitentiary in the United States."

Joseph E. Ransdell, a north Louisiana attorney who would later become a U.S. senator, stated in a trial in 1898 that a friend had told him that he had seen forty-two convicts buried at one camp in either 1885 or 1886, and "the deaths were nearly all caused by overwork, exposure and brutality." James kept his books closed from public and official scrutiny and there were no official reports from the prison for the years 1885 and 1886. However, the Prison Board of Control admitted two years before Ransdell made his charge that 216 convicts died during 1896 alone. And until the lease system ended in 1901, the death rate averaged about 10 percent, with a total of about eight hundred deaths during the system's last seven years. On the basis of his research, Mark Carleton of Louisiana State University estimated that as many as three thousand men, women, and children convicts, most of them black, died during that infamous thirty-year period between 1870 and 1901.

During the last full year of the lease system, 1900, there were a total of 989 prisoners in the state's leased penal system—149 whites and 840 blacks. The lot of those still alive at the end of the year improved considerably with the resumption of state control. The more brutal methods employed under James's rule were abandoned and the mortality rate dropped dramatically. While Carleton warns that much of the available information is questionable, Henry L. Fuqua, chief administrative officer of the penal system, reported to the legislature in 1918 that the death rate for convicts had dropped to 35.3 per year between 1901 and 1917.

The next available statistic on the convict death rate is contained in a 1940 prison report, which stated that between 1931 and 1935 the number of deaths had increased, under the general management of R. L. Himes, to an average of forty-one per year. In his history of the Louisiana penal system, Carleton states that prison officials, "squeezed between a Depression and their own venality, may well have resorted more often to brutality in order to make the penal system self-supporting." On May 11, 1941, the New Orleans *Times-Picayune* reported that a study of prison records revealed that 1,547 floggings, "with 23,889 recorded blows of the double lash," were inflicted on prisoners during 1933 alone.

Thousands have died in the Louisiana penal system. The gnawing question is where they have been buried. Information on this is even more scarce than information about what happened to the prisoners over the years. The problem is that the prison system, until recent times, operated in violation of state laws, with a criminality and violence that matched and often exceeded that of the prisoners in its custody. Like any criminal, the system cloaked its activities in secrecy.

Since Major James kept his books and operations closed from public and official scrutiny during his murderous reign, there is no way of knowing who died, how, when, or where between 1868 and 1900. Information was obtained during the penal system's transition from the lessee to the state, but no major report came out of the prison until 1918. And even that report offered no precise information as to the number of convicts actually imprisoned at any time between 1893 and 1917. It produced only muddled "averages" for prison population, deaths, admissions, discharges, and so on, some of which don't jibe with reports from other sources.

No more official reports were issued about the prison's activities until 1932. As far as records and public information went, Angola ceased to exist during the 1920s. For the most part, what happened during that period is and will remain unknown. And aside from the brief report issued in 1932, Angola was once again removed from public scrutiny until 1940, when an anti-Long administration assumed the governorship.

It is a dark stain on the state's history that no one, probably, will ever know what happened to those locked in its penal system throughout those secret years. Prisoners could die and be buried and, except for a few notable points in time, their fate was of little, if any, significance to the public or to state officials. Penal authorities could easily keep their activities—even murder—secret, given the public's apathy. Unfortunately, the public's concern for inmates' welfare and its enthusiasm for their rehabilitation have always been inversely proportional to the number of black convicts perceived to be within the system. Prior to the Civil War, when the convict population was primarily white, the state and even the lessees chose manufacturing as a means of utilizing inmate labor. When the inmate population became predominately black following the Civil War, the public soon confused the crime problem with the "Negro problem"—a perception that still lingers today.

With the infusion of so many blacks into the state's penal system, the public's concern about inmate welfare waned considerably. Consequently, the state's penal system became essentially a business enterprise using inmate labor and operated either by lessees or by politicians for the sole purpose of turning as much profit as possible off the blood, sweat, and tears of convicts. Given the racial prejudices prevalent following the Civil War, penal philosophy became a matter of dealing with "niggers," and the system became one tailored for Negro labor—backbreaking work on levees, farms, and plantations. Human misery and suffering became the cornerstone of the state's new penal system.

The further one moves back through time, the less likely it is that a prisoner's body was claimed by his family and given a private and decent burial. While prison officials today can pick up a telephone and immediately contact the next of kin in the event of a prisoner's death, communication wasn't always that simple. It was a long time before telephones or automobiles became a meaningful reality for the lower social class, the class from which the bulk of state prisoners have always come and the ones least able to afford the expense of transporting and burying a body. Given that reality, the frequency with which inmates' bodies remained unclaimed and the prison had to dispose of them must have been much greater, if not routine, prior to the 1900s.

So, where were the inmates buried?

It is reasonably safe to assume that prisoners who died between

1835, when the state penitentiary was located in Baton Rouge, and the Civil War were buried in a paupers' cemetery in that city. During that era of crude communication and transportation, it's highly unlikely that the body of a prisoner without family in the Baton Rouge area would have been kept somehow until the family received a mailed death notice and could come to pick up the body. With the same technological and economic realities governing the lives of people from 1868 to 1901, a time when prisoners died like flies under the rule of the lessee, it must be assumed that prisoners were buried wherever they died—and that could have been anywhere, since Major James worked his inmates all over the state.

Given the high mortality rate of those working under James's whip, it stands to reason that a lot of inmates died on the Angola plantation between 1868 and 1901—and the logical inference can be drawn that most of them were buried on the plantation grounds. It was common practice in the South for plantations to maintain their own cemeteries for family members and slaves, and it's unlikely that Angola was any exception.

The earliest recollection of the existence of a prisoners' cemetery dates back to the early 1920s. Jack Davis, a former Angola postmaster, grew up in and around Angola during that period. He recalls an inmate cemetery, popularly known as Boot Hill, located on a small knoll near the infamous Red Hat Cellblock.

At some point in the early 1930s, all of the Boot Hill graves were transferred to their present location, now known as Point Look-Out. C. C. Dixon was working at Camp F at the time and recalls that "they would dig up one grave and take it over there and bury it, then go get another one. They'd take one at a time—and they just kept at it until they finally got through with it."

Dixon and Davis recall that, ironically, during a period of strict racial segregation throughout the South, including in the Louisiana prison system, prisoners were buried together in the same cemetery without regard to race. As Gresham points out, that was something that didn't happen in the free community. Obviously, the only places in Louisiana where blacks and whites achieved equality during that era were Angola's Boot Hill and Point Look-Out.

The overwhelming majority of the Point Look-Out graves are marked by tombstones bearing prison numbers in the ten thousands, twenty thousands, and thirty thousands, all of which were issued to incoming prisoners between 1920 and 1940. "It's my guess that most of them died shortly after their number was issued," Assistant Warden Gresham says. "If you look at the number of deaths during those years, then it's my guess that some of those people weren't here very long."

It is also worth noting that prisoners generally served short sentences during those years. A 1980 *Angolite* study of records from that era revealed that even murderers serving life sentences generally got out of prison in less than eight years. (A 1969 report by the Louisiana Commission on Law Enforcement and Administration of Justice stated that the "average Louisiana inmate" during the 1960s was freed after only two years in prison. It has been within the last decade that Louisiana inmates have been required to serve far more years than traditionally required.)

Judging by the prison numbers and the years of their issuance, Point Look-Out experienced most of its burials during the 1920s, 1930s, and 1940s—a particularly harsh and brutal era, when official administrative secrecy veiled prison activities. And, according to William "Wooden Ear" Sadler, the first editor of *The Angolite,* who came to Angola in 1935, the procedure for burying the inmates was as mean as the world they were forced to exist in. In 1977, he recalled 1935 burial practices for *The Angolite:*

When an Angolan died or was killed, his body was taken to the ice house, next door to the power plant at Camp E, and kept cold for a period which did not exceed three days. The man's next of kin, if on record, were notified. If there was no next of kin, the man would be buried in the penitentiary cemetery (Point Look-Out) . . . halfway between the front gate and Camp I on the old Camp B road. The burial crew, three black trusties from Camp A, would bring their two-wheeled cart pulled by a mule to the ice house. A much-used pine coffin was in the cart. The body would be turned over to them. The crew would wrap the body in a canvas sheet, put it in the coffin, and drive the long, slow road to the cemetery. Once there the crew would dig a hole, not necessarily six feet deep—more often just deep enough to conceal the corpse. The coffin would be suspended over the hole, the bolt on the underside would be slipped, the bottom of the coffin would swing open (it was hinged on the other side), and the sheeted corpse would tumble into the hole. . . . Two of the crew would reach down into the hole and pull the canvas shroud off the body. It could be used again. . . .

While it is quite evident that the prison utilized Boot Hill, and then Point Look-Out, as a burial ground for prisoners whose bodies were not claimed, there are questions that beg explanation—and the 296 graves at the cemetery only compound the mystery. The average annual death rate between 1901 and 1917 was officially reported by prison authorities to be 35.3. Yet there is only one grave from that period at Point Look-Out, that of N. H. Waller, Number 1073.

It is not likely that the bodies of all the inmates who died between 1900 and, say, 1940 were claimed by friends or relatives and buried elsewhere, outside the prison. As Gresham points out, "They didn't know anything about embalming and they couldn't very well ship bodies all over the place. It wasn't practical to ship bodies long distances back in those days. It would take days to get anywhere by wagon." So it's logical to assume that the prison probably had to bury most of the inmates who died—and a lot of them died. Yet there are not enough graves at Point Look-Out to accommodate the number of inmates who died during that harsh era. Where were the dead inmates buried?

"We don't know," Gresham states frankly. "We don't know where they died at—whether here at Angola or elsewhere. If we knew where they were housed, we could guess where they were buried."

The most reliable indication of who died where and how, and the possible site of their burial, lies in the manner in which prison authorities distributed convicts through its work assignments system. The classification system employed by penal authorities was simple and determined along racial lines. Levee work, in that pre-bulldozer era, was arduous and deadly and, according to historian Mark Carleton, was where most of the recorded deaths between 1890 and 1900 occurred. After 1901, the prison assigned only black inmates to work on the levees. The second most onerous and brutal work assignment was the sugar cane plantations, and these assignments were also primarily given to black inmates. Therefore, over two-thirds of the prisoners, primarily blacks, were not even at Angola. Given the brutal nature of their work assignments, most of the deaths among prisoners in the early 1900s probably occurred at the levee camps or the sugar plantations. There may be more truth than fiction to the tales that the state's massive levee systems were built atop inmate workers. Those inmates certainly were not shipped back to Angola for burial at Point Look-Out.

Imprisonment and penal operations in Louisiana are no longer the crude, primitive affairs they used to be. Federal court recognition of prisoners' rights, and enlightened and sophisticated penal management have put an end to the harsh and brutal practices of the past. Medical care, which was once almost nonexistent for prisoners, now exists; and inmate violence, which used to tear at the very fabric of the prison world, has long ceased to be a major factor in the inmate mortality rate. Men now die of old age or illness. "Today's circumstances being what they are, more of our prisoners are dying of natural causes," Gresham says, "and are more likely to die in a hospital away from Angola than here."

The prospect of dying in prison is a nightmarish fear that haunts every prisoner like a ghost. "Dying anywhere isn't a pleasant thing," Warden Ross Maggio points out, "and those dying here die pretty much the same as people in nursing homes. While dying in prison is perhaps not the same as dying at home, we try to make it as comfortable as possible for them. In fact, that was a major consideration in the creation and operation of the Old Folks Ward at the hospital—to have a more comfortable situation for the elderly prisoner, with nursing care and medical attention readily available."

But that knowledge offers no consolation to a prisoner faced with the prospect of dying in prison. It's dying away from home, alone, with strangers, in the callous atmosphere of prison, being treated and cared for, more often than not, by an indifferent hand. It's grossly different from dying in the warmth of home, in the bosom of friends and relatives, which eases the sting of death somewhat. There is nothing in the prisoner's world that can soften the finality of death. A longing look out a window reveals a world of guns, curses, and noise as callous as the concrete it's made of. There is no warmth, beauty, or meaning—no last pleasures, touches, joys, words. In prison, there is nothing—you suffer alone and you die alone, feeding the fear and misery of those who must watch you die.

Roy Fulghum was a close friend of James Cripps. Fulghum, a patient at the prison hospital, couldn't attend Cripps's funeral, but he watched him languish on the prison hospital ward until Cripps was transferred to Charity Hospital in New Orleans. He shared Cripps's frustration during the initial stages of his illness as the doctors tried to find out what was wrong with him. They slept two beds apart on the hospital ward. After Cripps was transferred to New Orleans, Fulghum also made a couple of medical trips to Charity Hospital, and he inquired each time about his friend's condition.

"I was told that he was unconscious and had a bad heart and that they couldn't operate on him," Fulghum recounts. "The next trip I made the following week, I asked about him again and they told me, 'Roy, your friend is not going to make it.' " When word of Cripps's death finally reached Fulghum at the prison hospital, "it seemed like a part of me died."

A little later, Fulghum watched another friend, Charles "Little One" Collins, who slept three beds away from him, die. Cripps had died alone. In contrast, Collins's wife visited him a week before his death, although she couldn't stay with him.

"He suffered day and night," Fulghum recalls. "I sat there in my wheelchair the night he died—he was hollering about how hot it was. I told him the air conditioner was on."

Fulghum had to watch his friend's agony and death, then watch the hearse take Little One away the next morning. That kind of thing can get to you. "You're sitting there, helping your friend to die, looking at him and knowing that the same thing could happen to you," Fulghum says. "It starts to bugging your mind, and sooner or later you can't even think right. Sometimes I have nightmares. I lay in my bed and cry, like Little One did."

There is no respite from the pain of imprisonment. When Fulghum is transported to a hospital outside the prison for medical treatment, he travels with leg irons hobbling him around the ankles and with his wrists handcuffed and chained to his waist—and a painful black lock box also on his wrists to prevent him from picking the handcuff lock. He goes fully shackled, as did Cripps and Collins (despite the cancer eating Collins away). It didn't matter that Cripps and Collins were dying. They had to lie on their stretchers weighted down by the chains that bound and held them prisoner.

"It's the general policy that when a prisoner is shipped out of Angola, whether to go to court or to another hospital, that he is shackled," Maggio says. "My first responsibility is to make sure that a prisoner is secure when we send him out of the prison into the public. The fact that a man is dying doesn't mean that he won't attempt to escape or that he can't do anything. If the leg irons and handcuffs would interfere with the man's medical care, they are not put on the prisoner. And while it's a general policy to shackle everyone, there have been numerous exceptions to the policy and I expect that there will be more in the future. It all depends upon what the medical staff says about an inmate's condition."

Cripps died in shackles, chained to his bed in the Charity Hospital in New Orleans with the cold steel biting into him, as other prisoners have died before him. The mere idea drives needles of fear into Fulghum. "Who wants to die like that, chained up like some kind of animal?" he asks. "I certainly don't want to die like that."

He's trying to avoid the possibility. Though he's been in prison twenty-four years, time that would have crushed most family relationships, Fulghum's family is still sticking with him and fighting to prevent his dying chained to a hospital bed. His family is trying to secure a medical discharge or furlough from prison for him. "I'm hoping and praying that they can get a medical discharge or furlough, or whatever it is," he says. "My people are willing to take care of me, give me a home, medication, and whatever I need."

From his hospital wheelchair, there is little in Fulghum's immediate world to give him reason to hope. He watched Collins die, waiting for a medical furlough that never came. Looking a few beds away from him, he watches a nurse and an inmate-orderly tending to Joe Brown, another patient. "He's got no legs from the knees down—nothing," says Fulghum. "They've got to take care of him—bathe him, and everything else like that. He went up on the Pardon Board asking for a break, to be allowed to go home, but they said he ain't served enough time. Hell, how long they expect the guy to live? I think that any man who has been here years and got bad health, regardless of who you are, should be discharged. I mean, as long as there are people who're willing to take care of you."

Maggio believes in the concept of releasing terminally ill and aging prisoners on medical furloughs "so long as there's someone to release them to who's able to take care of them." But he also points out: "It depends on the man. If an eighty-year-old man killed someone and came up here, we can't very well ship him right back into the community the next day. The community and the judge obviously want him in prison, which is the reason why they shipped him to us in the first place. So, they wouldn't appreciate us shipping him right back the next day because of his age. Hell, I don't know how you would address a case like that."

Maggio has recommended inmates for medical furloughs in the past. "If and when the medical department recommends a terminal case to me for medical furlough," he says, "I recommend it to the Department of Corrections. They take it from there."

Fulghum is one of the more fortunate ailing, elderly prisoners. He knows it. "I've got everything," he says. "I'm one of the lucky ones."

Ailing and elderly inmates are a fast-growing problem. They constitute a class of prisoners with peculiar problems and needs. Many, if not most, of them require special attention and medical care, and a slower pace of life than the rest of the prisoner population. Most are unable to work, and they are more prone to depression and suicide than any other group. Yet, in most prisons, there are no special programs to deal with the aged—they simply vegetate in prison.

There are notable exceptions. Some prison systems provide special accommodations for the aged and ailing. The federal prison system operates two minimum-security prisons solely to house its ailing and elderly prisoners. The state of California has a similar 150-man facility in Chino, where elderly prisoners are permitted to live at a slower pace, away from the stress-filled and violent worlds of the other prisons. Louisiana is in the process of addressing what should be done with old and sick prisoners. Upon assuming office several months ago, Governor Edwin Edwards appointed a Forgotten Man Committee to study the prison system and recommend reforms. One of the priorities of the committee will be to study the increasing number of ailing and aging prisoners in the state; as Corrections Secretary C. Paul Phelps is fond of pointing out, if the state doesn't do something about them, the Department of Corrections will soon be operating the largest old-folks' home in the state.

Across the border in Texas, the aged and chronically ill don't fare as well. There are almost three hundred elderly inmates in Texas prisons; the oldest is an eighty-five-year-old man serving a seventy-five-year sentence for murder. The Houston *Chronicle* reports that almost all of the aged Texas inmates "need daily medical attention and at least one-third of them require hospital-type care. . . . Despite these clearly defined problems, there are no specific programs or facilities within the TDC [Texas Department of Corrections] to help the aged convicts do their time or deal with the outside world upon their release. . . . The Texas prison philosophy is to mix convicts of all ages in maximum-security prisons."

"The way we treat old folks out here is outrageous, but the way we treat them in prison is criminal," Don Taylor, a member of C.U.R.E. (Citizens United for Rehabilitation of Errants), a national prison-reform group, told the *Chronicle*. "We treat them far worse than what they did to get down there."

While prisoners generally fear the prospect of dying in prison, few of those who do actually end up buried here. Most are retrieved by relatives. Only eight prisoners have been buried at Point Look-Out during the past five years. A study of five of them, selected at random, reveals a pattern.

"What we're looking at are individuals with low educational levels, who were born and raised outside of Louisiana, and whose family lived outside the state," Gresham summarizes. "They were individuals who had been in constant conflict with the law and spent considerable amounts of time in jails and prisons, away from their families, throughout their lives. And that's important because individuals who are in constant trouble are less likely to be able to maintain close family ties through long periods of separation, and it appears that this is what happened in their cases, because they had families. So there was an evident deterioration of family ties. In addition, they were all either single or divorced, which means no immediate family ties, and they had no visits. Now, when you put all of these facts together, the accumulative effect is that it appears that these people had earlier in their lives lost their initial closeness with other family members."

While the families of two of the inmates refused to claim their bodies, Gresham points out: "The families of the other three men were unable to claim the bodies because of financial difficulties. They wanted very much to claim the bodies, and burial was delayed in a couple cases to give the families more time to try and work out some financial arrangements. In fact, some of the family members came to the prison for one of the funerals."

"You have to understand the background that prisoners primarily come from," Angola's chaplain, Gary Penton, explains. "They generally come from poor families, people already caught up in the trauma of life—people who don't have much, don't expect to have much. They do well to keep the old car running, for instance, just to go to work if they've got work to go to, and it's a very real hassle just keeping their own life together. Then they may live out-of-state, as in the case of Cripps. . . . Then you suddenly thrust upon them the expense of having a body shipped, prepared for burial, and the general cost of dying, which is pretty high. They cannot handle it, especially if they're ailing and elderly people living on fixed incomes. Cripps having to be buried here is a good example of that."

"There are going to be those men who don't have anybody in their lives, anywhere," Penton points out. "And it's not a case of rejection but of simply not belonging. They've been here for so long that their folks have all died and what other family ties they might have had simply disintegrated with the passage of time, their being locked away from them for so long—just the natural growing away from each other when people are apart. It's a natural process.

"When I was in the military," Penton continues, "I had to spend a year on a remote radar site in the Aleutian chain off the coast of Alaska, covering the chaplain duties. When I returned home after one year, my wife and I had to get reacquainted. We'd sort of grown apart. She had taken on added responsibilities and learned to function on her own during my absence, and I had to kind of wiggle back into her life when I returned. When a person copes without someone for so long, it becomes somewhat difficult for them to make a spot for them in their life again, especially when they've become involved with life and are burdened with so many other responsibilities and demands upon them. You've simply grown apart."

"And, too, if you're the kind of person who has been in and out of trouble and in and out of jails and prisons throughout your life, you don't have the time and the opportunity to develop close and lasting relationships to begin with," Gresham points out.

"A lot of the family relationships of people in prison were already strained or shattered or even broken before they even came to prison," Penton explains. "That's one of the factors in your ultimately having no belonging—having nobody to really encourage you, nobody to frown at you, so to speak, because they love you! Care about what happens to you. When you add the natural disintegration of relationships that go with long confinement, it just all goes down the drain.

The same thing happens in marital relationships of people in prison. It's just that the evidence of that natural disintegration in this instance is an unclaimed body—the other is divorce. The fact of death doesn't change what has already taken place. I think that it probably accentuates the dread that a man has—he already knows that there are tenuous ties."

Penton, a former air force chaplain, has been a chaplain at Angola for five years. The burial of Cripps was his first prison funeral, an experience he cites as his saddest since he's been at the prison.

"The fact of death is no major fear or dread or terror for me," he says. "That's a natural part of life. But the death where there is nobody to love you, to mourn your passing, no tears, that's sad. Standing at the head of his grave, I found myself identifying with him and those gathered around. I can relate to the pain, the fear. A man who is as much a family man as I, a man who feels the need for human warmth and belonging, I can appreciate the value of family relationships. He and his nonbelonging represent the fear of not only the inmates but that of every living human, of being alone in life. It's a very human fear. It's just that with the inmate it's worse, more intense, because he doesn't have that much control of his life, his being. Life in prison is much more intense. When you're excited, you're really excited, and when you're depressed, you're really depressed. And your fears are very, very real to you, whether they're real or not; they run that much deeper. Oh, I understand their fear."

[June 1984]

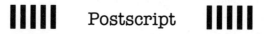 **Postscript**

On the morning of May 31, 1984, two weeks after being interviewed, Roy Fulghum was informed by prison authorities that he had been granted a medical furlough to his family, effective June 1. On the same day, Edmond Ruffing, a seventy-two-year-old resident of Angola's Old Folks Ward, serving a life sentence for murder, was buried at Point Look-Out. A first offender, he

continued

had no family and never received a visitor during his seventeen years of confinement. Fulghum died on December 29, 1990, at the home of his sister.

Following publication of "Dying in Prison," Warden Ross Maggio ordered Assistant Warden Roger Thomas to research old prison records in the state archives and determine the identity of every person buried at Point Look-Out. As a result of Thomas's efforts, names were placed on every tombstone in the cemetery.

MAGGIO RETIRES

|||||

Wilbert Rideau

EDITORS' NOTE

The 1983 gubernatorial campaign was a no-holds-barred contest, and at its conclusion clemency was the major issue. Incumbent Dave Treen boasted of having granted only forty acts of clemency to prisoners as compared to the thousands given by challenger Edwin Edwards during his previous tenure as governor. The debate was dramatized when one of Edwards's pardon recipients murdered the candidate's brother, Nolan Edwards. Notwithstanding this, Edwards defended his clemency policy, calling clemency a traditional and integral part of the justice system, and charged Treen with abdicating his gubernatorial responsibilities. Edwards promised that, if elected, he would seek legislation removing the governor from involvement in the clemency process.

Edwards won by a historic landslide. He announced the reappointment of C. Paul Phelps as head of the Department of Public Safety and Corrections. Shortly after taking office in March 1984, Edwards appointed a Forgotten Man Committee, a citizens' panel to help him keep his campaign promise to remove the governor from the clemency process and to also study the situation of Angola's then 1,200 lifers and address the problems created by the long-term confinement of prisoners.

Angola warden Ross Maggio strode into the main prison's visiting room, where some thirty inmate leaders had been assembled for an "important announcement" by the warden. Maggio had just finished meeting with his administrative staff. In his usual style, he wasted no time and got straight to the point.

He was retiring. "This isn't something I'm doing on the spur of the moment," he explained to the prisoners. "When I was asked to come back to Angola in 'eighty-one, I said I would but it would probably be no more than three years. I've given this move a great deal of thought and decided that it was time to go on to something else. I've done everything I set out to do when I came here in 'seventy-six and 'eighty-one, and I hope I've made some progress for you in your day-to-day living. I'm not the Pardon or Parole Boards, but I have a lot to do with how your life goes in this place. Everything I did here, I did it because I thought it was best for the overall penitentiary and not any one particular group—both at the inmate and employee level.

"I wish the best for you," he continued. "There are some things on the horizon that may help some of you, if all goes well. I feel that I've contributed to some of the things happening right now and, hopefully, they will work out. I've talked to the Forgotten Man Committee, which was appointed by the governor to study your situation, and that's the most I can do. I've told them that, when it comes to releasing men from the penitentiary, the administration should be allowed some input since we know you better than anyone else. Unfortunately, some people don't share that view and that is why we haven't had that much input in the past. But, hopefully, that may change. I want you to know that I wish the best for you. Good luck."

There was a brief exchange of questions and answers before Maggio turned and walked away. The inmates applauded, calling to him: "Don't forget us, Warden." He paused, looking back, and there was a noticeable softening of his usually granite features. "I won't." And he was gone. The departure marked an end of an era—one during which the inmates and Maggio had traveled a long road together. But despite any differences, the inmates and Maggio parted with mutual respect that transcended their circumstances. That respect was as much a tribute to the man as all the achievements of his career.

Ross Maggio began his career with the Department of Corrections as its agribusiness director in 1967, when he was twenty-eight. The prison's major crop at the time was sugar cane; it was grown and harvested by the inmates, who toiled in the fields under the brutal supervision of an army of shotgun-toting convict-guards. Maggio did not like the sugar cane operation and he was determined to play a role in changing it. His effort was instrumental in eliminating the sugar cane crop and reshaping the prison's agricultural priorities in order to bring the prison into the twentieth century.

"I'd hate to think that we were still in that business right now," he reflected to *The Angolite*. "During the sugar cane era, everything existed to get that crop in. Wardens came and went based on what kind of cane harvest they produced. Academic, vocational, and recreational programs were simply not important. The only thing that mattered was whether that sugar mill rolled, because if it didn't, then the officials did—right out the front gate. . . . You simply couldn't make any improvements in the prison as long as that situation existed. The only hope the prison had for progress was the elimination of the cane crop—and we succeeded in eliminating it and replacing it with soybeans, which is currently the prison's basic crop. By breaking the hold of the cane crop, we were able to move forward and I'm proud that I played a role in eliminating the crop."

In 1976 Maggio was appointed warden of Angola by Corrections Director C. Paul Phelps. At age thirty-six, Maggio was one of the youngest wardens in the nation, and at the time, the Louisiana State Penitentiary was, for all practical purposes, the state's penal system. Far removed from civilization, the prison had traditionally been a power unto itself, often able to buck the will of the Department of Corrections and go its own way. But the winds of change were blowing—a new penal system was being developed that would encompass many prisons and diverse agribusiness operations.

During the three years preceding Maggio's appointment to the wardenship, forty inmates had been stabbed to death and 360 seriously injured from knife wounds. Violence was woven into the very fabric of the prison's daily life. Inmate cliques controlled much of the prison and its operations, while a grossly understaffed security force was divided into warring factions vying for power. A local federal court was so shocked by conditions that it declared Angola cruel and unusual punishment and ordered sweeping reforms. Instead of fighting the court order as other states had done, Louisiana officials embraced it and entrusted its enforcement to Maggio. At the time of Maggio's appointment, Corrections Secretary Phelps told *The Angolite* that the department was tired of the Angola situation and determined to put an end to it, especially the violence. The situation called for a man "who will deal with the prisoners and personnel on any terms that they want to deal on."

"I want to create an atmosphere here that will allow any man who wants to improve himself the opportunity to do so, without having to worry about whether he will live to walk out of here," Maggio told *The Angolite* on his first day as warden.

Introducing the concept of a "floating administration," Maggio ordered all of his wardens out of their offices and into the prison to supervise its operations firsthand. Beefing up his security force, he cracked down hard on violence. Unlike other prison wardens, who locked up all prisoners to prevent violence, Maggio methodically identified and went after inmate clique leaders and potential troublemakers, locking them up or transferring them to positions in the prison where they were ineffective. Rule-abiding prisoners were left alone.

"Inmates are not that much different than citizens in the free community," Maggio told *The Angolite*. "Ninety-five percent of them, when they knock off from their jobs and go to their dorms, want to be able to relax, read a book, listen to the radio, or write a letter. They don't want loud noise and tension around them. The majority of the problems you have in here are caused by a relatively small percentage of the inmates—and it's the same ones over and over."

Personnel cliques were dealt with through dismissals, forced resignations, forced retirements, and transfers that made them ineffective. Maggio hired and fired more personnel than any previous warden. He reshaped the entire power structure of the prison. Blacks and Cajuns benefited from his administration, rising to positions never before held by members of either ethnic group. He placed administrative emphasis upon a prison-wide recreation program, creating a gymnasium and laying the foundation for what would become the largest organized prison recreational program in the nation. A multimillion-dollar dining hall was built. A prison training academy for new officers was established, marking the first professional training ever given to correctional officers in this state.

Maggio will probably be most remembered for his enforcement of the DOC's philosophy that every able-bodied prisoner would work. When Maggio arrived at Angola in 1976, several thousand inmates lay idle. Maggio put them to work, and in the face of some stern criticism, he made it clear that he would not tolerate idleness. His critics charged that he was placing work before rehabilitation. He shrugged this off, saying that rehabilitation could never be achieved through massive inmate idleness, that idleness produced only a bloody harvest of violence and strife.

The violence and bloodshed came to a screeching halt. During an eighteen-month period in 1976 and 1977, there was only one stabbing death and fewer than ten stabbings requiring hospitalization. At a time when nationally respected corrections officials were surrendering to the "inevitability" of prison violence, Maggio converted the bloodiest prison in the nation into the safest.

"I feel that I was instrumental in making Angola a safe place," Maggio explained to *The Angolite*, "but it was no one-man deal. I played a role in a big organizational effort. A significant part I played was recommending the number of correctional officers needed to adequately staff Angola. We have a lot fewer problems in this prison than in others, because we are adequately staffed. In 1976 Judge West accepted my staff recommendations and it worked out fine."

Maggio admits that, unlike previous wardens, he had the necessary resources to turn Angola around. The legislature gave the Department of Corrections an almost blank check to implement the court order. That allowed Maggio to hire and train an army of correctional officers who would ultimately number about 1,700. The increased security supervision effectively curtailed former inmate freedoms.

However, the drastic changes, especially the intense security supervision and imposition of the work ethic, did not go unchallenged by the inmates. In May of 1977 a substantial part of the eight-hundred-man Big Yard population staged a work stoppage in protest of some of the new policies. Maggio quickly nipped the protest in the bud. Security officers armed with machine guns surrounded the inmates and locked them up in cells and a makeshift holding area. Maggio promptly transferred several hundred inmates to other units. The inmates returned to work the next day. That was the only disturbance of Maggio's career, one that created his reputation of refusing to negotiate under threat or pressure.

While the strike was broken quickly, charges of insensitivity and a propensity for too much security followed Maggio throughout the rest of his career. "I've had a little criticism about using too much security during executions and other things," Maggio told *The Angolite*, "but I was never criticized for having too little. I'd rather have too much security than not enough. A good example of that point is the New Mexico prison riot. Security had information that something was coming down but they only had seventeen men on duty the night of the takeover by the eleven hundred inmates. Had I been in charge, we would've had two *hundred* and seventeen men on duty, because I believe in being prepared before something happens, not afterwards."

Much of the criticism leveled against Maggio after the 1977 work stoppage stemmed from his transfer of a large number of inmates to Camp J, an ultra–maximum security disciplinary unit. "Yes, I drew some criticism from some organizations I would call left-wing liberals about Camp J," Maggio admitted. "But it was those same reform activists who wanted the violence cleaned up in the prison, who cried about all the people being killed here. They don't understand the realities of prison. You have to have a unit like Camp J to lock up violent inmates—those who kill, rape, and strong-arm.

"As warden," Maggio continued, "I had two basic responsibilities. First, to protect society, and second, to have a safe, peaceful prison. This prison was out of control; it was literally being shredded by violence. Unlike the liberals who wanted to stand around wringing their hands in despair, someone had to have the courage to step in and put a stop to it. I made it clear that anyone—and I didn't care who they were—caught with or using a weapon would be transferred to Camp J. I was not going to tolerate letting a handful of thugs terrorize the rest of the prison population. The responsible, rule-abiding prisoner didn't end up at Camp J; he didn't have any problems with me. But, yes, the killers, the homosexual rapists, and the strong-armers caught plenty of heat from me—and I don't regret enforcing that philosophy to the letter, despite the criticisms."

In late 1977 Maggio announced that he would be leaving Angola to become warden of the Hunt Correctional and Diagnostic Center at St. Gabriel, then still under construction. For the next year, he personally supervised the construction of the multimillion-dollar facility that would serve as the intake center for everyone entering the state's prison system. It marked the first time a warden in Louisiana had been given an opportunity to create and organize a prison from the ground up. The facility opened in 1979, and Maggio settled down as its first warden. But not for long.

In October 1981, following a major administrative political upheaval, the DOC asked Maggio to return to Angola as warden. While the task facing him in 1976 had been to end the violence, instill a work ethic, and implement the federal court order, the major problem confronting him in 1981 was a seething hopelessness among prisoners. It was a problem that would test his abilities, requiring the exercise of day-to-day management with the delicacy and balance of a trapeze artist to keep prisoner dissatisfaction at a minimum.

During his second tenure, Maggio demonstrated that he was a professional warden. When the Republican administration proposed double-bunking as a means to cut costs by avoiding the building of new prisons, wardens across the state generally embraced the concept—and there was a lot of political pressure to do so. But Maggio opposed double-bunking, believing it would compromise prison security and the safety of Angola's employees and inmates. And when the Republican DOC proposed the idea of turning the prison's food service over to private contractors as a cost-cutting measure, Maggio once again refused to accept the idea, believing it could lead to some serious inmate unrest at the prison.

But there was little that Maggio could do about prisoner hopelessness, the solution to which was not within his power. Hopelessness was the direct result of a system paralyzed and intimidated by law-and-order politics and the removal of incentives and meaningful release mechanisms for long-term prisoners. A tough law-and-order conservative himself, Maggio had previously adhered to a policy of never requesting the release of any prisoner. But along the way he had acquired respect for those rule-abiding prisoners who tried to make the best of their situation and improve themselves in the process. And as the situation worsened, Maggio began speaking out on the state's obligation to assist inmates desiring to rehabilitate themselves.

Maggio believed in what he was telling the public. In October 1982, two inmates barged into his home, subjecting his family to several hours of terror. Taking Maggio and his mother hostage, the inmates attempted to force him to drive them out the front gate, but the escape was thwarted when Maggio rammed his truck into the gate. One inmate was killed and the other wounded. DOC officials went before the news media, citing the incident as an example of the nature of the inmates at Angola. The next day Maggio reined in his security force and prevented them from taking any reprisals against the inmates. And he told the press that the escape attempt had been an isolated incident and was not representative of the rest of the inmate population.

Shortly afterward, at a time when the Republican governor was refusing to grant clemency to Angola prisoners, Maggio stated publicly that, if asked to do so, his staff could pick as many as four hundred inmates who were rehabilitated and could safely be released into society. The request never came. Earlier this year, Maggio addressed the newly appointed Forgotten Man Committee on behalf of some three thousand long-term prisoners at Angola, calling for meaningful changes in the system to allow for release consideration for deserving inmates. He had come a long way—from the get-tough warden who would not request release for any prisoner, to the single most powerful voice speaking out on prisoners' behalf.

With the election of a new state administration, the prison monster has been quieted and hope is here once again. Now, Maggio is stepping out of the penal picture. He had an opportunity, like no warden before him, to stamp his personality on Angola, and he influenced the state's penal philosophy with his insistence on control, work, clean prisons, and strong recreation programs. His career was extraordinarily successful; even his detractors concede his expertise.

"Being a conscientious warden," Maggio told *The Angolite,* "is not being a warden eight hours a day through a forty-hour week. A conscientious warden is a warden seven days a week, around the clock, day and night. There are two ways to run Angola. You can grab the tiger by the tail and hold on for dear life, or you can grab it by the head and try to make it do what you want it to. Of course, when you do that, you're going to get a few scars and bites on you. Still, I'd rather hold the head than the tail.

"The warden is not the Parole or Pardon Board," Maggio added, "but he does dictate the quality of day-to-day life for the inmate population—the work you do, your recreational activities, the food you eat, the time you get up and go to bed, and the kind of prison you live in. Those are the kind of things a warden controls—and as simple as it may seem, that's a measure of his ability to manage. But not every warden places emphasis on those kind of things."

Maggio leaves at a time when the state penal system is at a crossroads. The state is suffering serious financial difficulties, the governor has created committees to try to institute reforms, yet the legislature doesn't feel compelled to loosen the screws. "There's some pressure to cut money from the prison system, as there always is when there are fiscal problems," Maggio says. "I hope that we never see a time when the prison budget is arbitrarily slashed. That would be a mistake that may reap short-term gains but create long-term problems.

"And I hope we never slide back into a situation where politics gets involved in the day-to-day operations of the prison," he added. "Angola experienced those kind of practices before, and it was continuously plagued by trouble. I've been fortunate in that I never had to contend with politics in my day-to-day decisions in running the prison. It needs to stay that way. But, of course, a warden will always have to contend with politics at a larger level—the legislature, the governor—because they reflect what the public wants."

Maggio is retiring with no regrets. "In all honesty, I can't think of any," he told *The Angolite*. "I can think of some minor things that I didn't get to do—like expanding the rodeo arena and little things like that. But the big things I wanted to do when I came here, I've done. I wanted to turn this place around, and I did. Of course, sometimes what you think was good, other people don't even notice that it was done—and, on the other hand, sometimes you have done something you don't think much of, but someone else will attach importance to it. But I know what I've done—and, in the final analysis, it was the best I could do."

The forty-five-year-old Maggio, whose retirement becomes effective October 8, left on July 8 to take advantage of accumulated vacation time. Asked if he thought the system would let him get away, given his experience, he smiled. "I don't see why not. They change presidents every four years, and the country keeps going."

[August 1984]

 Postscript

Frank Blackburn returned to Angola as warden. Maggio eventually entered the field of private corrections.

THE WALL OF REALITY

|||||

C. Paul Phelps

EDITOR'S NOTE

Inmates of the Louisiana State Penitentiary have maintained a keen interest in the workings and recommendations of the Forgotten Man Committee and the Prison and Jail Overcrowding Policy Task Force. A month after these groups' recommendations had been submitted to the governor, C. Paul Phelps, secretary of the Department of Public Safety and Corrections, accompanied by Forgotten Man Committee co-chairwoman Jane Bankston and Angola warden Frank Blackburn, appeared before a special meeting of inmate leaders to explain the recommendations of the two groups and the political realities attached to them, as well as answer any questions. The following is Phelps's verbatim talk to the leaders.

During the transition period, after Governor Edwards was elected, we talked to him about the formation of two study groups—one, the Forgotten Man Committee; the other, the Prison and Jail Overcrowding Policy Task Force. For those of you who don't know, the committee was a take-off from Governor Earl Long's Forgotten Man Committee following the prison scandals of the late forties. The committee, of course, was made up solely of volunteer citizens and their task was to look at the prison system with an eye toward long-term inmates, people doing long sentences, and see what the state should do, what its official policy was going to be, and make recommendations to the governor.

The Prison and Jail Overcrowding Policy Task Force took a little different track. It was made up solely of people who were policymakers in the criminal-justice system—representatives of the Supreme Court, Court of Appeals, district courts, city courts, sheriffs, district attorneys, councilmen and others, but all people who are involved on a day-to-day basis in making policy for the criminal-justice system. Also on it were people like Senator Fritz Windhortz of New Orleans, who is chairman of the Senate Judiciary Committee, and Rep. Bruce Bolin of Bossier Parish, chairman of the House Criminal Justice Committee.

Both committees worked independently of each other, though there was some overlapping in terms of membership. Both committees met extensively, grappled with the issues, and came out, not surprisingly, with very similar recommendations.

The Forgotten Man Committee made several recommendations dealing with long-term incarceration and sentencing. They recommended that something be done in the area of sentencing reform. They recommended that we reevaluate a life sentence—what it was and how long it should be. They also recommended that everybody be reviewed by the Parole Board after twenty years. I don't know how they arrived at the twenty-year figure—maybe they just picked it off the wall or figured it was as good a starting place as any.

The task force, on the other hand, dealt with the broader issues of the criminal-justice system. Their number one recommendation was that the state reestablish its criminal-justice data base. In 1980 the state, in its infinite wisdom, pulled the plug on the data base and we flushed about $800,000 worth of federal money down the drain. So, we're trying to reestablish a data base that will tell us who's in the system, how long they stay, when they arrived—all the things that you've always wanted to know about the criminal-justice system and been afraid to ask.

The one thing that was uniform to both committees was that, if we continue the way we're going, we're going to bankrupt the state. Both committees made very strong recommendations that the probation and parole system be beefed up and that we move toward a program that would be tantamount to intensive supervision on the part of probation and parole.

Now, for those of you who might not be aware of why you're here . . . the state, in its coping with crime on the streets, back in the early seventies, late seventies, and into the eighties, adopted the position that the only way it was going to punish people was to lock them up.

And we've done such a good job of it that Louisiana is now number one in the nation in terms of the number of people it has locked up per 100,000 people. This philosophy of incarceration was based primarily on the availability of a lot of money—the oil money, and there was a lot of it. Legislators were willing to set a significant portion of it aside to build new prisons. And during the last Edwards administration, the Department of Corrections spent $250 million building new prisons and renovating old ones.

By the end of the first Edwards administration, the state was generating 50 inmates a month more than it was letting out. Then came the Treen administration, and the state adopted the policy that it was not going to build any more prisons. The Treen administration felt that they could squeeze more people into existing facilities and solve the problem that way. Well, they did squeeze more people in. During the same time that they stopped building, they systematically enhanced and supported every bill that came along that either did away with goodtime, did away with parole eligibility, did away with pardon eligibility, or lengthened sentences. They were so successful that, in four years' time, they were able to increase the incoming prisoner rate from 50 a month to 115 a month.

During this period, I was working part-time for federal judge Frank Polozola on the jails and jail overcrowding and the constitutional issue of how full a jail could be. We were able to bring under court order everything we found that had a lock on it. So Louisiana is now the only state in the Union where every jail, prison, detention facility, holding cell, anything that has a lock on it that we know about has a constitutional capacity. That was arrived at by discussion with the fire marshal and the health officer—which is good. So, we now know how many beds there are available in the state.

The problem is that the state is using up the jail beds at the rate of fourteen hundred a year. So, as Department of Corrections prisoners back up into the parish jails, the judges, district attorneys, and sheriffs must have a meeting every Friday to decide who they are going to let out of jail so that they can arrest somebody on the weekend. Then, on Monday, they meet again and decide who they are going to let out of jail so that they don't violate the court order.

At the same time, as you are aware, the price of oil has dropped significantly. And every time the price of oil goes down a dollar, we lose millions in state revenue, which directly affects state operations.

So here we are getting ready to start the legislative session of April 1985 with a declining revenue base and an increasing prison population and a known number of beds to lock people up in. We've done a lot of groundwork and, if editorials meant anything, we would be in good stead. Every major newspaper, with the exception of the Lake Charles area, has basically supported what I have been saying and what the Department of Corrections has been saying: that to continue to lock everybody up as the only method of punishment is fiscally unsound and not something that the state can afford to do.

We were fortunate on the task force, in that we got Stephanie Alexander to come to the meetings. Mrs. Alexander is the commissioner of administration and, as such, handles the money matters for the state. She makes the recommendations to the governor as to how the money should be parceled out. One of her recommendations is that the Department of Corrections is to be funded at 99 percent. Of course, that's not really a big deal—99 percent of a standstill budget translates into our going from $180 million this year to $214 million next year as our expansion program goes on. But the really significant thing she did was to increase the number of probation and parole officers by a hundred. This is very encouraging because this is the first time that we have had that kind of support.

The package that the administration is going to turn in will include some additional studies and will also include, for the first time, the probation and parole officer increase. Now, I know that what you would like to hear is that the administration is going to push for a major change in sentencing. I don't believe that is going to come this year. The reason that I don't believe it is because it has not become apparent to the legislature yet that they have to make very, very difficult, hard choices this time up. Last year we lost our intensive-supervision and second-offender probation proposal by a vote of 72 to 21. But this session, the legislature is going to come face-to-face with the fact they are now going to have to make some choices that they have never had to make before due to the fact that the Public Safety and Corrections budget is now in a death fight with Highways, Education, and Health and Human Resources for money. Those are the three things that affect most people in the state outside of corrections. When they realize that, in order to fund this get-tough policy, they are going to have to take money away from education, take it away from bridges, and take it away from the Department of Health and Human Resources, they will—in my opinion—be left with the idea that they must change the system.

The only way to change the system is to enhance probation and parole. The task force grappled with a number of things that other states are doing to deal with overcrowding: their early release programs, emergency release, or what have you. But when you look at what happened in those states, it has not had any long-term value. It has not accomplished what it set out to do. My plan is to increase the probation and parole capability to the extent that we can control what happens to people who are either not sent to prison or who are let out early. The Parole Board has been much more liberal in the exercise of their parole authority than they have in the past and they are living on very thin ice because the probation and parole caseload is in excess of 150 [per officer], and there is no possible way that anybody is going to supervise that many people.

Now, while the administration is not willing to sponsor some of the more difficult legislation, I have the permission of the administration to seek other sponsors. My commitment from the administration is that, when I find my sponsors and get the bills introduced and sponsored, the administration will support them. They are not going to oppose them by any stretch of the imagination. But, if I sit here and tell you that we are going to pass everything that we introduce, I'd be lying to you.

We will introduce legislation to make it possible for everybody who is doing a life sentence to be considered by the Parole Board at the end of twenty years. I don't have to tell you that getting it passed is not going to be easy. It is not easy to change public opinion. As you know, the Baton Rouge *Morning Advocate* has been running polls and people are saying that they are willing to pay more money to keep people in prison longer. But I don't buy that. I don't think that they are really willing to pay that kind of money. They say they do, but they don't yet really appreciate what kind of money is involved. You see, the legislature is basically convinced that there is no cheaper way to run a prison system, that there is an absolute bottom-line below which prison administrators are not willing to go. We are not going to reduce staff to the extent that we skirt disaster in terms of riots or loss of internal control. Of course, I realize that there are two sides to the fence. But while some might not mind, I don't believe that any of you who have any hope of a future are interested in the Department of

Corrections reducing its staff to the point where we go back to the days of the 1970s, when Angola was one of the bloodiest prisons in the world.

Asking people if we should build more prisons to lock people up is sort of like asking about the flag, motherhood, and apple pie—everybody is for it. Unless they are directly involved, one way or another, or are particularly informed, the typical attitude will be "Yeah, let's lock everybody up. That sounds like a good idea. Put them in prison." However, the reality only comes into focus when it's time to pay up, and every political jurisdiction lately that has tried to pass a tax to build new jails has failed. So, it's almost a schizophrenic thing. People are willing to say, "Yes, I'm willing to lock everybody up," but when it comes time to put the money where the mouth is, they have second thoughts.

The Legislative Fiscal Office estimates that it will cost $240 per each Louisiana taxpayer to continue doing what we are currently doing. Well, when the head of a household sees that his family has to put that much out every year, and it's going to keep increasing, there's a very good chance he'll arrive at the same conclusion I have—and that is, I'm not willing to put up that much money because they're coming right behind that and asking for me to put up some more money for education. We've just got to get our priorities back in line again, and it's going to take a while. It's going to take some change in public attitude.

Each passing day, you all get older, and the fiscal weight gets heavier and heavier. You weren't in super good health when you came to prison, and the delivery of medical care in prison is very expensive. And, if we have to keep you in prison until age sixty-five or seventy or however old you are going to be, it's going to prove very expensive because we're going to have to pay to care for you while you're in prison, then have to pay to care for you when you get out because you'll have outlived your family and resources and will be too old to care for yourselves. We'll be stuck with the expense of caring for you for your entire lifetime. That may well be the price of punishment but, for we taxpayers, it's sort of like cutting off our nose to spite our face.

You all may get the idea that I'm very callous, but I'm talking dollars and cents that, at some point in time, we need to redefine how we're going to punish people and how much money we're willing to spend to keep somebody in prison to satisfy a very small group of people. Each of you, I presume, knows a small group of people who would like to see you kept locked up for two lifetimes maybe. Now, for somebody like me who doesn't have that kind of vengeance for any individual—and I like to think there are substantial numbers of people like myself—I'm beginning to become very concerned about how long *I'm* going to pay to keep *your* vengeance people happy.

Unfortunately, when we talk of changing public attitude, we're necessarily talking about a long-term proposition. However, I've been very, very encouraged by the change of attitudes that the District Attorneys Association, the Sheriffs Association and the District Court Judges Association have experienced. And too, there's a difference about this upcoming legislative session, and it has to do with simple economics. The thing that is different this time is that money is such an issue now that the legislature can no longer put their head in the sand and say, "Well, we'll vote to build more prisons." The money is not there. They cannot do that anymore. And when they run into the wall of that reality, they will have to, by the force of necessity, start talking about changing the costly and impractical way we are going about the business of punishing people.

[April 1985]

||||| Postscript |||||

Phelps implemented all of the Forgotten Man Committee's recommendations in 1985 to the Department of Corrections. All of the committee's recommendations designed to address system problems were rejected by the legislature, including the measures that would make long-termers eligible for parole after serving twenty years, and the removal of the governor from the clemency process. Eighteen months after it had convened, having made no progress, and having been abandoned by the governor, the committee officially dissolved itself in frustration.

The Prison Overcrowding Policy Task Force, which Phelps had counted on to alter the penal direction, instead recom-

continued

mended a vigorous prison construction program at both state and local levels. It recommended that the state pay 70 percent of the costs, with local governments kicking in only 30 percent. This fueled an unprecedented jail- and prison-building binge.

Also contrary to Phelps's expectations, the legislature did not address its fiscal insanity, but voted instead for tougher, longer sentences, more prisons, and an increased corrections budget while cutting back on social, educational, and other much-needed state services. This plunged Louisiana's bond rating to the lowest in the nation, forcing the state to raise taxes and borrow money to make ends meet.

BUTLER'S PARK

Wilbert Rideau

This looks like it's going to be the best thing to happen here since they put inmates in blue jeans," Ernest Warren says of his new duties. An Angola security officer, Warren assists on varying days with a new and innovative feature of the prison's inmate visiting program: outdoor visiting.

Announced earlier this year by Corrections Secretary C. Paul Phelps, who described it as the first step in the administration's long-term plan to institute incentives to induce and reward good behavior among the prisoner population, the program further improves the conditions of inmate visiting at Angola. Traditionally, inmates at the Louisiana State Penitentiary have been permitted only two methods of visiting, the manner being determined by custody status. Maximum-security inmates must visit with a screen or glass partition separating them from their visitors. Medium- and minimum-security inmates are permitted contact visits: The inmate and his visitor simply walk into the visiting room, select whatever table they desire, and are free to touch or embrace. The new program adds another dimension to visiting, and the first stage of it is already a reality.

A spacious tree-shaded park, nestled against sloping hills on the outskirts of the employee residential area, has been created at the prison for eligible trusty inmates to have picnics with their approved visitors. Barbecue grills have been installed to allow the inmates and visitors to cook their own meals. Administrative emphasis is upon a relaxed atmosphere and on allowing inmates and visitors the freedom to do things together as a family.

"People tend to forget that, regardless of the reason the inmate is in prison, he's somebody's father, son, husband, or brother," Buddie Dale Weber points out. Weber, a security officer, is on-site coordinator of the program at the park. "If the inmate is to eventually leave here and be reintegrated into free society, we have to prepare him for it by helping him to maintain and preserve his family ties. Having an inmate visit his family across a table in a crowded and noisy visiting room leaves a lot to be desired. Out here in the park, a father can play tag with his kids, they can move around, the family can cook and do something together as a family. This type of visiting is a much more meaningful way to let the inmate remain a husband to his wife, a son to his parents, a father to his children. In addition, this kind of visiting is less stressful for the visitors—who, we must remember, are taxpaying citizens who haven't committed crimes. I think this is definitely a step in the right direction for the Louisiana State Penitentiary."

The visitors are grateful. "This is the first time in seven years that we've been able to all be together as a family with Layton," Murl Creel states, watching her son and his child chase a butterfly. "It's such a great change from sitting in that visiting room. It feels good to be able to get out like this and we're really enjoying it."

Danny Welch had told his mother, Mary, about the new visiting program. But, she admitted, "I still didn't know what to expect. You can't really picture it in your mind until you come here and actually see it. And, having seen it, it's still hard to believe. It's so much more than I anticipated."

"The visitors love it," Weber states. "Once they've come out here, they'll go to any length to be able to come back and visit like this again. In fact, the inmates are now getting pressure from their wives and families as a result. They know that they can only come out here and visit like this as long as the inmate is behaving himself while he's in prison. And I hear the visitors talking to the inmate as they're leaving, telling him in no uncertain terms that he'd better stay out of trouble so that they can continue to visit like this."

"It's true," Louis Dabon, a trusty, acknowledges. "Right after the first visit in the park, my wife served notice on me that, if I cause her to lose this privilege, I'm in trouble."

Eligibility for a picnic visit in the park is more or less in the hands of the inmate. His custody status and prison conduct record determine whether or not he and his visitors are eligible for the new program. Currently, the inmate is required to be a Class A trusty and must not have had a "write-up" (disciplinary infraction) within the past year.

"I don't know of anything better than this to give an inmate a reason to keep his business straight," Warren says. "It works out good for the system, the inmates, and all us employees who'll benefit from the inmates behaving themselves."

"That's the purpose of the program," Deputy Warden Hilton Butler admits. He created the outdoor-visiting program. "It's to give the inmates and visitors something good to look forward to while, at the same time, making the prison more trouble-free."

"The park was Hilton's idea," Warden Frank Blackburn states. "He felt that the trusties of Angola deserved something for their efforts and good behavior and, as you know, there's not very much we've been able to do for them. Ever since Hilton told me about it, I've liked the idea and encouraged him to do it. And I'm proud to say that it's turning out very well."

"I think it'll do a man a lot more good to be able to visit and picnic with his family out there rather than being jammed up in the visiting room," Butler explains. "Some of the inmates going out there haven't cooked and eaten with their families in ten, fifteen years. Now, they can have a picnic, run around and play with their kids. I think it'll contribute to keeping the families closer together. It'll also help the inmate by giving him a better attitude while encouraging other inmates who don't qualify to straighten up their act, make better men of themselves and work toward trying to get the same privilege. It's also a good disciplinary tool because, once they've had a visit in the park, they're not going to want that privilege canceled by getting a write-up."

The program has had its impact. While Danny Welch points out that the new privilege won't cause any dramatic changes in his behavior, since he makes it his business to stay out of trouble anyway, he admits that the knowledge that a write-up will cancel the privilege "does make you a little more careful to make sure you don't get one." He believes the program will prove a definite incentive to other inmates: "Once they see the park and visit like this, they'll realize it's definitely worth working and looking forward to."

Outdoor visiting in the park begins with the onset of warm weather and runs "until the weather gets too cool for people to be out there comfortably," Butler explains, pointing out that Louisiana's winter rarely lasts more than three months.

Unlike the regular visiting program, which restricts visits to two hours or less, the new program allows inmates to be with their visitors in the park for six and a half hours—from eight in the morning until two-thirty in the afternoon. Visitors eligible for picnic visits are required to arrive at the prison gate between eight and nine-thirty. Those arriving late must take their visit in the visiting room under normal procedures. Given the time factor, visitors have to put forth a little extra effort to get to the prison within the appointed time, but many are willing to make it. A Texas couple drove twelve straight hours from Brownsville to get here in time to have a picnic visit with their son. A New Orleans woman whose car broke down in Baton Rouge hired a taxi to get her to the prison on time. While the early hour might be somewhat inconvenient, the visitors have no complaints. As Mary Welch, also from New Orleans, states, "It was worth having to get up at four in the morning to get here in time. The surroundings, the atmosphere—it's all so different and nice. This is the most wonderful thing that could have happened to us. Visiting like this lets us really feel like a family."

To be scheduled for a picnic visit in the park, an eligible inmate must submit a written request to Butler, proposing a specific date on which his visitors can come. Since a year without a disciplinary infraction is the criterion for eligibility, administrative assistant Nettie Voorhies pulls the inmate's file for Butler's review. "I do make exceptions," Butler admits. "If the inmate had a minor disciplinary infraction, something like dropping a cigarette butt on the floor or not cleaning up around his bed or something—I don't hold that against him. For example, one inmate requesting a park visit had two write-ups for gambling, but hadn't had a write-up for several years before then. I went on and approved him for the program. I'm flexible and I'm willing to consider the nature of the infraction. But disciplinary infractions involving refusal to work or insubordination with my officers are the kind I'm not going to give consideration on."

While the regular visiting program operates five days a week, eight hours per day, the outdoor visiting program, in its infancy and restricted to Class A trusties, operates on only a small number of days per month, those days being determined primarily by the number of requests for such visits. Eligible inmates are allowed only one picnic visit per month. (A plan to extend the allowance to twice per month is currently being considered.) The park contains twelve tables, and visits there are not scheduled until there are enough approved requests to justify opening the park to accommodate them. The problem is that Class A trusties constitute only a small segment of the prison's inmate population, and a substantial percentage of them are men who've been confined here many years, men who've experienced the natural corresponding decrease in number and frequency of visitors that goes with the passage of time. And, with disciplinary reports barring some from eligibility, the number of inmates currently participating in the program is small.

Eligible inmates requesting an outdoor visit are encouraged to give an alternate date. "If he asks for just one particular day, he might be the only person requesting that date," Butler points out, "and we can't open the park just to accommodate him. But if he gives us more than one date, that allows us to maybe be able to schedule him on the second date when we might have enough requests to justify opening the park."

The stricter regulations governing behavior in the prison's visiting rooms do not apply to the outdoor visiting program, where the emphasis is on a relaxed atmosphere and freedom. Aside from requiring that everyone stay within the perimeter of the park, "we only ask that each set of visitors respect the others," Voorhies explains. "Each inmate is responsible for his visitors and children. We rely upon those who have the privilege to want to keep it and not mess it up for themselves or others."

A disciplinary infraction incurred at any time, anywhere in the prison, can result in removal of the inmate from the program. Given the importance of visiting, the loss of outdoor-visiting privileges, in addition to the normal punishment meted out by the prison's disciplinary court, makes a disciplinary infraction particularly costly. "That's why I'll consider the nature of the write-up and make exceptions for minor ones," says Butler. "You have to understand that I'm giving the inmate something special. All I'm asking in return is that he stay out of trouble, something he should do anyway. I don't think that's asking for much. So I want him to understand that he automatically loses all of this if he messes up. The only consideration he's going to get and the only exception I'll make is if the infraction is something minor, something I can understand and maybe ignore. Other than that, he's going to be taken off the program. If he's not, I'll be defeating the purpose of the program."

Butler's enthusiasm for the new program is common knowledge. He paid for the first round of charcoal for the barbecues out of his own pocket, asking that visitors donate whatever they wish to a fund so that a steady supply could be available for everyone utilizing the park. He often visits the park, going from table to table, greeting the visitors and asking their input on ways to improve the park. He wanted to install swings and provide playthings for the children, something many of the visitors also suggested, but he's having to reconsider. "I'd love to do it," he says, "but I'm having to give it a lot of thought because I've got to consider the possible civil liability involved if one of the kids got hurt. That's something I'm going to have to discuss with Mr. Phelps and our lawyers before I install anything." Recently, he permitted one visitor to donate small plastic playthings to the park for the smaller kids.

The new program has been greeted with enthusiastic support from Phelps and Blackburn, visiting personnel, and "a lot of prison personnel who you wouldn't ordinarily think would like the idea," Butler says. "Even staunch hard-line security people tell me that they think it's one of the best things to ever happen for the inmates here, and they've offered to do whatever they can to help make it a success. Everyone wants to see it work. For instance, when we had to come up with a way of letting visitors cook without allowing them to bring groceries into the prison, Randy Whitstine, who works at the commissary, agreed to leave his home on his days off to go open the store and fill orders for the visitors. There've been times when I've told him that he didn't have to, that I would personally go get the groceries, but he wanted to do it. And that's the kind of support we've been getting, and from a lot of people—the maintenance department and its inmate workers, my staff, officials, personnel, and even inmate organizations who've offered to buy things that might be needed at the park. Everybody seems supportive. If there's somebody who's not or if they have a problem with the program, they're not letting me know about it."

The program began with trusty prisoners, but it will not end with them. Picnic rights for Class A trusties represent only the first stage of a much larger program. "I definitely intend to extend it to Class B trusties and medium-security inmates," Butler states. "They'll both be integrated into the program at the same time and place, and it'll operate more or less just like it does for Class A trusties in the park. The only difference will be the location." He's considering creating a parklike area adjacent to the front of the main prison visiting room. He had initially planned to start the program for medium-security inmates next spring, but "the program for the trusties is working so well that I'm actually trying to get something started for medium-security inmates this fall," he says. "But if I can't pull it off, I'll definitely have it ready for them by spring. Those who are interested in participating in the program can get ready for it—all they've got to do is give me a year without a serious write-up."

Butler anticipates no problems in extending picnic visits to medium-security inmates. "We're still going to have inmates strip-searched following their visits, just as we do now on regular visits in the visiting room," he points out. "We don't want any contraband flowing through here. Of course, there's always the possibility that, after a while, someone might toy with the idea of trying something. After all, there are some people who'll go through a lot of hassle to get some dope. But that's no real problem, because that kind of prisoner is not likely to be eligible for the program to start with—he's not the kind who can stay clean of a disciplinary report for an entire year. After considering all the angles and based on my thirty-three years' experience with prisoners, I don't expect any increase in the flow of contraband, or any other type of problems."

Butler feels the full potential of the program won't be realized until medium-security inmates are incorporated into it. That's when it is expected to become a full-fledged affair, operating on a daily basis. Medium-security inmates constitute the majority of the prisoner population and the largest percentage of inmates receiving regular visits from friends and relatives. "I think we're going to have a lot of people in the program," Butler speculates, "and the more, the better. I hope we have so many people and that the program gets so big that we have to keep expanding the picnic area, because if there are a thousand inmates participating in the program, that's a thousand prisoners who are staying out of trouble and not causing problems for anyone— that's good news.

"I think this program has the potential of being one of the best incentives for good behavior that you can come up with, given the circumstances and what we have to work with," Butler says. "It's something to help the inmates, something that once they get it, I don't think they're going to want to lose it. And that will reduce disciplinary problems, make the prison more trouble-free, and, in the long run, be good for the security of the institution."

The outdoor-visiting program might be an idea whose time has arrived. Jack Donnelly, warden of the troubled Washington Correctional Facility at Bogalusa, the state's newest prison, recently visited the park site and has requested all available information about the program. He's considering creating a similar one at his prison, which has been plagued by a lack of adequate incentive mechanisms. Butler and his idea were paid the ultimate compliment at a dinner in his honor attended by officials and numerous inmate leaders. Warden Blackburn, at the request of the inmates, officially proclaimed the park site's name to be "Butler Park."

[August 1985]

  Postscript

Layton Creel, Louis Dabon, and Danny Welch served their sentences and were released. Sgt. Ernest Warren retired, Buddie Dale Weber no longer works at the park, and Nettie Voorhies transferred to a prison closer to her home. Frank Blackburn retired in 1987 and Hilton Butler was named warden the same year.

In 1987 picnic visits were extended to medium-security inmates. The now-expanded picnic visiting program is administered by the prison classification department. Similar programs now exist at most Louisiana prisons.

THE PELICAN PROTECTOR

|||||

Tommy Mason and Wilbert Rideau

Duty is a very personal thing. It is what comes from know-ing the need to take action and not just a need to urge others to do something.

—MOTHER THERESA

Year's end 1986 saw the official dedication of the John B. Rabalais Waterfowl Refuge at the Louisiana State Penitentiary. The refuge is believed to be the first wildlife sanctuary within the perimeters of a prison anywhere in the nation.

The story of the refuge began some four years ago, when Lieutenant Bobby Oliveaux discovered a pelican trapped in a trout line at Lake Killarney. He freed the unfortunate bird, but the pelican had suffered serious injuries to its wing. Oliveaux saw to it that the bird was treated and nursed back to health. Once healthy, the bird was still unable to fly because of the damaged wing, so Captain John B. Rabalais took him to Camp F, where he was adopted and cared for by the prisoners, who named him "Pierre."

Rabalais and Ron Wikberg, a lifer, decided that Pierre should have a mate or be relocated to an area where a mate was available. With the blessing of Warden Frank Blackburn, Wikberg spearheaded the project, contacting the media and people throughout the region. Pierre, one of the most unusual of jailbirds, quickly became a focal point of the media. He was featured in *Louisiana Conservationist* magazine and was the subject of television reports.

As a result of the media attention, a mate was found for Pierre. Dr. W. S. Bivens, of the Louisiana State University's School of Veterinary Medicine, and two students had treated a gunshot-wounded pelican they named Samantha, and she needed a place to rest and heal. Through the combined efforts of Bivens and Fur and Refuge Division chief Johnnie Tarver, Samantha was brought to Angola. She immediately hit it off with Pierre. A variety of other feathered creatures gradually joined the two pelicans at the pond, including two more injured pelicans, compliments of the Audubon Park Zoological Gardens. To ensure the peace of the Camp F pond for its increasing waterfowl population, Rabalais persuaded Warden Blackburn to prohibit all hunting and fishing there.

On December 2, 1986, on a sunny but chilly afternoon, a host of prison personnel, prisoners, local and state officials, and friends and relatives of Rabalais gathered in front of Camp F to dedicate the John B. Rabalais Waterfowl Refuge as a testimonial to the man and his thirty years of service at Angola. Warden Blackburn served as emcee for the event.

Prior to acknowledging the dignitaries present, Deputy Warden Hilton Butler recounted his longstanding friendship with Rabalais. "John and I go back a long ways," he told the audience. "It was kind of like it is now—we were real short-handed. I was captain then and John had just started work for me. He wanted to get married and I told him to go ahead, I'd work in his place—so I pulled his shift for him to get married." He joked, "To this day, I don't know whether I did Mrs. Dora a great favor or not."

Wikberg, who had worked with Rabalais to create the sanctuary, told the group: "Today, at this dedication, mankind is solemnizing two important events. It is reaffirming concern for our wildlife and environment, and it is paying tribute to a special human being and friend. In my opinion, there is no man that is more deserving."

The high point of the event was provided by attorney Jack P. F. Gremillion, who, as attorney general, first met and became associated with Rabalais long ago when Rabalais was working in the prison's record office. "I have always cherished his friendship, and I will value it as long as I live," he declared. Calling his old friend up to stand beside the podium, Gremillion presented him with an official certificate on behalf of J. Burton Angelle, secretary of the Louisiana Wildlife and Fisheries and of The Jeffersonians (a civic organization), appointing him to the honorary position of "Premier Pelican Protector."

A simple man of simple tastes, Rabalais accepted the honor with both pride and humility. He was never a soft man, but his face bore the lines of age and wisdom and mirrored a hint of the compassion that lay beneath the gruff exterior. He was a man for his times, and a man of few words: "I have always said, and I still do, that anything can be accomplished by anybody willing to work together. This refuge is a perfect example of that belief." Visibly moved by the honor, he thanked everyone for participating.

Bishop Stanley Ott of the Baton Rouge Catholic Diocese blessed the refuge, pointing out that the "pelican is a symbol or a sign of the Eucharist. A pelican's mother will give of her own blood to her young in order to feed it; and the pelican is a beautiful symbol of love, of unselfishness, and of total giving. . . ."

Assistant Warden Roger Thomas closed the ceremonies, observing: "We've had quite a few of these grand openings in recent months. I'm happy to see that this has been one of the nicer ones. It demonstrates that there is more to Angola than bars and guns. We are not only in the business of rehabilitating inmates, we are now going to be rehabilitating birds."

Tarver, representing the Wildlife and Fisheries Department, told *The Angolite,* "I've been looking forward to coming here to see for myself the results of everyone's efforts, and I'm pleased by what I see. It is most likely that this is the first such sanctuary ever created inside a prison setting—an event for which Louisiana is proud." Sheriff Bill Daniels of West Feliciana Parish, on hand to extend his congratulations, said: "John has been a big asset to the corrections system and is deserving of this honor."

Rabalais told *The Angolite:* "The dedication of the refuge in my name is an honor I will never forget. The event was a very touching, emotional, and proud time for me and my family. Although the honor was bestowed on me personally, it is an honor which is shared by many people who participated in the venture. The refuge signifies much more than a place for different birds and animals to live together in peaceful coexistence. It confirms that employees and inmates in a maximum-security institution, as well as all people, can work together under unusual circumstances to develop positive programs in any environment. I personally dedicate the refuge to all employees and inmates at Angola as a symbol of cooperation, dedication, honor, respect, and accomplishment. Words cannot express the gratitude I feel for the efforts of all the inmates and staff who were responsible for developing the refuge and for dedicating it in my name."

Rabalais's family was touched by the event. His wife, Dora, who heads the prison's Legal Programs Department, stated: "It is of great significance to all of us at this particular time in our lives. The dedication ceremony was a very moving and memorable time for all of us." She added, "While John portrays a gruff, tough, professional exterior, those of us who know him know that he is a kind, dedicated man of courage, honesty, and integrity who has a special place in his heart for anything or anyone suffering a disadvantage. I cannot think of a more fitting tribute for John's thirty years of dedicated professional service to the Louisiana State Penitentiary. I hope that the honor bestowed on John will serve as a reminder to all employees that corrections is not a thankless profession and that the refuge will serve as a symbol to both staff and inmates that they can work together to accomplish positive goals."

[February 1987]

Postscript

Captain John B. Rabalais died in 1987. The wildlife refuge is still maintained. The pelican still lives in a nearby waterway.

A LABOR OF LOVE

|||||

Tommy Mason

Prison is a hard, smothering place where men become stagnant. Prisoners are bombarded with the public's notion that they are animals who are not to be trusted, who will prey on law-abiding citizens, and who are incapable of rising above their mistakes.

In spite of these stereotypes, many people are willing to extend a hand to men behind bars, and help them to rise above their worst failings. At the Louisiana State Prison, in April 1987, a group of musicians did just that by staging a concert for them. The entertainers were the Neville Brothers, Charmaine Neville & Real Feelings, and the Pfister Sisters.

Seven years earlier, Chuck Colson of Watergate fame brought Johnny Cash to perform at Angola through the organization Prison Fellowship. That was the first concert since 1974.

Ironically, following the show in 1974, spirits were high and there was much expectation for future concerts. However, state politics were gradually moving right. The result was no concerts, and on the occasions when interested entertainers tried to come, the key administrators were not willing to allow them to put on their shows.

The seed for the 1987 concert began, coincidentally, when *Angolite* editor Wilbert Rideau spoke to a civics group from the New Orleans area. It happened that Lynne Batson and Aaron Neville, of the Neville Brothers, were in the audience. Neville is the head of the Uptown Youth Cultural and Development Center, a nonprofit volunteer organization he founded in 1980, whose mission is to help young people become self-reliant, contributing members of society rather than waste their lives on crime, drugs, and alcohol. His brother Charles served time in Angola during the 1960s.

Lynne Batson has her own legal practice and has worked with the Nevilles for about nine years as their unofficial spokeswoman. When she discovered how long it had been since a concert had been organized for Angola prisoners, she decided to take action.

"The Nevilles were one hundred percent in favor of doing the concert," Batson said. "The Pfister Sisters, a local harmony group, were interested in coming, and so was Charmaine Neville and her group, Real Feelings."

At Angola, R. Hilton Butler, newly appointed warden of the prison, liked the idea and designated Assistant Warden Roger Thomas to oversee the project.

There were problems. "I guess I did foresee some of them," Batson told *The Angolite*. "It was hard to make people see the amount of expenses that were incurred in doing something like this. The musicians, of course, were donating their time, but we still had equipment to move and to arrange."

Roger Thomas admitted: "I knew it was going to be a tremendous amount of hard work." But, he said, "concerts provide an outlet for the inmates. It's done all over the country. I never heard of anybody who had a strong objection to someone coming in and performing for inmates. I've always been for things that benefit inmates as long as it doesn't interfere with the security operations of the penitentiary."

Wilbert Rideau sought out the leaders of inmate clubs to come up with donations to cover the expenses of trucking, paying roadies, and other fees. The Angola Amateur Boxing Association, the Pardon Finance Board, the Angola Jaycees, the Lifers' Association, the Drama Club, and also the Social, Educational and Athletic Club donated money to the event.

Prisoners were involved in almost every aspect of the production. Terry Deakle, Jerry Bell, and a crew of prisoners worked to design a stage that would accommodate the equipment and entertainers. Thomas was also appreciative of the cooperation he got from security. "You couldn't ask for a smoother operation. It was done through the coordination of security, the administration, and the inmates. This thing went off without a hitch."

*   *   *

Charles Neville, an inmate at Angola some twenty years ago after being convicted for possession of marijuana, flew in from Oregon to make the concert. Charles is quick to chide those people whose attitude is "If you're going to wind up in the penitentiary, that's going to be the end of your life." He admits that for some people, coming to prison *is* the end. "However, the fact that you have served time doesn't end your life."

Now a talented saxophonist, he acknowledges that his time behind bars provided him with both the opportunity and the motivation to refine his musical technique. "The one thing that happened to me is it got my technical skill together on the horn," he told *The Angolite.* "When I came, I could play, but I hadn't ever sat down and spent hours and hours every day practicing scales." While at Angola, Charles had time to do that, and he had the determination to do it. "When I left here, I could go anywhere and play with anybody. Really that was the beginning of the big change in my life."

The effort Charles Neville put into getting the most out of serving time, and his desire to overcome the mistakes of the past, opened up a vast new world to him upon his release from prison. When he was paroled, he went to New York, where his brother Aaron was enjoying success with his big hit "Tell It Like It Is." Charles has traveled the world, established himself as an outstanding musician, and now lectures at Oregon State University.

Twenty years have passed since Charles Neville was an inmate at the Louisiana State Prison, but he has forgotten neither the experience nor the people who are behind bars. Eighty percent of Angola's population is black, and Charles says, "I would like to talk to people here about stories and toasts and things like that which used to be passed down from generation to generation in black families." Charles has hopes of obtaining a grant that would allow him to preserve the stories that have enriched the black experience.

An accomplished musician, a father and grandfather, Charles Neville has an identity, a sense of direction. "I think of myself as a person now, a useful functional part of any community," he says. "What you do determines what you are, not what you have done. "I know that there are some people here who are really A–number one people. They are real people, they just had bad breaks in life." He says: "I just like to say for everybody, you are going to get out of here; this is not the end of the line, but when you get out, that's the beginning."

*   *   *

While Charles Neville's experience may be unique, his was not the only prison story. Holly Bendtsen of the Pfister Sisters was also at Angola nearly twenty years ago. Her dad was a basketball coach out in California, and during the summer of 1968 he was the recreation director at Angola. Holly recalled, "The real funny [thing] was the day my dad walked into the *Angolite* office. The guy working there was his old college roommate. He was an inmate."

Bendtsen and her mom and dad and sisters lived outside of Angola's gates that summer. "That's the first place I ever saw James Booker play," she recalls. "Booker was leading a band at the time, and Charles [Neville] had been in the band the year before."

In the late sixties prison was a very hard place, and women were not part of the overall prisoner routine. "We didn't have that much contact with prisoners," Holly said. "We had people that would work with you at your house or with my dad, and then we had a fellow that used to help my mom around the house."

Bendtsen remembers one prisoner in particular. "His name was Acie. He used to be a gardener. He'd been here forever." After his release, Bendtsen says, "He just came back. There was nobody in his family left alive, there was no place left for him to go."

Bendtsen learned of the concert from the Nevilles. "Charles was here before, and I'm kind of another kind of alumni."

Charmaine Neville is Charles's daughter, and a talented entertainer in her own right. As a young child, she never visited her father in prison. "Matter of fact," she comments, "I didn't even know he was in here, until he was already out. They kept that kind of secret from me."

Once out of prison, Charles told his daughter about his experience. "He told me stories about Angola. First they were kind of scary, but as I got older, I understood."

Performing at a prison was a first-time experience for Charmaine. "At first I was kind of nervous about it," she told *The Angolite* before the show. "I'm not nervous now that I'm here. I think the guys are really going to enjoy the show. I know I'm going to give them a really good one, because I've never been here before, and I know they haven't had any kind of entertainment in a long time. We're going to make it as good as we can."

*   *   *

Cyril Neville, at thirty-eight, is the youngest of the Neville Brothers. He began playing music professionally at age sixteen, but he says: "Music has always been a part of my life. My older brothers rehearsed in my front room, so I have always been exposed to it."

Cyril has very strong feelings about having the opportunity to perform for the men at Angola. "I feel like the same way I would feel if I got invited to South Africa to play for the brothers and sisters over there." He says of the prisoners at Angola: "They got a lot of people that I went to school with and grew up with and everything. It's an honor to be able to come here and lighten the load some."

The groups did not receive any payment for performing at Angola. They didn't expect any, but Cyril says: "Well, it's not really for nothing. You could say this is a labor of love. We might not personally get a chance to meet any of these people, but I will always feel good in my heart that I was able to do something to show that I care."

By far the most well-known of the Nevilles is Aaron. He has been in the music business since the early fifties. His grandmother comes from the Caribbean islands. An uncle founded a New Orleans–based dance group, the famous Wild Tchoupitoulis.

"We are a musical family. That's the only way I can put it," Aaron told *The Angolite.* "Even our kids. I got a grandson. He's just two years old. He just hears music and he's got to move."

What the Nevilles play isn't "message" music. It's just music. "We just do what comes from the heart," Aaron explains. "We got a unique style which comes from Mardi Gras, Fats Domino, and four individual brothers, plus our rhythm section—then we pool everything."

For all the Nevilles, the trip to Angola was a special occasion. "We are getting ready to go back overseas, and I figure this is about giving a blessing," Art Neville says. "Put it like this: If it wasn't for the grace of God, this could be me."

"It was really important," Aaron said, "because we are playing for some people that aren't going to get a chance to see no live entertainment."

‖‖‖   The Concert   ‖‖‖

The Pfister Sisters—Holly, Yvette, and Suzie—opened the show. The arena, filled with well over a thousand prisoners, was alive. The prisoners were excited and the entertainers were warming to their audience. Charmaine Neville and Real Feelings took over from the Pfisters. Charmaine took off with the tune "My Momma Don't 'Low No Gettin' Down Funky Down Heah," and by the end of the song she was soaked in sweat, and the prisoners were in a frenzy. She took the

The inmates in the stands cheer for the Neville Brothers (Courtesy The Angolite)

audience higher and higher, and the prisoners screamed, yelled, and applauded with each gyration of her hips or change in her voice. She brought the prisoners out of the prison world into a fantasyland where there was only pleasure and joy.

As Real Feelings closed their act, Charmaine threw kisses, and waves, and smiles with the sweat pouring off her. She took her towel and began to dry herself; then off she strode toward the fence. The towel sailed into the air, over the fence, and toward the prisoners. A wave of humanity moved in unison toward the towel, but a guy from the fifth row snatched it out of the air. More towels were given to Charmaine to toss into other sections of the arena. When the towel supply ran out, prisoners began to hurl caps, scarves, handkerchiefs, shirts, T shirts, any little item that could be autographed and used for a souvenir, into the arena. No sooner had Charmaine autographed a bundle of clothing than other prisoners hurled their belongings toward her.

Act three was the big event, the Nevilles. The Brothers took up where Charmaine left off. They greeted old friends. "What ya' know, Dut?" rang out. "Robert Norwood" and "Checo" were a couple of the names that burst through the air.

The Nevilles opened with songs from their new hit album, then performed many tunes from the past. They performed a moving rendition of "Hey Pocky Way," and a stirring version of the gospel tune "Amazing Grace" signaled the close of the show.

"I loved it, I enjoyed it, and I want to come back," said Suzie of the Pfister Sisters. Aaron Neville told us: "It was so great, we're going to come back again and do it."

[June 1987]

The Neville Brothers at Angola, from left, Cyril, Aaron, Charles, and Art
(*Courtesy* The Angolite)

▍▍▍▍ Postscript ▍▍▍▍

This story prompted Pardon Board chairman Lawrence Hand to suggest that Charles Neville had paid his dues and should file an application for a pardon. Charles was granted a full pardon by Governor Edwin Edwards. The Nevilles offered to return, but an administrative effort is only now being made to bring them back to Angola. There has been no concert at the prison by professional entertainers since the Nevilles in 1987.

THE LONG-TERMERS

|||||

Ron Wikberg

Roaring out of eight years of political retirement, Earl K. "Red Rooster" Long was the man of the year in 1948. In the gubernatorial election, he laid claim to 66 percent of the vote, and the governor's mansion. Gone were the horrible Depression years. The Second World War's oil economy was still keeping the state coffers healthy. Long began massive road and school construction, raised teachers' salaries, old-age pensions, and homestead exemptions, and paid bonuses to war veterans.

Nineteen forty-eight was also a year for executions as Louisiana sent five people to their deaths in the electric chair, bringing the body count to 104 since 1930, an average of 5.8 executions per year. The last to die that year was Edward Spriggs, on June 25, following a conviction for aggravated rape in Iberville Parish.

These events sparked little interest in rural Tensas Parish, where twenty-six-year-old James "Black Mattie" Robertson, a Narcola native lived. He was a laborer who worked odd jobs in and around Ferriday. In July of 1948, shortly after the Spriggs execution, the wife of a white sawmill worker in Tensas Parish was raped. Robertson was indicted and tried for aggravated rape, but a mistrial was declared when the jury failed to bring in a verdict. In April, 1949, Robertson was indicted again and pleaded not guilty. On the same day, his lawyers asked that the not guilty plea be set aside, and the presiding judge appointed the coroner and a psychiatrist to assess Robertson's mental status. Four days later, the lawyers entered a "not guilty by reason of insanity" plea. In May, the coroner and psychiatrist determined that Robertson was insane, and in June, he was committed to

James "Black Mattie" Robertson in 1951, on
entering Angola (Courtesy The Angolite)

the state hospital, where he was held for two years.

In May 1949, he was examined by a second psychiatrist at the state hospital, who concluded that he "presented a psychopathic personality, but at the same time, he was not psychotic." On October 4, 1951, he pleaded guilty, and five days later, shortly after the massive inmate protest that brought the deplorable prison conditions at Angola to national attention, Robertson entered the penitentiary.

Forty years later Black Mattie has earned the distinction of being Louisiana's longest-confined prisoner. If there is any anger, it is well hidden. With unexpectedly good humor, Robertson recalls another man sentenced to life imprisonment from Tensas Parish. "Ole Eugene came here in 1954 and he went home about three years later," he informed *The Angolite.* A check of records confirmed that Eugene, Number 44814, came to Angola on December 29, 1954, and was paroled on November 21, 1957, serving only two and a half years of a life sentence for aggravated rape. In fact, records also show that Robertson is the only lifer still in prison from Tensas Parish of those sentenced to life imprisonment for either murder or rape in four decades.

Black Mattie worked for years in the prison's notorious sugar-cane fields and spent ten years in the prison tag plant making license plates. More recently, because of his age and physical condition, he was assigned orderly duty. "I always liked to work and I try to give them a good day's work," says Robertson. With only thirteen disciplinary reports since 1951, a laudable accomplishment in itself, Robertson has also upgraded his academic standing. "One thing I am proud of is that I can write and read my own mail," he explained. When awarded trusty status in 1976, Robertson felt that he might gain his freedom.

"I went on the Pardon Board in 1976 and they [recommended my time be cut] to 50 years, but Governor Edwards never signed it. I went back in 1981 and Governor Treen's Pardon Board recommended my time be cut to 105 years, but Treen never signed that. In 1988, Governor Edwards signed the earlier Treen recommendation and that made me eligible for parole," Robertson recounted. On March 16, 1988, the board denied parole. "They put a check mark in every box on the denial form and I still don't know why they turned me down. I felt so sure they would let me go home, I told my people not to come to the hearing," he said. "The victim is dead, the judge, DA, and lawyer are dead, and much longer in here and I will be dead too," says Robertson. Both parents have died during his record-breaking prison term. His only brother resides in California and Robertson hasn't seen him in a long time.

What would keep one man in prison for forty-one years yet allow another to go free in two and a half years when both committed the same criminal act, were convicted and sentenced in the same courtroom, and received the same sentence?

Former parole board chairperson Dorothy Henderson told *The Angolite:* "Parole was denied in this, and another case on March sixteenth, because of strenuous objection from law enforcement and judicial officials, and particularly because of the peculiar circumstances surrounding the commission of the crime." Telephone queries to the offices of Seventh Judicial District Judge Charles R. Brackin and District Attorney James D. Caldwell were not returned.

At sixty-six, Robertson has reached an impasse. "I've seen over five

Black Mattie in 1989 (Courtesy The Angolite)

hundred murderers go home in less time than I got in, some who killed several people. I just don't know what to do now. Edwards's board [recommended] me, but Edwards refused to sign it. Then Treen's Pardon Board [recommended] me, but Treen refused to sign it. Then Edwards comes along and signs the Treen recommendation, but the Edwards Parole Board turns down what he signed. It don't make no sense. The reason I don't know what to do is because I just don't know what is wanted of me anymore."

Every prison has them: long-termers, usually lifers, who remain in prison many years awaiting freedom while others with similar offenses and sentences are seemingly routinely released. Some are sentenced the same year, even in the same courtroom, yet one achieves freedom while the other remains imprisoned for as much as fifteen or twenty-five additional years. Codefendants convicted of the same crime, even brothers having equal culpability in a criminal offense and receiving the same sentence, are treated differently. One grows old behind bars, while the other wins his freedom, marries, raises children, acquires retirement tenure, and lives a normal life in the community.

The reasons some long-termers remain behind in prison while other prisoners are freed are varied. Some are obvious; others defy reason.

It has long been a common belief that money could buy a prisoner freedom in Louisiana that could not be earned through meritorious behavior; dollars worked when nothing else could. This aspect of doing justice has always been officially denied. However, former chairman of the Louisiana Board of Pardons Howard Marsellus, who is now serving time himself in a federal prison, admitted last year that pardons and commutations of prison sentences were sold during his tenure. Lack of money must be cited as a very real factor in the continuing confinement of a substantial number of long-termers. It is not unreasonable to assume that some, if not most, would not still be in prison were it not for the chains of poverty.

Conduct in prison is sometimes a reason for long-termers not being favorably considered for freedom. In some cases the prisoner commits an offense in prison and receives an additional conviction and sentence. Such is the case of Parnell Smith, fifty-six, who is the second-longest-confined prisoner in Louisiana. He is now in his thirty-sixth year of imprisonment.

Smith arrived at Angola in 1953 to serve a life sentence for a murder he committed in 1952. Smith, then twenty, had been assaulted, stabbed four times in the neck, head, chest, and back. He was hospitalized for nine days. Two weeks later, on New Year's Eve, he walked into a nightspot, his wounds still bandaged, only to meet the man who had stabbed him. The man reached into his pocket. Smith pulled out a gun, fired once, and departed. The man later died. Smith pled guilty to murder and received a life sentence.

In 1954, inmate Louis "Capone" Lee confronted Smith in the Camp A dining room, threatened him with violence, and pushed him, all in front of witnesses. In a brief knife-fight later, Lee died. Smith was taken to St. Francisville for jury trial, and in spite of a self-defense argument he was sentenced to death. The conviction was overturned on appeal, but following a second trial, the death penalty was again imposed.

Twenty years later Smith was the longest-held prisoner on death row, earning a place in the *Guinness Book of World Records*. Coming within hours of execution in 1960, Smith remained on Angola's death row until December 2, 1976.

"I have always regretted those incidents because I did not wish nor did I intend to kill anyone. I just did not want to do that," Smith explained. "I still suffer from one of the stab wounds from 1952. I just wanted to stop from being threatened and hurt. This place was rocking and rolling in the 1950s. If you did not stand up as a man, you would end up being treated like a woman. Getting killed at Angola was a way of life here then."

Parnell Smith in 1954 and in 1988 (Courtesy The Angolite)

Diagnosed with diabetes in 1983, and having undergone surgery to repair one of the old stab wounds, Smith is on a permanent "light duty" medical status. He has worked mostly as an orderly since leaving death row. He never knew his father, his mother died in 1982, and he has not seen his only sister since 1952. His only brother visits him once a year.

In 1977, Smith's attorney applied to the Board of Pardons for clemency, gaining a recommendation to commute his sentence to forty years. It was never approved by the governor. In 1981 the board recommended a commutation to ninety-nine years, which still awaits the governor's action.

Smith was unsure why some people, including those who murdered while in prison, are released while others remain in prison for the same crimes. "I guess some are just lucky and some aren't. The lack of money hurts too, because with money you can make your own luck," he said.

Fifty-year-old Henry L. Patterson, serving a life sentence for a Caddo Parish murder, has not acquired any additional conviction during his twenty-seven years of imprisonment—yet his behavior cost him. He got caught up in the prison jungle and, for a long time, was lost in it.

Arrested in March 1961, tried in May, and received at the state penitentiary on May 31, Patterson and codefendant George Saxton had been repelling a bully at a nightclub Patterson was overseeing at a friend's request. The six-foot-four-inch, 250-pound troublemaker was getting the best of youthful Patterson when Patterson struck him on the head with a piece of the wooden bar. The man died from the injury; later, it was determined that he had a prosthetic plate in his skull.

Towards the end of the trial, it looked as if the all-white jury would recommend the death penalty. If both men pled guilty, they would get a life sentence, and the existing custom was to release lifers after ten years. They opted to plead guilty.

Patterson would go on to serve more time for a Caddo Parish murder than any other murderer sentenced to prison from that parish. Saxton, Patterson's codefendant, was paroled on February 8, 1968, having served only six and a half years. Patterson is now into his twenty-eighth year at Angola. Another lifer from Caddo Parish, who arrived in 1961, was also released after serving less than eight years.

Moreover, the four lifers received from Caddo Parish in 1962 and 1963 have also been released after serving less than ten years.

The conduct record Patterson built at Angola left much to be desired. "I never wanted nor started any trouble but, when I got here, Angola was a jungle," Patterson explained. "The security captain told me, 'son, get yourself an ole man, do what he say, and be a good prisoner,' Well, the problem with that was my mama raised me to be a man and I wasn't about to disrespect her by letting these people up here turn me into a galboy, a prison whore. No way—that wasn't gonna happen, and I was ready to do whatever it took to make sure it didn't happen, not to me. No way."

Patterson established a reputation as a man not to be messed with. "I ain't never figured it out. I got lost in the wild and violent ways of Angola during the bad years. You had to fight to survive. I think I hurt myself by trying to keep up with the fittest instead of trying other ways of coping. But I was young, ignorant—but I had no malice in my heart. I had to be macho to survive and maintain my manhood.

"Prior to 1980, no one really gave me a chance to better myself, to help get me out of the rut I was in. Security Warden Walter Pence got interested in me and gave me a break. I've done well ever since. I am very grateful for that," Patterson says. He entered cooking and baking school, earning certificates from both. He was made a trusty in 1981, and for the last seven years has cooked and baked at the prison hospital. Having served twenty years longer than his codefendant, he hopes the new administration will recognize his vast improvement.

His last family visit was from his mother, in 1985. She died shortly thereafter. Patterson, an only child, has not seen his father since 1958.

While poor conduct can keep a man confined longer than others with similar sentences, it is not an overriding factor because, barring death, just about everybody gets out of prison eventually, even those prisoners who kill others while in prison. Such is the case of James Dunn, who arrived at the state penitentiary in 1960. On January 2, 1963, he killed inmate Coy M. Bell, who was serving time from East Baton Rouge Parish. Dunn was convicted and given a life sentence. In 1969, he picked up another conviction, this time for attempted manslaughter, with this additional sentence to be served after the others. In 1987 Governor Edwin Edwards granted executive clemency to Dunn, freeing him after twenty-seven years.

What keeps Patterson confined but allows Dunn to walk free is that

Dunn pursued his freedom relentlessly, acquiring the assistance that enabled him finally to win his release. Patterson did not pursue his freedom as zealously as Dunn, nor does he have outside assistance to lobby on his behalf.

Zeal is a crucial factor, even for those prisoners with reasonably good conduct records. Convicted of the aggravated rape of a white woman, Woodman Collins, now fifty-eight, was sent to Angola from Jefferson Davis Parish with a death sentence. Winning a new trial in 1964, Collins agreed to plead guilty to aggravated rape with a life sentence because he feared that if convicted at trial he would receive the death sentence again.* But he also had to plead guilty to a charge of attempted murder, for which the court gave him an additional twenty-year sentence to be served consecutively. Arrested April 7, 1960, Collins is now in his twenty-eighth year of confinement.

Angola records show that, of all the life-termers at Angola from Jefferson Davis Parish for either murder or rape from 1950 through 1972, Collins is the only one still confined.

Getting Collins to plead guilty in 1964 to attempted murder was apparently a legal strategy by the prosecutor to make it more difficult for him to obtain his freedom.

Collins's reliance on the "10-6 release" procedure was significant; he waited twelve years before realizing he would not be freed. He made no effort to secure his freedom during that time. His first clemency application, in 1972, was denied. "I know many inmates who came here after me, got more time while they were here, and done went home already. I don't know how they do that," Collins said to *The Angolite.* "A man has to change after being here a long time— you can look at the record to tell that. I don't think they look at no records when releasing a man. I ain't killed nobody in here, raped nobody in here, or escaped, but many have, and they all done went home," he said.

To upgrade his academic level, Collins entered school in 1983, but was later transferred to a camp where no classes were held. "I've been trying to get into vocational school, but they won't let me because I'm

*In 1926 a procedure was established providing for automatic review of a lifer's case by the state Board of Pardons after he served ten and a half years. In the wake of the U.S. Supreme Court decision in 1972 declaring capital punishment as then imposed unconstitutional, this "ten-six" procedure was dismantled by the Department of Corrections.

a lifer," Collins explained. He was awarded trusty status in 1985, and because of his age and high blood pressure, he has a "light duty" medical duty status.

Collins has had only one visit in the twenty-eight years he has been in prison. Both parents have died, and the only time he's left the prison grounds was to attend his mother's funeral in 1975. He has eleven siblings, but only a sister keeps contact. He doesn't even know where his other brothers and sisters are. He hasn't seen one brother since 1960.

An application for clemency in 1987 was rejected. "I guess they think a man can't rehabilitate. If I was a man who couldn't change, I'd have been in a lot of trouble since I've been here. I just don't know why I am so different from all those that have already gotten out," he adds.

What makes Collins different from others who lacked personal zeal but walked out is that he has been abandoned without outside assistance, circumstances common to many long-termers. In dealing with a system that responds only to intelligence, zeal, resources, and pressure, prisoners like Collins are at a definite disadvantage. The criminal-justice system in Louisiana is not required to track prisoners to ensure they receive meaningful release consideration. Once someone is in prison, it is the responsibility of the Corrections Department to detain and care for the prisoner; unless instructed otherwise by appropriate authority, the department will do so until the prisoner dies. No part of the system has the legal responsibility to assure equity in the release of long-termers, and there is a need to track long-termers who, for varying reasons, do not seek release.

Jack Lathers, fifty-seven, falls into that category. He was arrested January 26, 1957, at the age of twenty-six, for a murder in East Feliciana Parish. He was convicted and sentenced on January 30, and received at Angola on February 1, 1957, to serve a life sentence—a judicial process that took only six days.

In 1962, Lathers applied for clemency and was denied. Afterwards, he worked hard, kept a low profile, maintained a good conduct record, and became a self-taught plumber, welder, and lift station operator for the main prison maintenance department. He was a quiet man, respected by both prisoners and prison personnel.

He did not apply for clemency again until 1987, a quarter-century later. The Pardon Board recommended a reduction of his sentence to

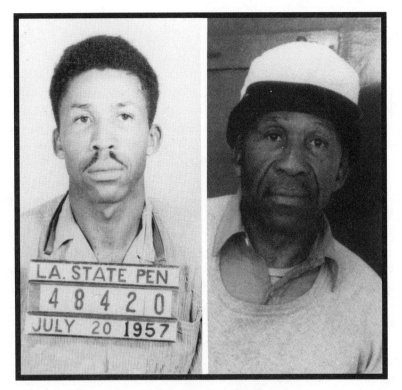

Jack Lathers in 1957 and 1988 (Courtesy The Angolite)

fifty years. Asked why he waited so long to ask for clemency, Lathers told *The Angolite,* "I just gave up. They wouldn't do nothin' for me anyhow." He adds: "The DA, the judge, and my lawyer said to plead guilty and I would be there [in prison] ten years and six months if I kept my record clean. I did but they never let me go. I only had a few write-ups many years ago, for leaving socks on my bed and stuff like that. Now the judge is dead, the DA is dead, my lawyer is dead, and nobody knows I'm still here, I guess."

A look at the records of lifers received from East Feliciana Parish indicates that Lathers and five others were convicted in the 1950s. Two died in prison and three were released after serving an average of ten years. Another life-termer from the same parish, who arrived in 1968, gained his freedom after serving eleven years. When asked why he is still imprisoned after thirty-one years, Lathers said: "I don't know. I killed a black. I am black. Nobody raised no Cain in the case and I ain't heard of nobody protesting [my release] at all."

Lathers has not had a visit in almost six years. While he gets occasional mail from siblings who "send me things now and then," both parents have died since his confinement. He's only been off the prison grounds once since 1957. "I went to New Orleans Charity Hospital with a piece of metal in my eye," he said. "I did not know where I was—everything had changed. It looked so dirty. No one takes care of things like they used to."

Lack of personal zeal and outside assistance characterizes the case of fifty-three-year-old Louis "Pulpwood" Ducre, now in his thirtieth year of imprisonment. Ducre is the only lifer sentenced from St. Tammany Parish in the 1950s who is still in prison. He was convicted of aggravated rape of a white woman in 1958 at age twenty-four. His case was never appealed, though he underwent a jury trial. "I don't know why he [the lawyer] didn't appeal—ain't nobody ever said nothing about it to me. I always thought my appeal had been denied," Ducre said to *The Angolite*. No record of Ducre's appeal could be found in court reports.

With no serious disciplinary infractions, Ducre is a first offender who has an excellent work record: Thirteen years at the sugar mill, eleven years at the prison warehouse, and now work as an orderly in the hobby shop.

Ducre gets an occasional phone call or letter from surviving siblings, but has not had a visit since 1972. Both parents have died. "That was the only time I was out of Angola, in 1975, when I went to my mother's funeral," Ducre said.

In 1980 the state Pardon Board recommended that his sentence be reduced to forty years. Asked why he did not check on his appeal or apply to the Pardon Board more frequently, Ducre said: "I guess I just didn't try to help myself. I didn't know how and I didn't know anybody important to ask for help. All the others that came here with me have left a long time ago and I figured my time would come too." His trust that the system was fair was badly misplaced, and it cost him. He should have learned from another St. Tammany case that justice was neither equal nor fair. On December 23, 1962, Luther Davis murdered two people; he arrived at Angola on September 2, 1964, to begin serving two life sentences. For whatever reason, he received executive clemency from the governor and was paroled on January 7, 1970, after serving only seven years.

Louis Ducre in 1958 and in 1988 (Courtesy The Angolite)

Strong community or victim opposition also plays a role when some long-termers find it difficult to obtain freedom. Occasionally adamant opposition is maintained for many years, as in the case of Moreese Bickham, now in his thirtieth year behind bars.

Probably one of the worst offenses is the killing of a law enforcement officer. Bickham was convicted in St. Tammany Parish of killing two deputy sheriffs on July 12, 1958. Then forty-one, he worked for the town of Mandeville, reading utility meters. "I lived in a white community and the two deputies involved were sort of security watchmen around the neighborhood. I used to come and go as I pleased with my work crew. They didn't like me out at night—in those days it was tough on blacks at night. The mayor was always having to keep those two off my back. They just hated me, I guess, because I was successful and living where I was," Bickham told *The Angolite*. "Just to give you an idea like it was, when they were picking my jury, there was a black on the list. The judge said, 'Oh, no, we ain't having no blacks on this jury.' He was kicked off, too," Bickham said.

The killings outside his own home, himself shot in the fracas, the media attention afterwards, and his eventual death sentence in 1961 would haunt Bickham for the next twenty-five years.

Bickham was released from death row in 1973 following the 1972 U.S. Supreme Court decision invalidating the death penalty. He had come within fifteen hours of the electric chair on one occasion. A year after leaving death row, he was awarded trusty status and embarked on an achievement program. At age sixty-four, he raised his academic level to the eleventh grade. At age sixty-six he entered the vocational school for auto mechanics, and in two years earned a certificate from the state school system.

During this period, Bickham joined the Methodist church; he became its pastor and president for nine years. An active force in the prison religious community, he has made many trips to speak to church groups in Baton Rouge and Port Hudson. In 1978, he was taken out of the prison for his ordination as a minister by Methodist church bishops.

The Board of Pardons rejected Bickham's application for clemency three times in the 1970s and once in 1981, on the basis of opposition from the Mandeville community. However, with a petition supporting Bickham signed by five hundred Mandeville residents, and strong support from the religious community, in 1982 the Pardon Board recommended a sentence reduction to forty years, which has yet to be acted on by a governor.

With both parents and two sisters now dead, and a brother who has been paralyzed for many years, Bickham only receives visits from his aunt. Following a heart attack and a year of convalescence, Bickham now tends two beds of rosebushes at the main prison, shuffling from one plot to the other. "I go when I want, do what I want, and work when I can," he says. "My medical situation isn't too good and they let me come and go as I need."

When *The Angolite* asked "Pop" Bickham why some life-termers stay in prison while others are released, he said, "There ain't no real answer. The Bible says that the good must suffer with the bad." Bickham is seventy-one.

Opposition from law enforcement, as distinguished from general community objection, is another hurdle many long-termers must overcome. When they don't, the governor and Pardon and Parole boards will often override judicial and law enforcement opposition and release the inmate. But the force of opposition from law enforcement can, and often does, keep some in prison while others go free.

Louisiana's philosophy in the release or continued confinement of long-termers sometimes defies reason. Given today's heightened political sensitivity to victims' rights, victim opposition is often recognized as official reason for the continued confinement of a prisoner. Occasionally, however, there are cases in which the victim recognizes that an offender has been punished enough and officially requests that the long-termer be given mercy and freedom. Sometimes the system listens, sometimes not.

In August 1962, Donald "Frog" Buffett and an accomplice were arrested and charged with the armed robbery and aggravated rape of a Lincoln Parish white woman. Within three months of arrest both men pled guilty and were sentenced to life imprisonment plus twenty-five years, to be served consecutively, "They said I would eligible for parole in ten years," the forty-three-year-old Buffet told *The Angolite*.

The Oakland, California, native was eighteen years old in 1962 when he arrived at Angola. Buffett recalls, "I had to fight every damn day. I told them they weren't going to get these drawers [i.e., pull his pants down to rape him]!" His disciplinary record shows that between 1962 and 1972, during the rougher prison years, Buffett received most of his misconduct reports, while between 1974 and 1985 he had relatively few, and in 1987 and 1988 he's remained report-free.

When Buffett's victim learned a couple of years ago that he was still in prison, she sent two sworn, notarized affidavits to the Louisiana Board of Pardons and the governor, with a copy to Buffett and his parents. The document, in part, stated: "Although he did commit a crime against my person, it is genuinely believed that he has served a sufficient period of confinement, and that after a sufficient period in excess of twenty years, any further confinement would only serve to outline the seriousness of the offense, and not deprecate the offense with respect to Donald Buffett."

He applied for clemency four times, receiving three favorable recommendations from the Board of Pardons since 1975, but no governor has ever acted upon them. A current recommended sentence reduction to sixty years has been pending since 1986. It would make him eligible for parole after twenty years.

Buffett is now in his twenty-seventh year in prison. Prison records reveal that four life-termers entered Angola from Lincoln Parish between 1949 and 1979. Buffett is the only one still in prison. Of the three lifers already released, whose offenses included both murder and aggravated rape, they averaged only 8.6 years on their life sentences before being freed. Expressing concern, Buffet says, "I didn't think people could be this way. It is like an Alfred Hitchcock movie. When I went to court on a writ in the early 1970s, the judge told me this was the wrong way to get out, and that I should apply to the Pardon Board. Well, I did that and it still hasn't worked."

Buffett has not had regular visits since 1976. His last visit was in 1980. His mother is too old to travel and he has not seen his father since 1960. "I have contact with brothers and sisters by mail and telephone and they send me what I need. But I sure would like to see my mother before she has to leave this world," he says.

While Buffett's situation is not a common one, it is not unique. The most coveted and rarest assistance a long-termer can garner is from his prosecutor. In one particular case known to *The Angolite* (the inmate prefers to remain anonymous), the prosecutor who sent the individual to prison two decades ago has since requested, in writing, that the lifer be released. Additionally, in 1980 the Pardon Board recommended to the governor that the inmate's sentence be commuted to thirty years, which would allow him to be freed. This long-termer is still awaiting the governor's action.

The number of people behind bars with long sentences, or little or no chance of parole, is increasing. The spring 1987 *Jericho* (the Unitarian Universalist Service Committee quarterly) reported that the National Council on Crime and Delinquency, and numerous other independent research sources, note that the United States hands out some of the longest prison sentences in the world. Some states mete out sentences double or triple the national average. Louisiana leads the nation in harsh criminal penalties.

According to *Crime and Justice Facts, 1985*, published by the federal Bureau of Justice Statistics (BJS), the average time served on a life sentence in the United States in 1982 was five years and nine months. In 1986 that average only increased to six years and nine months. The study also revealed that a quarter of those lifers released in 1982 served only three years, while three-fifths of those released served seven years or less.

In a 1987 BJS study reporting results from twenty-eight jurisdictions that utilized probation, the city of New Orleans reported that, of 2,600 homicide convictions, 8 percent were given probation, 8 percent a combination of jail and probation, and 84 percent were sent to prison. Of those serving a life sentence, servitude averaged sixteen years, almost triple the national average.

Reacting to public concerns about crime, the Louisiana legislature of the 1970s passed law-and-order measures that lengthened prison sentences, reduced earnable goodtime credits, restricted criteria for parole and clemency, and, for some offenders, completely eradicated release eligibility. Prior to the seventies, a life-termer had a good chance of earning freedom through the clemency process if he accrued a record of hard work and good conduct, and a prison file of accomplishments showing rehabilitation.

In Louisiana, sentences of life imprisonment are imposed for first-degree murder, where the jury does not recommend a death sentence; second-degree murder; aggravated rape; aggravated kidnap; certain habitual-offender violations; violations of certain drug laws relating to distribution; and the killing of a child during delivery. Regardless of how long he has been in prison, unless his sentence is commuted to a fixed term no one sentenced to life for any of these crimes can be put on probation or paroled, nor may his sentence be suspended.

Even before the "10-6" release procedure (described on page 225) was established in 1926, life sentences in Louisiana rarely exceeded ten years. In preparing a September 1984 report, Angola Assistant Corrections Warden Roger Thomas found records showing Amos Washington, Number 001, who was received at the Baton Rouge penitentiary on February 13, 1866, with a life sentence for burglary. After being granted clemency, he was released April 28, 1877, having served eleven years. Amanias Spooner, Number 2646, arrived with a life sentence for murder. He was pardoned after six months. Vina Martin was received July 13, 1877, with a life sentence for murder. On July 9, 1884, after serving nine years, he was released. State judge Thomas J. Ford, Number 6982, arrived with a life sentence for murder in June 1885. He was given clemency on March 8, 1895, serving less than ten years.

Some steps have been taken to look at the problem of long-term prisoners and the role of lifers in the current overcrowding crisis. When then-governor Edwin Edwards was inaugurated in 1984, he formed two study groups: one, the Forgotten Man Committee; the other, the Prison and Jail Overcrowding Policy Task Force. Composed solely of volunteer citizens, the committee was to determine what policy could be made regarding long-term inmates and to present recommendations to the governor.

The task force was made up entirely of policymakers in the state's criminal-justice system: sheriffs, district attorneys, councilmembers, and other officials involved in the day-to-day business of jails and prisons. In several areas, both committees reached similar conclusions. One was the recommendation that life sentences at some point be reevaluated for parole-release eligibility.

Jack P. F. Gremillion, Sr., a former state attorney general, remembers the 10-6 rule, but also sees a need to keep some offenders confined longer. "We need some procedure," he told *The Angolite,* "since the ten-six lifer provision has been eliminated, whereas a prisoner who has served twenty-five years in prison with a good record of rehabilitation—and I'm not married to that specific length of time—should receive prime consideration for clemency, unless the state can otherwise rebut the clemency with overwhelming reasons."

Nearly 3,800 of Louisiana's sixteen thousand prisoners are either life-termers or those with the equivalent of a life sentence. Most are confined at Angola, the state's only maximum-security penal facility, which now houses 4,700 inmates. In 1978 there were only 640 lifers at the penitentiary. According to corrections records, the number of lifers rose to 1,200 by 1984, and at year's end 1987 Angola's lifer population had jumped to nearly 1,800.

"The prison crowding problem faced by Louisiana has developed in part from the practice initiated in the mid-70's of excluding increasing numbers of inmates from parole eligibility based on their crime or their offender class," the Forgotten Man Committee said in its 1985 report to the governor. Fifty-two percent of those in custody are currently barred from parole, and many of those serving lengthy sentences are not even eligible for goodtime release. The report added: "Unless their sentences are commuted by the governor, many of them are destined to live out their lives behind bars."

The committee eventually submitted to the governor and legislature twenty recommendations, thirteen of which directly impacted on long-term prisoners. When its recommendations were rejected, the Forgotten Man Committee, frustrated and dejected, disbanded.

Lifers and other long-termers are still released, though in the past decade that number has decreased drastically. Louisiana statutes dictate that persons sentenced to life imprisonment cannot be considered for parole or other release unless the life sentence has been commuted to a fixed number of years.

Referred to in the prison world as a gold seal, a commutation can only be obtained by first making application to the Board of Pardons for clemency. Following its investigations, notification to law enforcement court officials and the victim or victim's family, and a public hearing (which the prisoner is not allowed to attend), the Pardon Board votes to grant or deny the relief requested. If it is denied, the prisoner is required by board rules to wait one calendar year before reapplying.

If the application is granted, the board in theory sends its recommendation to the governor's office. The recommendation is then approved or disapproved by the governor. Realistically, however, the board's recommendation sits untouched, sometimes for years, before being addressed. Some recommendations are never acted upon at all. Seldom does the governor personally disapprove the board's action in writing, and the prisoner can wait years before learning the disposition of his clemency recommendation. During that period of limbo, the prisoner can't make another application to the board because one action is already pending and the board could deny a second.

The Edwards administration was nearing an end when Executive Counsel C. W. "Bill" Roberts said that at least 464 clemency applications had been approved by the Pardon Board but would never get to the governor's desk because the administration had not asked for them. Roberts said, "I'd like to review them all, but I just can't," explaining that he was reviewing those that legislators, members of Congress, preachers, and others had asked to receive special attention.

Why would clemency recommendations by the Pardon Board never make it to the governor's desk? *The Angolite* was informed that during Governor Edwards's last term, his office instructed the Pardon Board office not to forward recommendations, but to retain them until his office called for them. This decision confirmed that politics and patronage play a large role in the Louisiana clemency process.

Those cases reviewed by the governor were those in which important and politically potent people had interceded. In 1980 Louis Ducre received a Treen board recommendation that his sentence be reduced to forty years; in 1987 the Edwards board recommended that Lathers's sentence be reduced to fifty years. The Pardon Board recommendations for both men, who were alone in the world and without political connections, sat in the board office—until *The Angolite,* while researching this story, had their cases brought to the attention of Governor Edwards during his last days in office. The governor approved both recommendations and the men have since been released from prison.

Also criticized by both prisoners and corrections employees is the rule that prohibits employee input into the parole and clemency process. The lack of participation by corrections professionals, who surround the prisoners twenty-four hours a day, also contributes to some prisoners being overlooked. "I believe that these correction people should have some say-so in the release process," says fifty-seven-year-old Andrew Joseph, inmate president of the Lifers' Association. Serving a life sentence for murder, Joseph told *The Angolite:* "These people know more about us than our family knows. They're with us all day and night, year after year, and let's face it—they know how we think, what we believe in, how we act and respond to different life situations, and even what vices we may have. They know our different philosophies on life. All this information is necessary for any board or other official to make a reasonably fair determination to grant or deny freedom from prison." Joseph added: "It is impossible to get a handle, an honest appraisal, on an individual if you don't know what motivates a person and what makes him tick."

"The state has no philosophy for pardons," former Corrections Department head C. Paul Phelps told the Baton Rouge *Morning Advocate* in 1981. "The historic origin of pardon is the king's right to correct a wrong. But in Louisiana, governors have operated the clemency process for political expediency, as a reward for good behavior, or for the convenience of the state—and once in a while to correct a wrong."

The current inequity plaguing criminal justice in Louisiana, which is primarily caused by political and/or corrupt influences, was criticized by U.S. District Judge Frank Polozola of the Middle District of Louisiana. On August 3, 1987, at the American Correctional Association's 117th Correctional Congress, Polozola, a tough law-and-order conservative in criminal-justice matters, told thousands of penal administrators that "politics has no place in the criminal-justice system and particularly in corrections. . . . Those who have the responsibility for maintaining prisons cannot and should not allow politics to enter any of their decisions or procedures for incarcerating or releasing inmates. Those in the Executive Department who review pardons or paroles have an equal responsibility to ensure that one standard of justice is administered in a fair and impartial manner."

Serving a life sentence creates problems for the prisoner that are very different from the pains of general confinement. Loss of contact with family and friends poses a problem for all inmates, but for long-term prisoners, it is feared that these relationships will be lost forever. The prospect of maintaining them over a long period is dim, and most studies have established that only a few long-termers are able to keep high levels of outside contact. Many lifers' entire extended families die during the prisoner's long years of prison confinement.

"The older you are in prison, the fewer people you have left on the outside who care about you or are in a position to do anything about taking care of you," Phelps pointed out. "So, if we kept everybody until the age of sixty-five, we really wouldn't have any place to turn them loose to."

Friendships inside the prison are also restricted because long-termers have so little in common with the average inmate serving a lesser sentence.

The ranks of elderly prisoners are growing. These inmates have no real prison work assignments, and expectations of productivity are nil. They are more or less allowed the illusion of semiretirement, going about the prison without the restrictions placed on younger inmates. More often than not, elderly long-termers are assigned to minimum-security status. Those not confined to wheelchairs or using crutches are expected only to go to the dining room, participate in outdoor recreation, clean up their own bed area, and perform other menial tasks.

The growing number of geriatric inmates requiring above-average care has forced corrections administrators to consider special facilities. Sociologist Sol Chaneles, of Rutgers University, is editor of the *Journal of Offender Counselling, Services and Rehabilitation*. In the

October 1987 issue of *Psychology Today,* Chaneles said: "By the year 2000, the number of people over 65 is expected to increase to 21 percent of the general population. In prisons," he added, "I estimate the increase will be 50 percent. Many of those 65 and over, the fastest growing segment of the elderly population, will require complex, round-the-clock care, creating new cost burdens."

In 1985, Louisiana spent $9.1 million of its corrections budget on prison health care, according to the U.S. Justice Department's *Sourcebook, 1986.* In Pennsylvania, the cost of prison health-care services went from $1.23 million in 1973 to $16.7 million in 1986. Eyeglasses, dentures, hearing aids, prosthetic devices, surgical procedures, and other medical needs of the elderly are just some of the services required for the aging prisoners.

American Correctional Association (ACA) executive director Anthony Travisano told *Compendium* that a natural life sentence removes the control factors from an inmate's day-to-day actions. "If I ask you to do absolutely nothing except take care of yourself for the next 60 years, one day you're going to go balmy on me. It's not the life sentence," Travisano said, "it's in the day-in, day-out drudgery of having nothing to do."

Locked up for all but nine years since 1935, ninety-three-year-old Isa Mae Lang was forced from prison to an old folks' home in Frontera, California. Convicted of killing her landlady in 1935, she fell ill in 1960 and was released to a nursing home. Four years later she told the Parole Board she wanted to be with her friends in prison, instead of sharing a room with five senile women. Her request was granted, and Lang moved back to prison. In 1983, her health again forced her into a nursing home.

Some long-termers refuse parole. John Davis, of South Carolina, spent half his 106-year life in prison before dying of cancer. His sentence began in 1922, after he was convicted of "night burglary," then a capital offense. Near the end of his life he was offered parole, but chose to remain at the Watkins Pre-release Center, where he was the only inmate allowed to come and go as he pleased.

There is a growing perception among the more recently arrived life-termers and long-termers that they have little or no chance of release even if they establish a clear record of rehabilitation. This perception alone augurs difficult years ahead for prison administrators.

"I have hardly no hope of ever going home," says Patrick DeVille, twenty-seven, a mandatory lifer sentenced in 1981. DeVille adds: " 'Cause I look around at all who are here and ask, What makes me so different? I may even die here of old age. I was eighteen when arrested, a first offender, and some of these old-timers have been here ten years before I was born! They got perfect records and can't get anything." Concluding that there is little to hope for, DeVille said, "A man can't earn freedom by being good, working hard, and doing right in prison because there are too many here to prove it doesn't mean anything."

In his seventh year of a life sentence imposed when he was thirty years old, Lafayette Ballard, thirty-seven, voiced similar sentiments: "There just ain't no hope," he said. "It's a graveyard. Once they send you here with a life sentence, it's all over." Ballard was recently awarded trusty status because of his good conduct record and demonstration of responsibility. "If these other long-termers can't go free, I'll never go free either. They just throw away the key," he said.

The American public has a legitimate expectation that satisfactory retribution be exacted from those convicted of crime. But traditionally, most offenders have been sent to prison with specific release dates. And various release mechanisms, predicated on a longstanding philosophy of redemption, have been provided for long-termers, those with long sentences or no specific release date. The nation and its justice system were founded upon the basic principles of fairness and equity. Those citizens charged with a crime are constitutionally guaranteed a fair trial and equitable treatment by the system. But in Louisiana, considerations of race, class, politics, and corruption have been the major factors influencing who is punished and for how long.

All of Angola's wardens for the past two decades agree: "There is something wrong with a system with such a high per capita lockup rate," says C. Murray Henderson, warden from 1968 through 1975. Henderson added: "By nature, people in Louisiana are no different than people in other states. By law, the clemency situation in Louisiana only allows for a lifer to be freed through the governor. In Mississippi, a lifer can be released in seven years; Florida, five years; Texas, eight years; and in Iowa, in one day unless it's first-degree murder, which is then eleven years." Henderson said the Iowa model allowed clemency responsibility to be handled by the Parole Board which traditionally bases an inmate's release on merit. "The board is highly respected by all levels of Iowa society. I agree with the current administration that clemency decisions should be made on individual merit. Unless this philosophical change is made, lifers will continue to be lost in the shuffle, and the rising population will become more expensive, resulting in throwing away badly needed resources."

Ross Maggio, Angola's warden from 1976 to 1977 and from 1981 to 1984, said: "There are men at Angola who have made a true change, who have reevaluated their lives and set out on a positive course. I can't attempt to say who or how many there are. I wouldn't attempt to say that *x* percent of the inmates are rehabilitated, but from my own personal contact with individuals inside the prison, I can say there are men here who have definitely made a change in their lives."

Former Angola warden Frank Blackburn (1977 to 1981; 1984 to 1987): "There is no system to releasing lifers and long-termers; of who goes or who stays in prison. As a prison administrator for many years I personally knew of twenty-five to fifty long-termers that I would release immediately, because there is no doubt they are rehabilitated. I feel other Angola wardens would agree. . . . There are just too many people in prison today as tax burdens that should not be there. If politics can be removed from the clemency process and a degree of input [added] from the prison administration in deciding who is released and who is not, the risk factors, if any exist, would be considerably lessened."

R. Hilton Butler, Angola warden from 1987 to 1989, expressed hope for a more lenient parole and clemency process. "If we don't, our system may come apart at the seams. I don't advocate a throw-open-the-door policy. But there are some inmates we could release and better supervise on parole. Parole is not leniency. It's just a different level of supervision that is somewhat less strict than prison supervision. We just have to develop a rational philosophy of who to let out and who to keep in."

In an effort to determine the average cost of imprisoning an offender for life, the National Council on Crime and Delinquency conducted a study based on the crime and incarceration rates in nine states, including Louisiana, and the current costs of prison construction and annual maintenance of prisoners. In its report, released

James "Black Mattie" Robertson with Angola
Warden Hilton Butler on his release from prison on
July 10, 1989 (Courtesy The Angolite)

April 14, 1988, the council stated that "to build and house an inmate for thirty years, about the average time for a life sentence, costs the taxpayer over a million dollars."

[June 1988]

▌▌▌▌ Postscript ▌▌▌▌

The plight of James "Black Mattie" Robertson and the dilemma of long-term prisoners were much publicized as a result of *The Angolite*'s article. Prison officials and experts called upon the state of Louisiana to address the problems and prevent hopelessness among the prisoner population. The following long-termers profiled in this article received executive clemency and were released in 1988: Parnell Smith (after thirty-six years), Jack Lathers (thirty-one years), and Louis Ducre (twenty-nine years). After a record forty-one years in Angola, James Robertson was paroled July 10, 1989. As of July 1991, the number of Angola prisoners who had been confined twenty years had reached 250; the majority of these men were between the ages of forty-five and seventy-four. Louisiana now has 1,231 prisoners over the age of forty-five, of which 343 are fifty-five years of age or older. The number of prisoners serving life sentences has risen to 2,260.

"The Long-termers" received the 1989 Certificate of Merit from the American Bar Association Silver Gavel Awards Committee, which cited the article's public service contribution when it bestowed the award.

HOLLYWOOD COMES TO ANGOLA

||||||

Wilbert Rideau and Ron Wikberg

Leigh Murray was an intern reporter at WABC-TV in New York when Joyce Mattox commandeered a helicopter and broke her boyfriend, Jesse Glenn Smith, out of a Tennessee prison. The story was front-page news. Its elements captured the public imagination. It was the first successful helicopter escape, and Mattox, a South Carolina housewife, surrendered everything for love of an outlaw.

Murray, also a South Carolina native, took an intense interest in the story. "It was a modern-day fairy tale," she said. "This was a story where the woman really makes all of the action happen. She's got to, because all the men are behind bars." When Mattox was sentenced to forty-two years in prison for her act of love, Murray felt she got a raw deal.

"I tried to contact her right after it happened, but she was in jail, in court, and nobody could get close to her," Murray recalled. "I wasn't thinking of doing a movie. I wanted to write a book." Three months later, when Murray was in Los Angeles, she again attempted to contact Mattox. "Her family told me she was in a federal prison in California, but they wouldn't tell me which one, so I called the FBI and every federal prison in California, trying to locate Joyce. Finally, one of them said yes, she was there." The authorities relayed a message to Mattox, who returned Murray's call about two hours later. Mattox agreed to meet with her and that was the beginning of a relationship that led to a television movie based on Mattox's story and made Murray a producer. And during the first week of December, scenes of the movie were shot at Angola.

The $2 million movie of Joyce Mattox's story, entitled *The Outside Woman,* is being produced for CBS. Sharon Gless *(Cagney & Lacey)* is playing Mattox, with Scott Glenn *(Wild Geese II, Urban Cowboy* and *The Right Stuff)* portraying her convict boyfriend. Max Gail of *Barney Miller* also stars.

Producer Jim Green explained that the movie could have been filmed almost anywhere, except for the helicopter escape. "We called the prison in Georgia, told them what we needed to do in their prison, and they said no," Green said. "We called a prison in Arkansas and they said maybe—they wanted to read the script. We came to Angola and met with Warden Hilton Butler. The first thing I told him was that we are going to break three prisoners out of here and are going to use a helicopter to do it. I figured that if he was going to throw us out, he would do it right then."

"Go ahead," Butler responded. "That should be exciting."

The movie's crew and actors consisted of about sixty people, who stayed at a hotel in nearby St. Francisville, and were bused the twenty-two miles to the prison each morning to begin the day's shoot. "As movie crews go," sound mixer Richard Birnbaum said, "this is a fun crew, a very good crew." Sharon Gless tended to stick to herself, but most of the others kidded, played, took photos with the inmates and locals, and signed autographs. Louisiana State Penitentiary security caps and *Angolite* magazines were popular souvenirs.

But despite the fun, the production proceeded on a tight schedule, and Murray followed the process like a mother watching her baby. "It's like watching your dream come true." She smiled. "I'm on cloud nine." And she's learned a valuable truism about success: "It's being there at the right time and being ready to take that chance."

Being successful also involves hard work and sacrifices. Scott Glenn, who's been in the entertainment business for twenty years, lives in the mountains of Idaho with his family. When he's not acting, he likes to write poetry, rock-climb, parachute, cross-country ski, and play with his two kids. How much time does he get to do the things he likes? "Not much," he said. "Realistically, hardly any time at all. In the past year, I think I got to jump two days, got to cross-country ski maybe a week. I've been away from home six months this time. As an actor, you struggle so long and so hard just to get a job, any kind of job at all—and it's not just me, it's like a universal kind of thing—that once you start working, you get terrified that your last job is the last one you're ever going to have. And I'm realizing that, over the last few years, I've been like a slave to work, and now I'm just trying to slow it down some. I've got kids and they're growing up. I don't want to just work my whole life away. Just as soon as we finish up here, I'm gonna go home."

Assistant Warden Roger Thomas coordinated the prison staff and worked closely with the movie crews. "I know this business is supposed to be glamorous," he observed, "and I'm sure there is some glamour to it at some stage, but I haven't seen it. All I've seen is hard work. Hell, we don't work inmates as hard as they work these actors."

Max Gail observed that working on a movie is much like a prison because it involves a collection of mostly strangers who congregate in one location and must get along. "It's very much the same thing," he said. "You've got a wake-up call, you've got a time to be on the bus, you've got a time you got to be there on the set, and you've got to do the job, no matter how long it takes. This past Saturday, we worked about nineteen hours. On *Barney Miller,* we used to work around the clock all the time. You just stay at it until you get it done. We've got [an assistant director] who is the equivalent of your warden, who makes arbitrary decisions—Do this, Do that, Don't ask why, Just do it 'cause I say do it. . . . But don't get me wrong. I'm not going to say it's the same experience, 'cause I get to leave whereas you guys have to stay with it.

"Some people think about getting into acting," he continued, "and they want what they imagine the results to be. They look at the glamour or whatever and say, I can do that. They don't think about the price you pay. But it's worth it. Acting allows you to escape the humdrum routine of modern life. It allows you to do your thing. I guess I'd rather pick up some form of expression and change somebody's mind than pick up a gun and change their body. . . . Of course, sometimes there's a minefield because of all that money and all the different motivations that bring people to it. Because of the way the country is—the more money, the happier—but money just brings you another set of decisions to make and things to deal with." Gail is widowed, with a five-year-old daughter in kindergarten. "This is the first time since her mom died that I've left, taken off to do something."

This was also the first time Gail had ever filmed within a prison. "It's been a learning experience," he stated. "I didn't have any real set attitudes about prison before, but I feel like I know more now about what's going on. They've told me this isn't the typical prison and there aren't any gangs here. And that's a good thing, because if somebody is spending all their time just protecting their ass, then there's no way, really, that they can get at any kind of growth or insight into what wrong choices they made or whatever the hell it is that got them here."

Angola was not the first prison Glenn had filmed in, nor was Jesse his first bad-guy role. Some actors hesitate to play villains; Glenn doesn't mind. "They're the more interesting parts, usually," he said. "You get to go through changes playing people who are on the downside kind of things. And there's a public fascination about them. You watch people go into a zoo. They laugh at the monkeys, but when they get to the snake house they're fascinated. I think the other side of it is there's the sneaking suspicion that they're kind of the same as the bad guys, that they just either haven't been in the wrong set of circumstances to lead them to do the things the guys in here did, or else they did and haven't gotten caught, or it's just a case of you seeing yourself in them. And when you say 'circumstances,' it's not that people are here because they're innocent of never doing anything bad. I think the fascination has to do with the reality that, Shit, if I had turned the corner and looked in a different direction, I could be sitting here just as easily. It's just a case of being lucky, and I know I've been lucky."

The film *The Outside Woman* would provide Roger Thomas with one of the high points of his life. As fate would have it, the last day of filming was Thomas's birthday. When he arrived on the movie set, he discovered that the crew had given him a personal dressing room, complete with a star on the door. That afternoon, he was given a small speaking role as a security officer. This was heady stuff for Thomas, who once studied theater and aspired to be an actor. But his biggest birthday surprise was yet to come. With perfect timing, Lieutenant-Governor Paul Hardy, accompanied by Tesa Laviolette, head of the state's Office of Film and Video, showed up to observe Thomas's acting debut and wished him a happy birthday. As dark settled over the prison, a voice crackled over the radios on the set: "That's a print." The movie was done. A rousing cheer went up from all the movie crew. It was over.

[February 1989]

THE OMEN

IIIII

Wilbert Rideau and Ron Wikberg

The most powerful force governing the behavior of prisoners at Angola is Hope, the belief that, at some point, they might be among those fortunate enough to win clemency from the governor and escape the prison existence. This perception produces decades of responsible and productive behavior by the inmate who strives to "earn" a second chance at life. This is the foundation upon which Angola has traditionally functioned, and governors, who control Hope, have generally understood this, and historically they have kept hope alive.

But there has been a revolution in Louisiana: the Roemer Revolution. Since Buddy Roemer took office in March 1988, promising to restore integrity to the scandal-plagued clemency system, no clemency has been granted to anyone at Angola. And he has become the first governor since at least 1892 to not grant clemency to anyone during the Christmas season. Indeed, he has compiled the most dismal clemency record of any Louisiana governor. For all practical purposes, the clemency system has not existed since Roemer has been in office, a reality certainly not designed to inspire hope among the hopeless. And a recent rash of desperate acts by long-term prisoners is causing much speculation among Angola inmates and personnel about the natural law of cause and effect. One doesn't need a degree in psychology to realize that even the most sane and law-abiding of men will be moved to irrational and desperate behavior if hope is removed from their existence. Prisoners are no different.

On April 15, 1989, Francis "Corky" Clifton, a fifty-two-year-old lifer at Angola, escaped. It was several days before the prison's chase crew apprehended him. Normally, it's obvious why a prisoner would attempt to escape—but for a prisoner like Clifton, escape was un-precedented.

Warden Hilton Butler, who has been at Angola forty years, could not recall the last time a prisoner like Clifton had attempted to escape. "That's very, very unusual," he acknowledged. "He was a trusty, living in one of the best places you could live in prison, and had the best job here. I talked to him, asked him why. He said that he just gave up hope. He told me there was no way that he could ever get out of the penitentiary the way things were, that he would just die here. So he ran off."

Two weeks later, on May 1, Steven "Poodle" Howard, a thirty-four-year-old Camp F trusty, escaped, also eluding capture for several days. A lifer, Howard had served ten years in an exemplary manner. "He had only two minor disciplinary reports in those ten years," Butler stated. Howard also was not the kind of prisoner who normally runs off.

A week after that, on May 8, inmates of Camp A's Farmline Number 21 were reporting for work when Donald Fink began running away from the guards. According to several witnesses, an officer yelled, "Where are you going?" Fink replied, "I'm going home," and broke into a run. Nearby guards fired a volley of shots. The thirty-nine-year-old Fink fell to the ground, bleeding. He was rushed to a Baton Rouge hospital and is now recuperating at the Angola infir-mary.

Serving a life sentence for murder, Fink was nearing his twenty-first year behind bars when he made his escape. "I talked with him the day before," said fellow lifer Jimmy Graves. "He had nothing going for him, no people helping him, nothing to look forward to. He just gave up. There was nothing to live for anymore. Hell, he just gave up! We all could see the dust flying as the bullets hit all around him."

"I feel Louisiana has taken away all the hope and closed all the avenues of possible release," said John Ortego, in his eleventh year of a forty-year sentence for armed robbery. "What Donald did—that was nothing more than a kamikaze move."

Acts of desperation are not unknown in the world of prison. But for three such acts to occur within less than five weeks is unprece-dented in modern penal history. Butler acknowledges that he has not seen a rash of such behavior from these kinds of inmates in his four decades at the prison. It defies all prison experience and expectations.

The Clifton-Howard-Fink escape attempts have caused some to reflect on an earlier incident and look at it with a new perspective. A month before, on March 15, McKinley Reddick, a trusty carpenter and model long-term prisoner, hanged himself at the rodeo grounds. Reddick had served thirteen years of a life sentence and was not the kind of prisoner to commit suicide. Nor was he given to irrational behavior. In Reddick's case, a girlfriend reportedly ended their relationship, pushing him over the edge. Where hopelessness ended and heartbreak began, no one knows nor ever will.

Butler, a career security man who's fought toe-to-toe with inmates and even executed some, is no bleeding heart. But he firmly believes the system should always extend hope to even the worst of men. "I feel that everybody should be reviewed and given some type of hope," he said. "You're not telling him you're going to turn him loose this time or any other—there are no guarantees. But the man's record should be reviewed by a bona fide board [and] when it makes a recommendation, something [should] be done. . . . Somewhere down the line, when a man shows that he's been rehabilitated or just gotten too old, something needs to be done for him, somewhere. If we don't, the situation is going to eat us alive."

Angola, Butler pointed out, "is the end of the road. This is where all the lifers, all the long-termers, and all the people other institutions don't want, wind up. There are a set of rules in the Department of Corrections that we're all supposed to go by, but I keep pointing out to everybody that Angola is different and has to be operated differently from other prisons because you've got a different type of convict. Most of them are lifers and long-termers, many of them with no hope of ever getting out.

"I feel that every man has to have some type of hope in life," Butler continued. "We're getting a lot of seventeen-, nineteen-year-old kids in here with life sentences or ninety-nine years for armed robbery and the like. A kid like that has no hope. If you're going to keep him locked up till he dies, then all he's going to be looking forward to is seeing how much trouble he can cause. That's because he don't have any incentive to do differently. Now, if he knows that people are going to be watching his record and maybe, somewhere down the road, making a recommendation for a commutation of his sentence, then he's going to try to improve himself and try to do better.

"There are a lot of people here who should never be released. They should die here," he said, but pointed out that "there are men here at Angola who deserve clemency. . . . I feel that I could pick some, turn them loose, and you'd never have to worry about them coming back. And if those who've kept good records and proven they are ready to go back in the free world and be law-abiding and productive citizens, were turned loose, it would save the state a lot of money."

"I agree with Warden Butler," Mike Gunnels, the prison's security czar, said. "There are some people here who, if freed, will never be back. If the governor would take a close look at what's happening in the penal system and, if he'd help some of the people who deserve help, it would do a lot to improve the situation. It would give inmates the hope that 'Someday, if I straighten up and keep my record clean, . . . maybe one day [I'll] get out of here.' Officials here at the prison are striving to help keep the hope alive, but there's only so much that we, as an administration, can do. We can see to it that the prisoners are treated fairly and decently in their day-to-day life. But for hope— only the governor can give them that. We have no control over that."

At a time when Louisiana can ill afford additional expenses, the unraveling of hope will ultimately increase prison operational expenses. Corrections professionals and prison officials have consistently cited the role of old-timers and long-termers in providing leadership, moderation, and even sanity to the caged world of prison. As the more trusted and safer risks, long-term prisoners have always played a significant role in prison management and operations, at considerable savings to taxpayers. But as hopelessness sinks its claws deeper and spreads like cancer throughout the population of long-termers, penal authorities face the prospect of having to reshape many traditional practices. They know that hopelessness breeds desperation, and desperation can make even the most rational person suicidal and/or dangerous. To protect against that ominous potential will prove costly.

"It'll get to where you don't make lifers trusty after they serve eight or ten years," Butler predicted. "And it's going to cost a lot more money to operate this place because a lot of the work that's done here by trusties is more or less done with little supervision. You take a tractor driver, you can't put an officer on every tractor. That's done mostly by lifers. The milk dairy, the cattle operation—there's so much up here that's done by trusties. And if we quit making prisoners with the better disciplinary records trusties, we won't have any tractor drivers, any dairy hands, any cattle hands, any mechanics—all this and a lot of other things would have to be done by paid prison employees, all of whom we'd have to hire. We already got problems trying to hire people. We're seventy employees short now. It's hard to get people to work at Angola."

While many prisoners and some employees see the recent rash of escape attempts as an omen of things to come, prison officials are reluctant to leap to conclusions or discuss the situation in public forums. But they are mindful of its potential.

Poodle Howard *was* desperate, as he acknowledged to *The Angolite* following his apprehension: "The reason I left when I did was because . . . I now have eleven years in and can see no end to it. Over the years I have been keeping my nose clean and doing the things that may help me get released. I had a good job, belonged to two clubs, was on their boards. I had plenty of income through my hobby craft. . . . I took on a lot of responsibility but was not happy. It was getting me nowhere. . . .

"I would sit back and look at the old-timers, like the ones [written about] in *The Angolite.* . . . They were also lifers with twenty, thirty years in and growing older. I did not want to turn out to be like them. . . . I have no lawyer, no money, or the help one needs to free himself. I feel as though I'm in a no-win situation."

Corky Clifton, too, explained his behavior to *The Angolite* after his recapture:

Why did I escape? I suppose it was for the same reason that men have fought wars and died for throughout history. I wanted to be free.

For twenty-seven years I have submitted to discipline, the rules, the harsh conditions, the torment of my children growing from babies into men—without ever seeing them. I've never had a visit from any of my family during these twenty-seven years because, being from Ohio, no one could afford the trip here to Louisiana.

I once thought, as most people do, that all you had to do in order to get out of prison was just be good and they'll let you out someday. One does not have to be in the prison system very long to learn what a joke that is.

If Jesus Christ himself was in here with a life sentence, he couldn't get out unless he had money to put in the right places.

I've always been a pretty stubborn person, so even though I was told how the political and Pardon Board system works, I freely submitted to all the prison rules and discipline. After twelve years with a perfect record—no disciplinary reports—I applied to the Pardon Board and was denied any consideration for relief. So I waited ten more years and applied again, with still an excellent prison record. This time they wouldn't even hear my case. In 1983 I applied to the board for the third time and the Pardon Board cut my time to fifty years. However, the judge and D.A., retired, simply called the governor's legal staff and told them they don't want me to be free—so, end of case. When I applied for my pardon in 1983, the D.A. published an article in the newspaper saying I was a very dangerous man that would kill anyone who got into my way. He said a lot of things which were all designed to turn public opinion against me and justify his reason for protesting my release.

In spite of having to endure the torment of prison life all these years without hope, I was still determined to better myself, no longer with any hope that a nice record would get me my freedom but because the years of discipline and hardships had molded my personality to the extent that I no longer desired to do anything criminal. I could not even inflict revenge on my enemies within prison.

I taught myself how to repair watches, and for more than twenty years I repaired watches for other prisoners as well as guards. I also taught myself how to paint pictures. At the 1988 Angola Arts & Crafts Festival, I won a second place for one of my watercolors. Aside from all my other accomplishments within prison, I have only two disciplinary reports in twenty-seven years. I proved my honesty and sincerity many times over. Every time I made a friend through correspondence, one of the first things they wanted to know is how come I'm still in prison. I'm always tempted to use up several legal pads trying to explain about the corrupt legal and political system here in Louisiana. But who's gonna believe a man can be kept in here all his life just because some big shot out there don't want him out? Well, I am one example of it, and there are hundreds more lifers in here, many of them I know personally, who are in here for no other reason than because some big shot out there don't want them to go free. The only way you can get around that is *money*—in the right places.

Since the sheriff, the D.A. and/or the judge can dictate who can get out and who can't, then what's the purpose of a pardon board? Why the waste of taxpayers' money? I spent many years in here struggling for freedom. There are many people here in prison, as well as outside, who believe I should be free, but the judge and D.A. say they intend to see that I never go free, as long as I live. How am I supposed to handle that?

I'm not Charles Manson or some other mass murderer. I didn't torture or mutilate some child. When I was twenty-three years old I killed a man in a robbery. That's bad enough. But the point is, hundreds of prisoners in here for the same, and even worse crimes have been pardoned throughout all the years I been here. The majority of them served only half or less time than I have.

Of course, it's no mystery to me why I'm still in prison. The judge and D.A. are keeping me here. But I say that's unfair; should, in fact, be illegal. They prosecuted and sentenced me twenty-seven years ago and that should be the end of their involvement in my case. They justify keeping me in here by claiming I am still the same dangerous man I was twenty-seven years ago. If this were true, then I would like for someone to explain why, when I escaped a few weeks ago, I did not steal a car, knock someone in the head, or break into one of the many houses I passed.

On the night of April fifteenth, when I finally made up my mind to escape, I knew the odds were against me. I was fifty-two years old and had already suffered two heart attacks. In those final few days before April fifteenth, I fought many emotional battles with myself. I had a lot to lose and I'd be letting down a lot of good people who'd put their trust in me. But desperation is pretty hard to win a rational argument with. My time was running out. Had run out, really, because I was certainly in no condition to run through that jungle in the Tunica Hills. But even against all odds, I went for it anyway.

I struggled through those hills, mountains really, for five days and six nights, sleeping on the ground, with no food and very little water. I ended up in Mississippi. I seen a lot of people and I even talked to a few.

After a couple days I knew it would be impossible for me to get away unless I stole a car or knocked someone in the head. Not far from Woodville, Mississippi, I came across a house trailer. I sat in the bushes watching the trailer from about fifty yards away. I watched a woman drive up and unlock the door and go in alone. A few minutes later, she came out and washed her car. I could have knocked her in the head, or even killed her, took her car, and been long gone. But I couldn't bring myself to do that.

I discovered that in reality I could no longer commit the crimes that I once did. So here I stood in those bushes, watching that house trailer, that car, and that lady—my ticket to freedom—and discover I can't pay the price. I can't think of any words that could truly describe the dejection and hopelessness I felt at that moment. There was no way I could continue on as I had those five days past. There was just no strength left in my legs to go on. Resigned to my fate, I walked several hundred yards to the highway and gave myself up.

So now I am left with only two ways left to escape my torment. Just sit here for God knows how many more years, and wait on a natural death. Or I can avoid all those senseless years of misery and take my own life now.

Having to sit in this cell now for several weeks with nothing—even being denied my cigarettes—I have thought a lot about suicide and it seems to be the most humane way out of a prison I no longer care to struggle in. Suicide, or endless torment. Which would you choose?

[June 1989]

 **Postscript**

The crisis regarding life-term convicts at Angola came to a head in the spring of 1989. David Carr escaped on May 22, 1989, shortly after learning his life sentence had been confirmed by an appellate court. On May 24 Jeffrey Clovis was stabbed and killed with a kitchen knife. Peter Sterling died in similar fashion on June 8, marking the third stabbing death within a six-week period. On June 19, Terrence Metoyer turned a routine court trip into a desperate escape attempt that ended with a high-speed chase and shoot-out that landed him in the hospital. A psychiatrist told the news media that Metoyer had attempted

continued

suicide in the past "because I got tired of living."

The rash of suicides, escapes, and murders at Angola prompted high-level, unpublicized meetings between corrections officials, including one between Governor Buddy Roemer and federal judge Frank Polozola. On June 21, 1989, an angry Polozola declared a "state of emergency" at the mammoth prison, criticizing Warden Hilton Butler and his administration. The judge appointed former Angola warden Ross Maggio, who was then a vice president of Wackenhut Corrections Corporation, to determine "whether the warden and others in charge . . . are operating it [Angola] in accordance with the Constitution and laws of the United States and the State of Louisiana and the Consent Decrees approved by the Court." Polozola also directed U.S. Attorney Raymond Lamonica and the U.S. Justice Department to conduct whatever civil and criminal investigations they deemed warranted.

Charging that drugs and mismanagement were at the root of the prison problems, Roemer dismissed inmate hopelessness as an "excuse." On June 24, 1989, Bobby Grigsby was found dead, hanging in his cell; and Roemer softened his stance on clemency, commuting the sentences of several Angola long-termers on July 1. He also ordered the state police to conduct a criminal investigation into activities at the prison and authorized several million dollars in additional funding for Angola.

Hilton Butler defended his management of the prison and charged that he was being made a scapegoat. He was forced to retire, filed an administrative appeal, and was fired. Security Warden Michael Gunnells and his main prison security chief were demoted and suspended. Both won their appeals and were restored to their positions. Assistant Warden Roger Thomas quit in disgust. Larry Smith, a Maggio protégé, was named acting warden, the first black to hold that position in Angola's history. Some prisoners were indicted for operating a scam on homosexuals outside the prison and for drug smuggling. Several officers also were indicted, for various acts of corruption. Security was tightened and, in order to attract more officers to work at the isolated prison, hiring standards were suspended; women were aggressively recruited. In response to the continuing inmate suicides, the mental-health staff was increased and two mental-health units were created.

On April 15, 1990, Larry Smith was promoted to Deputy

continued

Secretary of Corrections and John P. Whitley, a twenty-year corrections veteran, came out of retirement to assume the wardenship of Angola.

Francis "Corky" Clifton, whose miserable escape came to symbolize the hopelessness and seething desperation of Angola prisoners, died a year later.

Following two years of combined investigations, probes, analyses, politics, improvements, paranoia, and uncertainty, Judge Polozola ended the state of emergency on February 21, 1991. The prison and its operation were finally taken off the front pages of the state's newspapers.

There was little improvement in how prisoners live and feel. From the employees' perspective, however, the crisis was a boon, causing them to get a raise in salary and other perks. The influx of new employees eased individual workloads. Many got promotions. Private business interests also benefited from the sales opportunities and profits to vendors supplying the array of new equipment purchased to improve prison operations. The crisis escalated the opening and privatization of two new prisons.

In a letter dated May 13, 1991, John R. Dunne, Assistant Attorney General of the U.S. Justice Department's Civil Rights Division, informed Governor Roemer: "Based upon our extensive investigation, we have concluded that conditions at LSP [Louisiana State Penitentiary] deprive inmates of their basic constitutional rights. . . . The State's failure to provide prisoners with the core requirements of adequate medical and psychiatric care, and a safe environment violates the Eighth Amendment."

Louisiana had only three adult penal facilities in 1975. Today, there are twelve prisons, holding 14,200 prisoners, with an additional 4,300 housed in local jails because of lack of space. Louisiana currently enjoys the dubious distinction of having the third-highest incarceration rate in the country, topped only by Nevada and South Carolina. The state is broke, and basic social and educational needs of the citizenry are not being met.

The prisoners? They still hang themselves.

PRISONOMICS

|||||

Wilbert Rideau and Ron Wikberg

During the past fifteen years, the United States has indulged in an unprecedented lock-'em-up-and-throw-away-the-key binge, restricting or eliminating parole, increasing penalties, passing mandatory sentences, and demanding that every offender be locked up for longer periods of time, thereby stripping judicial discretion from sentencing to ensure that a maximum number of offenders go to prison. This has been the official response to public fear of crime. Vengeance is a simplistic solution with much appeal to the fearful and angry. It allows the public to exorcise its fear and "feel good" in punishing those who scare them, even when it solves little.

The current effort to deal with crime represents a tragic waste of society's resources, not to mention of people, because there is no correlation between crime and the incarceration rate. That reality has been exhibited by the California experience. The state of Texas used to have the nation's largest penal system—until California decided to "get tough" on crime by packing everybody off to prison. To avoid prison overcrowding, it engaged in a $4.5 billion prison construction program. According to the Houston *Post*, William Bennett Turner, a San Francisco lawyer, in a letter earlier this year, pointed out to Texas Assistant Attorney General Bob Ozer the futility of California's efforts during the past decade: "California has just admitted its 100,000th prisoner, the prison budget is $2.6 billion and expected to triple, all the prisons are terribly overcrowded, and there has been no impact on the crime rate."

Texas has also cracked down on crime and is now faced with the problem of having too many prisoners. Some urge the building of more prisons; others question the practicality of it. "The real problem is not how many beds we build," Seldon Hale, chairman of the Texas Board of Criminal Justice, told the Houston *Post*. "There is a thing called the Iron Law of Corrections. For every prison bed built, a judge and a district attorney somewhere will fill it." Unless there is a distinction made between who needs to be confined and who does not, the "Iron Law of Corrections" will keep the prisons filled to capacity no matter how many prisons are built.

The United States now possesses the highest confinement rate in the world, surpassing South Africa and the Soviet Union. According to a July 1990 U.S. Bureau of Justice Statistics report, over 1.1 million persons were confined in the nation's jails and prisons on any given day of 1989. By November 1990 an additional 457,797 were on parole and 2,520,479 more on probation. America entered 1991 with a record 4.1 million adults (1 of every 25 men and 1 of every 173 women) under direct control of its criminal-justice system. A total of 61 billion tax dollars was spent in 1988 on the nation's justice system, an increase of 34 percent since 1985. In October 1988, the system employed 1.6 million persons; that month's payroll was $3.7 billion. By any standard, meting out punishment has become Big Business.

William Chambliss, a George Washington University professor, studied governmental spending trends and reported that the United States is now spending more money on criminal justice than on educating its citizens. He cites that cities spend 20 percent more on law enforcement than education. In 1982 county governments started spending more on criminal justice than education, and by 1988 the gap widened to $2 billion. And while the federal government cut its education spending by 25 percent (adjusted for inflation), it increased its criminal justice expenditures by 29 percent.

Jerome Miller, president of the National Center of Institutions and Alternatives, which sponsored the Chambliss study, observed: "We're trading textbooks for prisons." He's right. According to the Bureau of Justice Statistics, state governmental expenditures for building prisons has increased by 593 percent since 1979. The state of California, which has been pursuing a multibillion-dollar prison-building campaign, recently laid off 10,000 school teachers, opting to spend its monies on prisons, which have little impact on crime rather than education, which can prevent crime.

Across the nation, 29 cash-strapped state governments have been forced to cut their budgets, reducing delivery of much-needed services to their citizens except in the area of criminal justice. The prison-building and lock-'em-up-and-throw-away-the-key momentum continues full-blown, fueled by demagogic law-and-order politics that even the more conscientious political leaders cannot now confront without risking serious political consequences. The corrections system is like a runaway train, the biggest growth industry in the nation.

What began as a response to the very real problem of crime has turned into something else due, in part, to an army of opportunists seeing advantage and/or profit in converting a system traditionally dedicated to "doing justice" into one dedicated to "doing business." The rapid growth of the justice system has spawned a corresponding growth in service and supply industries, providing profits and jobs. For example, Texas employed 4,500 correctional officers nine years ago; today, 18,000. Criminal-justice–related educational programs, once found only at certain colleges, are now featured at over 1,000 schools in the United States and Canada. Even companies have cropped up offering to confine prisoners for profit.

In 1984, Nashville's Corrections Corporation of America won contracts from the U.S. Immigration and Naturalization Service to house illegal aliens in Texas. Since then, over a dozen companies (such as Miami-based Wackenhut Corporation, and Pricor, Inc., of Murfrees-boro, Tennessee) have entered the private prison business, constituting an industry with about $275 million in annual revenue. Still a fledgling industry, it is a harbinger of things to come.

The massive growth of the criminal-justice system simultaneously bred a large commercial/political constituency or private lobby with a vested interest not in curbing or halting the flood of prisoners but in maintaining, if not increasing, their numbers. For all the law-and-order rhetoric about reducing crime, a solution to crime is not in their best interests. They benefit and prosper from continued growth. To commercial interests, increased criminal-justice operations and prisoners translates into increased profits; to economists and political leaders, growth means more jobs for the less educated, less productive segment of the populace at the expense of others of the same socioeconomic strata (imprisonment of three persons creates jobs for two in corrections); to law enforcement, there is increased power and appropriations; to the more politically mean-spirited, it means expansion of the net of governmental control over the less desirable element of society, the "inferiors" in life. Once unpopular, prisons are now regarded as recession-proof, tailor-made industries for small towns, which fiercely compete for them.

America has entered the era of "prisonomics" when justice becomes a business with everyone feeding at the trough of prisoners-for-profit. It forebodes a troubling future.

[August 1991]

BOOK
THREE

|||||

HOUSE OF THE DAMNED

Tommy Mason

This is a world without God—this is a world of hypocrites
affecting the language of justice and moral outrage.
—ALBERT CAMUS

The sounds of doors opening, the food cart rolling over worn concrete floors, and milk crates rattling, wake the slumbering prisoners. The first glimpse of sunlight filters into the death tier; dawn is breaking and the shift is changing. Throughout the tier, the condemned men stir. One lies numbly on his bed as reality seeps into his tormented mind. He fights to recapture the darkness of semiconsciousness. He tries to blot out the knowledge that another day has come. The prisoner lives on Angola's death row, sentenced to die in Louisiana's electric chair. Frustration gnaws at his gut. Loneliness embraces him daily, driving him deeper into a world of nothingness. Fear—a constant, never-changing fear—eats away at his sanity. Two years ago, three years ago, today, tomorrow—the same, all the same; there is no inkling that the torture will end. Hope has become merely a flickering candle whose light pales quickly before the all-engulfing feeling of devastation.

There was a time on death row when there was more to fear than the electric chair. Take, for example, the occasion when a rattlesnake climbed up a four-foot wall and flopped onto the floor of the tier. The entire tier was seized by a blind panic. As the poor snake slithered down the hallway, it had to negotiate a gauntlet of thrown shoes, broomsticks, bleach bottles, and dirty underwear. It created a new psychological terror for the condemned men to cope with: No one knew when the next snake would flop onto the tier and go unnoticed until it was too late. But the worst terror was born one day when Brodie Davis was sitting on the toilet. Suddenly, the tier was racked by cries of "Oh, my God, oh, git, git out of heah, oh, oh!" About that time a large, wet rat—it looked like a cross between a lynx and a Shetland pony—loped down the hallway in front of the cells. He had crawled out of the toilet while Brodie was using it. It took four orderlies forty-five minutes to chase down and kill the creature. Of course, death row suffered for the next six months with a serious constipation problem.

But that was another era, and death row is much different today, much stricter. It is located in the Reception Center, the first building one sees at the prison's front gate. The Reception Center also houses Close Custody Restriction (C.C.R.) prisoners; Admission Unit (A.U.) prisoners; and Reception Center (R.C.) prisoners.* All incoming prisoners stop over at R.C.-A.U. However, only a few of them, called orderlies, come in contact with the death row prisoners. They are selected to work along with two R.C. prisoners. They scrub the floors, wash windows, pick up and deliver laundry, and serve meals to the death row prisoners. The closest any other prisoner comes to the row is an occasional glimpse at one of the condemned men being escorted to the hospital, to the Major's office, or on some other prison appointment. The occasional callouts, and mealtimes, are the only contact a condemned prisoner has with other inmates. The dominant activity of death row is shower time. Since each man is given one hour in the hallway and there are fourteen men on the tier, shower time can extend late into the night.

A first look at the death row tier reveals a barren hallway. One seldom notices the three black-and-white television sets arranged along the tier to accommodate the fourteen prisoners housed on the row. Looking inside, the observer soon becomes the observed. The

---

*C.C.R. prisoners, for security or protective custody reasons, require long-term cell confinement.

A.U. prisoners are new commitments received at the prison.

R.C. prisoners are housed permanently at the Reception Center but afforded the same custody status and privileges available to the general prison population. They perform culinary, maintenance, and other routine labor.

prisoners have improvised "peepers" (a peeper is a mirror on a salvaged piece of cardboard or tablet back) that, when held at the proper angles, afford them a view of the hallway and anyone visiting the area. The peepers are used in cell-to-cell conversations as well. Men in isolated cells often grow weary of talking to walls, windows, and bars. A human face, even if viewed through a makeshift mirror, adds meaning to a destitute existence. Sixteen cells—one holds the shower—face the row of windows on the opposite side of the death tier. There is a view of a portion of the R.C. yard, of the Cyclone fence surrounding the Reception Center, of the hills and trees capped by traces of the sky.

Each cell on the tier has a bed (attached to the wall); a washbowl and toilet, which sit in a corner at the rear of the cell; and a wooden trunk for the prisoner's personal belongings. About the cell are pictures: a mother, wife, girlfriend, brother, or father. One sees the loneliness, the deprivation, and the desperation of the condemned. Lesser pressures have driven stronger men across the Rubicon into insanity in search of relief; a brief jaunt into a world of fantasy, where there is tenderness, passion, laughter, joy and—life.

Death row is really a world within a world. Like any other part of the prison, it has its own routine, rules, and regulations. Landry P. Mayeaux, a correctional officer with sixteen years' experience, supervises all Reception Center prisoners. "Death row prisoners are and should be treated as maximum-security prisoners," he told *The Angolite*.

Mayeaux's views, however, are not shared by death row prisoners. They feel that by being forced to live under the punitive and restrictive rules of C.C.R., they're being disciplined. "We just sent a petition to Warden Blackburn," David Dene Martin, a death row resident for two years, told *The Angolite*. "We're trying to point out that we're under C.C.R. rules and shouldn't be. We're not asking for much. For example, C.C.R. prisoners can't have plastic or glass containers because they have a long history of throwing feces and urine on each other; they abused the privilege and lost it. But we're not allowed to have the same items—even though we don't have a history of such abuse of the privilege. The privilege was arbitrarily and unnecessarily taken from us—simply because of what happened in another part of the prison we have no control over."

As must be expected, Mayeaux sees the matter differently—he

doesn't feel the rules governing death row are harsh and unfair. "They have privileges," he told *The Angolite*. "They have television. They have typewriters in their cells. They are afforded just about every privilege afforded to C.C.R. prisoners."

That is precisely the heart of the controversy. C.C.R. prisoners are placed in maximum security because of disciplinary infractions, usually violent ones. C.C.R. is a disciplinary unit, but death row is not. It is a housing unit where men under the death sentence must be confined. State law requires that condemned prisoners be kept in solitary confinement. There is nothing in the statute requiring that they be subjected to the kind of restrictions the administration imposes upon its disciplinary-problem cases.

"I don't care how you look at it," Martin explained. "We're under

David Dene Martin (Courtesy The Angolite)

a disciplinary punishment—and for no reason—and when you add that to our death sentence, you come up with a double punishment. We're denied all sorts of privileges—and some may not seem important to the average man, but in this deprived world, they mean a lot. Recently we just got a memorandum issued by Warden Blackburn to Camp J, C.C.R., and death row. Camp J and C.C.R. are disciplinary units, but because we're housed in the same building with C.C.R., we must have the same disciplinary rules imposed on us.

"And it doesn't get better," Martin continued. "It gets worse. They keep taking things from us. Let me give you an example: When I first came here, we could have bleach, but somebody in C.C.R. threw bleach on somebody else. So what happens? We lose our privilege to have bleach. How's that fair? How is it right? I get punished for what somebody else does! I'm here to be put to death—to face the worst of punishments—and they want to take my little bleach privilege. I mean, all I can do with bleach is keep my clothes clean—which the state cannot do—and my cell clean. I could understand prison officials taking my bleach if I threw it on someone else. But to take it from me because some nut threw it on somebody else is not only totally unreasonable—it's unfair."

Prison officials are basically bureaucrats. They play their cards close to the vest. Since they have so little success at preventing misbehavior, they rule by curtailing opportunity for misbehavior. It's a policy based on failure. In this particular instance, since the correctional officers in C.C.R.—who will quickly tell you they are professionals—cannot prevent a few inmates from throwing bleach, or feces, or urine on each other, the supervisors will react by taking away the bleach and any containers that can be used to throw anything. It is the simplest solution; fairness and reason never enter into the decision-making process.

The practice of making death row prisoners live under C.C.R. regulations actually began in 1970—and, again, C.C.R. prisoners are responsible for it. "I know the story behind the practice," a former death row prisoner told *The Angolite*. "It began with the way death row prisoners used to visit. Our families would visit us in front of our cells—they would sit on benches talking to us. They didn't have wire-mesh screens up then. They put the screens up first in C.C.R. and the prisoners up there were resentful about the way we visited and the way they had to visit. Their resentment kept building—they kept complaining to the officials. So, to resolve the matter, prison officials put up a screen for death row visitors. One thing led to another. Now every time they pass a rule for C.C.R., they simply extend it to death row."

"C.C.R. prisoners are not exactly punitive," Mayeaux told *The Angolite*. "I would say that they are there because they're undesirables in the population. I also understand that death row prisoners are not there for disciplinary reasons, but because of the law they cannot be put in regular population—so we have to keep them segregated."

Semantics can twist any issue lopsided. The fact is that C.C.R. prisoners are in a restrictive housing situation and their privileges are severely curtailed for disciplinary and security reasons. The law itself requires that death row prisoners be *segregated;* it does not require that they be denied access to bleach, a jar of instant coffee, or a plastic container. The prisoners form two distinct classes—yet one, the condemned prisoner, must suffer because the administration has serious problems controlling the other.

There are thirty-three states with capital-punishment statutes. Of those only one, Pennsylvania, has no death row. At least eleven other states house their death row prisoners with other selected prisoners. There are fourteen men on Louisiana's death row, but only six of them, Martin, Colin Clark, Timothy Baldwin, Robert Williams, Dalton Prejean, and Benjamin Berry, are under death sentence. The rest of the men were sentenced under the state's old death-penalty statute, which was declared unconstitutional by the U.S. Supreme Court. The threat of execution no longer hangs over the heads of these men. Still, they choose to stay on death row for reasons only they can understand.

"I don't know why they're on death row," Martin said. "I think most of them simply don't want to leave to face the prison—to have to get out there in the fields. I'd rather be out there in the fields, chopping cotton or anything, than to be sitting around in a cell. I'd rather do any kind of work than be in a cell.

"But it doesn't affect our relationships," Martin adds. "I mean, I think there should be a difference between us—and I think as more people come in under the new law, they're going to have to be taken off the tier. I'm hoping then that [the administration] may change our status back [so that we're treated differently from the C.C.R. prisoners]. I feel that they should anyway. There is some frustration about

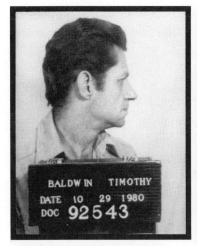
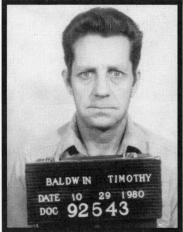

Timothy Baldwin in 1980, at the time of his conviction (Courtesy The Angolite)

Colin Clark (Courtesy The Angolite)

Timothy Baldwin (Courtesy *The Angolite*)

Dalton Prejean (Courtesy The Angolite)

it. Like when reporters or somebody comes to interview us, the only ones to come out to talk are the ones under the new law. The others just sit back there—they won't try to do anything that may help."

Eleven years ago Angola's death row was the center of a major legal battle. Inmates had filed a civil rights suit challenging conditions on death row and prison officials' practice of not permitting them outdoor exercise and recreation. A young, aggressive civil rights attorney named Richard Hand was appointed by federal court to represent the inmates. He was responsible for setting a precedent concerning the issue of lengthy periods in cell confinement without outdoor exercise. "The condemned men lived in dirty six-by-nine cells," Hand recalled for *The Angolite*. "Besides not having outdoor exercise, they were not provided any reading materials or legal materials. Some of the cells were vermin- and roach-infested. The food was tasteless and served to the men in an unsanitary manner. In effect, the men were being held in cold storage until the state or the courts decided what to do with them."

Death row prisoners still have the right to outdoor exercise. But it's a right they seldom use. "Death rows don't go out on the yard too regular," Steve Hamilton, a death row security officer, said. "They have the privilege but they don't take advantage of it. I talk to them and try to get them to go out, to get a little fresh air and sunshine, but they seldom do."

Hamilton has worked on death row for four and a half years. He stresses that he tries to do his job professionally and fairly. He has succeeded. "I can't find fault with the free people over us," Martin told *The Angolite*. "We got some good free personnel working over us. They don't give us any hassles. They seem to understand that we have a lot on our minds and they don't give us a hard time. Of course, it's a trade-off—we don't give them a hard time either. We treat them with respect and courtesy." Hamilton agrees. "The men on death row," he says, "are well-behaved. . . . We don't have any problems out of them."

The worst restrictions death row prisoners must live with are those placed on their telephone privileges. "We're only allowed one personal phone call a month," Martin stated, "and that is for only five minutes. It's really hard on me—and it's hard on other prisoners—because some of us can't get regular visits; our families live too far away. And there is so little you can say in five minutes, once a month."

The rule is harsh. It was implemented for prisoners in restrictive disciplinary units. Prisoners in regular population have daily access to the telephone. Living on death row, living under a death sentence, is harsh, but the confinement is made harsher by restrictive regulations designed to curb misbehavior in disciplinary units. The routine on death row seldom changes, winter, summer, spring, or fall. The prisoners don't have hobbies, crafts, or other activities to engage in, as other prisoners do. "I read, write letters, and listen to my radio," Martin explained. "We're restricted on the amount of books we can have in the cell at one time. I watch a nominal amount of television. Most of the other prisoners spend the entire day and night watching it. I can't do it—it's an idiot box. I exercise my mind by writing and reading."

The condemned prisoners can have their own radio, but no tape player. "But when you're locked down in the cell," Martin said, "the reception is not very good—and it's frustrating at times not being able to listen to music because of the reception."

Men on death row prefer to keep their problems off their minds, but there are discomforts that make escape from reality difficult. "During the winter," Martin explained, "we freeze, and during the summer we bake. We've got one fan at the front of the tier but it reaches only to the fifth cell. During the winter months, we're given two blankets, and for some it is enough. When I'm in bed, it's enough, but when I get up, I have to put everything else on." The prisoners have "store day" twice a week, Fridays and Saturdays. "We'll pick up store orders at dinnertime—ten thirty to eleven—and the store man will fill them out and they come back in the evening," Hamilton explained. "There's lots of stuff they can have, but they can't have any kind of glass jars. It's really complicated, a lot of it."

Death row prisoners have little to look forward to: mail call, a personal phone call, or a visit twice a month. Perhaps Louisiana's death row, more than any other, reeks of the menace of death. Two of its prisoners—Martin and Colin Clark—have come within thirty-six hours of dying. Each man must face the constant barrage of death dates, reprieves, and new dates. During his tenure over death row, Hamilton has talked with the prisoners about the execution dates. "I talk to them about it," he said, "when his date is set, but only if he wants to talk about it. If he doesn't, that's his right—but if he wants to talk, I'll listen to him, anything he has to say. I can't blame some of them because that's a tough situation, when you're under the death penalty."

The condemned men sit idly in their cells, waiting, hoping, and thinking. Days turn into months, months into years, and years into an eternity. It is a lonely and depressed life—a world of the damned and hopeless. Caryl Chessman once wrote:

> Life on the Row is a blending of the real and the unreal; it's a clash of internal and external tension, the tension of everyday living magnified a hundred times. You're a prisoner in a strange land. You are and you aren't a part of the larger whole around you. You form friendships and your friends die. You dream and your dreams die. . . . On Death Row life not only copies art, it creates a grotesque art form all its own that makes life its slave, death its master.

[August 1981]

 Postscript

Brodie Davis, who saw the rat first, was eventually freed. The eight men condemned under the old death-penalty laws, declared unconstitutional in 1972, were ultimately removed from death row.

In 1985, the Reception Center building, constructed in 1950, was closed for renovation and the condemned prisoners were temporarily housed at Camp J, the prison's supermaximum-security unit. In November 1989, the men were transferred back to death row quarters in the Reception Center building, where they remain today. One half of the building now houses offices of the prison administrative hierarchy, over two hundred officials and secretaries; the other half, C.C.R. prisoners and Louisiana's thirty-three condemned men.

Of the six on death row when this report was published in 1981, only Colin Clark is alive, having won a new trial and pleading guilty for a life sentence. Robert Williams was executed

continued

December 14, 1983; Timothy Baldwin on September 10, 1984; David Dene Martin on January 4, 1985; Benjamin Berry on June 7, 1987; and Dalton Prejean on May 18, 1990.

Major Landry P. Mayeaux retired from corrections in 1987.

Contact visits between condemned prisoners and their attorneys were eventually instituted in January 1991, following negotiations between ACLU National Prison Project lawyers and prison authorities. Contact visits with family members and friends are still prohibited.

THE DEADLIEST PROSECUTOR

|||||

Ron Wikberg and Wilbert Rideau

Joe Freeman Britt is district attorney for the Sixteenth Judicial District of North Carolina, which encompasses Robeson and Scotland counties. Following his election in 1974, Britt found his passion in life: prosecuting murderers and putting them on death row. "I love going into court, and there's no greater challenge in law than prosecuting capital cases," he said in a March 1987 *Southern* magazine profile of him. "It's good stuff, I'll tell you. It makes me high. It's the only thing I want to do in life."

During the past fourteen years, Britt has pursued his life's work with a passion, prosecuting forty-seven murder cases and winning death sentences in forty-four of them. He sees himself as an angel of retribution, and there is no room in his philosophy for redemption and no use for the lawyers who defend murderers. "I just stay the hell away from them," he told *Southern* magazine. "They're the enemy." Robert Jacobson states: "Trying a case against Joe Freeman Britt is like getting into a pissing contest with a skunk." Jacobson faced Britt in the arena of death when he fought to save the life of Velma Barfield, who in 1984 became the first woman executed in the United States in twenty-two years.

The fifty-two-year-old Britt has attracted considerable media attention during the past several years, even landing a CBS *60 Minutes* profile. The *Guinness Book of World Records,* impressed by his prosecutorial record, lists him as "the world's deadliest prosecutor."

Guinness and its editors, however, are dead wrong. If *Guinness* wants to recognize Britt for having racked up the most capital convictions (which we can't verify), that's one thing. But the number of convictions does not necessarily make him the "deadliest" prosecutor. Some of Britt's death-penalty convictions were later whittled down by commutation or reversal. More significantly, the bottom-line reality is that all of the subjects of Britt's capital cases are alive, well, and breathing—except the grandmotherly Velma Barfield, the *only* person actually executed as a result of a Britt conviction.

Now, if *Guinness* editors want to recognize "deadliness," that's a different matter and one that can only be measured by the number of cases that actually culminated in execution. If that is the yardstick, then the "deadliest" prosecutor in the United States is not Britt, but a Louisianian named Henry Newton Brown, Jr.

When Edward Byrne, Jr., died in the electric chair on June 14, 1988, following a failed clemency bid, it marked the end of Henry Brown's

Prosecutor Henry C. Brown (Courtesy The Angolite)

death row cases. He had five men on death row at the Louisiana State Penitentiary and, during the past four years, all were executed, one by one, four within the past twelve months: Ernest Knighton, Alvin Moore, Jimmy Glass, Jimmy Wingo, and Edward Byrne, Jr. There are no more condemned persons from the Twenty-sixth Judicial District of Louisiana, which Brown has served as district attorney since 1975.

While Louisiana has recently earned the distinction of being the "execution capital" of the nation, Brown's district, which encompasses the small rural parishes of Bossier and Webster, has won that of being the deadliest jurisdiction in the state. This is particularly odd when viewed against the historical backdrop of past execution practices. While the rest of Louisiana executed 134 persons between January 1, 1930, and December 31, 1977, not a single offender was put to death by the Twenty-sixth Judicial District. During the past four years, however, that district—more specifically, Bossier Parish (Webster has not executed anyone since the beginning of such recordkeeping)—has sent more men to their death than any other in the state and perhaps the nation. All five men were prosecuted by Brown, and each died as a direct result of his prosecutorial effort.

Nine men were sent to death row from the Twenty-sixth Judicial District during Brown's tenure in office. However, when the U.S. Supreme Court declared a part of Louisiana's capital-punishment laws unconstitutional in 1976, the Louisiana Supreme Court ordered all condemned persons convicted under the law resentenced to life imprisonment. Four of the condemned prisoners benefiting from this reshuffling of laws were Brown cases. But aside from that, Brown, unlike Britt, has not had a single condemned person elude his penalty.

Brown prefers to describe his success as "effectiveness." "I work hard on the cases I handle and go to trial with," he explains. He follows each case to its conclusion; he even witnessed the execution of Jimmy Glass. Louisiana governors have consistently refused to interfere in capital cases, but in the single instance in which a governor seriously considered sparing the life of a condemned man, the deciding factor was Henry Brown. "I spoke personally with Governor Edwards, who was inclined to grant clemency to Ernest Knighton," Brown confirms. "I was opposed to the granting of clemency." Knighton was executed on October 30, 1984, shortly after that telephone conversation.

There is little in Brown's forty-six-year life to indicate he would become so effective a prosecutor. He has never been personally victimized by crime, nor have any of his friends or relatives been touched by crime or violence—"not even a burglary that I can think of," he points out. His has been a pretty typical middle-class existence. He was born in rural Bienville Parish but, at age five, moved with his parents to Bossier City, where he attended elementary and high schools. "My mother taught school in Bossier Parish until her retirement, and my father was an engineer with the State Highway Department," Brown recalls. He attended law school at Louisiana State University in Baton Rouge, graduating in 1966. Afterwards, he served a tour of duty in Vietnam in the army infantry as a member of the 173rd Airborne Brigade. Discharged in 1968 with a six-year National Guard obligation, Brown returned to Louisiana, married, became a family man, and began the process of building a life and career. By 1972, he had become chief assistant to the district attorney. In 1975, he was elected district attorney.

Brown expresses no personal delight in putting people on death row. But "I believe in what I do," he explains. "I think it is the right thing to do. I was talking to a state representative from Shreveport not long ago and I was telling him that I didn't think you should put people who are prosecutors in categories of liberal or conservative, because I didn't think there was any category when it came to crime. I don't think that a Democrat or Republican wanted to be a victim of crime. His response to me was, 'Well, Henry, you're just a cop—that's all you are.' And I think that might have something to do with it. I probably have a cop mentality."

Brown works closely with the police, routinely relying upon them, even more than upon witnesses, when arguing against clemency in his capital cases. "We are all part of the same system," he says. "You know, the police won't do any good without a good prosecutor. A prosecutor without a good police investigation is not going to be effective. So we all work together."

Ironically, one of Brown's first major cases was the prosecution of members of his local law enforcement community. Jack Favor, a fifty-seven-year-old high-profile Texan and four-time world rodeo champion, had been convicted in 1967 of the 1964 double murder of a Haughton, Louisiana couple. In 1971, he filed a writ of habeas corpus alleging that his conviction was obtained through perjured testimony by the state's star witness and collusion between the authorities and that witness. The federal court, ruled in 1972 that Favor be granted a new trial or released. The state resisted and it took another federal court decision before the state retried him in 1974, at which point he was acquitted. In the meantime, Brown and his boss secured an indictment of the trial judge and the D.A. in the original case on charges they perjured themselves when they testified before the grand jury investigating Favor's complaint of collusion. The charges were ultimately dismissed.

"That was an example of everything that can be said bad about the criminal-justice system," Brown recalls. "It was really an example of corruption in the system." Favor, now seventy-four and in deteriorating health, spoke to *The Angolite* from his Arlington, Texas, home. He remembers Brown well. "Henry Brown is a pretty straight guy and a good prosecutor," he told us. "If you violate the law, no matter who you are, he will prosecute. I just don't think anyone can buy that guy off. He'll call a spade a spade. He's a helluva man, and I have a lot of respect for him."

Brown has prosecuted several other government officials with some success. "I think it's a bad idea," he says, "when someone in public office gets the idea that someplace is their turf. We are there to do a job and, if we don't do it right, we need to be thrown out."

Violent crime commands top priority with Brown, who points out: "We had a real violent era since 1975 in my district, lasting until 1984 when it drastically dropped." Whether his targeting of violent offenders has been responsible for the drop, he admits it "would be hard to really estimate. But, we haven't had any killings during the course of an armed robbery or a rape or other type of crime. The killings that we have had in the past year that I can recall have been barroom shootings, husband-wife stabbings—this kind of crime. We have not had any type of felony murder this past year. Our capital cases have been reduced greatly. I like to attribute that to the fact we have been very strong in Bossier on violent crime cases."

While violent offenders are targeted for vigorous prosecution, the death penalty is not sought for most murderers. "We have a lot that get life sentences because they don't qualify for the death penalty," Brown points out. Those cases that do qualify are "what I consider to be the most heinous-type crimes in my district." But, as Brown is the first to acknowledge, while people theoretically believe in capital punishment, they are often reluctant to impose it.

Allen Gaskin and James Thomley, convicted of murder in 1981, were two who escaped the ultimate penalty. "I strongly sought the death penalty" in that case, Brown states. "I was disappointed in the jury's verdict, but accept our system of justice. The defendants were seventeen years of age and this was a big factor with the jury's decision."

Perversely enough, Brown's inability to obtain death sentences for Gaskin and Thomley returned to haunt his prosecution of another case. Gaskin and Thomley, both white, were convicted of brutally raping and murdering a black woman, Virginia Smith. She was related to Alvin Moore, who was executed on June 9, 1987, for the rape and murder of a white woman. North Louisiana blacks saw the disparity in penalties as proof of racial injustice. Brown found he had to defend himself against charges of racism, which he claims were unjustified. "The attorneys representing Gaskin and Thomley asked to plead guilty to first-degree murder with life imprisonment," he explains. "I refused their offer and proceeded to trial seeking the death penalty. I believed then, and still do, that both Gaskin and Thomley deserved the death penalty. The jury returned a conviction of first-degree murder but, after a sentencing hearing, imposed life imprisonment. The defendants were seventeen years old. The victim of Thomley and Gaskin had been to a nightclub in downtown Shreveport until midnight and was walking with another lady in front of the Municipal Auditorium when taken by the defendants. In [the] Moore [case], the victim was in her home taking care of her three-month-old child. But I emphasize that I refused to allow Thomley and Gaskin to plead guilty [in exchange for] life imprisonment and strongly sought the death penalty."

Brown was also unable to obtain a death verdict in what has become a controversial case for him. James Monds, a surgical technician, was convicted of the brutal 1985 rape and murder of Vicki Thomas and sentenced to life imprisonment. Monds steadfastly maintains that he is innocent, and a substantial number of people agree. In September 1987 60 Minutes aired a report questioning not only Monds's conviction but also the nature of justice in the Twenty-sixth Judicial District. All this reflected negatively upon Brown, who insists Monds "belongs in the electric chair." And while Jack Favor believes in Brown's integrity, Monds says, "He just plays real dirty."

The criminal-justice system is subject to constant criticism, especially when capital punishment is at issue. Some see a flawed system that allows innocent people to be imprisoned and even executed; others believe it permits the guilty to escape punishment. Some charge that there are not enough safeguards to protect the innocent; others, that there are too many protecting the guilty. Brown believes the system is fair for everyone—defendant, victim, law enforcement, and the community at large. "I think it's fair," he says. "I think Louisiana's system is fair. It is like any system: You are going to have varying degrees of capabilities throughout. There is no one central decision-making process. For example, there is no one D.A. handling all capital litigation. There is no one defense attorney handling all capital litigation. And there are varying abilities among all these people. That's the way human life is. You deal with human beings and all of them have their particular limitations. Some have greater abilities in certain areas than others, and that is what the system is based on. Now if there is any unfairness, it might be that. . . . And you have the way people look at [a crime], too, which varies in different locations and also with the people handling the process, with the police, with the prosecutors, with the judges, with the district attorneys and with the defense attorneys as well as with the community itself."

A problem inherent in capital cases that is cited not only by death-penalty opponents but also by the American Bar Association is the difficulty of securing defense counsel to represent condemned prisoners in postconviction appeals. Critics charge that, as the judicial system moves to expedite death row cases and the number of executions increases, so does the likelihood that a condemned man will go to his death without having had legal representation at the most critical stage of the process. "Every person facing the death penalty should have excellent legal representation," says Brown. "In the Knighton case, I found that attorneys had not obtained a stay of the initial execution date. I brought this to the attention of the attorney representing Knighton, who sought and obtained such a stay. I cannot conceive of a case where a defendant facing the death penalty would not have an attorney, but if such occurred, I would insist on the court appointing an attorney. There is no lack of volunteers to represent defendants on death row, and a number of organizations have been formed to provide this type of representation. If such organizations did not exist, then the judicial system would have to appoint attorneys to ensure that a condemned person is represented throughout the entire process."

Prosecutors and defense lawyers alike frequently express frustration and criticism in dealing with the system in capital cases. Having been the prosecutor most effective in getting his death cases to the final stage, and having observed and defeated various legal defenses, Brown has advice for both sides. "The advice I would give prosecutors is to stay on top of the case and respond quickly to all pleadings filed by the defense," he states. "To defense attorneys, I would suggest they determine the legally strong features of their side and emphasize these points. I find defense attorneys emphasize too often their personal objections to the death penalty and consume valuable space on legal points with little chance of success. It reduces your effectiveness before the court to present erroneous points."

Though Brown vigorously opposed clemency in all of the cases that ended in execution, there is room in his prosecutorial philosophy for both redemption and clemency for prisoners, even lifers, who serve a satisfactory amount of time in prison in a meritorious manner. "I think, generally speaking, you are going to find a district attorney will object to clemency because they've had no contact with the person since he went to prison," he explains. "Now, in some cases, the district attorney will have seen what the person has done and will probably, might very well, withdraw his objection or not make an objection. But the problem is that most D.A.s have no idea of the man after he left. I had such a request come across my desk recently and the only thing I know about the man is when he committed the crime in Bossier Parish. I don't know about him in Angola. I don't know whether he has done something, changed his life around, and has become a productive and legitimate person in a community.

"I think the Pardon Board should respect my objection, but should also see it in the proper perspective—why I am making it and where I am coming from. . . . They need to understand that the district attorney has had no contact with that person since his crime and therefore his objection is based upon the crime itself. And, if they need to say, 'Okay, Mr. D.A., we understand why you are objecting, but we are going to look at this man since he's been down here and we are going to see whether there is any merit to him being granted clemency,' fine."

Brown states that he can accept the Pardon Board's grant of clemency over his objection. "Definitely," he says. "I don't consider my objection as having any validity other than my opinion, and they have an obligation to look at all the factors and they should override or reject an opinion if other factors warrant it. I believe that people can get their lives straightened away. I think a seventeen-year-old is usually a pretty stupid person. I was when I was seventeen—and eighteen-year-olds and twenty-year-olds, even older, there were numerous things that we all did back then that were foolish, and I think that a person can change and can straighten his life around."

While Brown believes in rehabilitation, he regards claims of it with a jaundiced eye. "Yes, people can be rehabilitated," he says, "but that is tempered with a suspicion that comes from the school of hard knocks. Too many folks get religion in jail. In fact, the jailhouse has converted more people than Jimmy Swaggart ever thought about doing. What I'm saying is, as a prosecutor, like the police, when you see the things that people do to each other, you begin to get a little skeptical about people. You get a little hard about people and their ability to change, because you saw what people do to each other. So you have a little skepticism, but it doesn't mean that you are totally shut out to the idea that people can change. It's more like a 'Show me' attitude. But I think, definitely, that people can get their lives straightened away, particularly young people."

[August 1988]

 Postscript

Following this story, state and national news media reported on Henry Brown's distinctive career. In 1990, after serving as district attorney for fifteen years, Brown was elected a judge of Louisiana's Second Circuit Court of Appeals.

THE HORROR SHOW

|||||

Ron Wikberg

*One of the ill effects of cruelty is that it makes the bystand-
ers cruel.*

—THOMAS FOWELL BUXTON

As Louisiana governor Charles E. Roemer III was signing the state's
lethal-injection law in 1988, putting an end to forty-eight years of
executions by electrocution, chances are he wasn't aware of two
significant and related events—one old and one new. At the time he
was signing Act 717, the electric chair, used to end the lives of over
five thousand people, was celebrating its hundredth birthday. And
other legal pleadings to postpone the September 19 execution of Frederick Kirkpatrick were in the final stages of preparation for filing in
St. Tammany Parish court. All three events would put Louisiana into
the national limelight.

The new law affects only those sentenced to death after January 1,
1991, thus leaving the thirty-two condemned men remaining on Louisiana's death row to face the electric chair with Kirkpatrick's execution next on the schedule. But while Louisiana was changing its
method of execution for the first time in half a century, lawyers for
Kirkpatrick were, for the first time, claiming that those executed in
Louisiana's electric chair remain conscious and that the electric chair
that had already executed nineteen people was riddled with design
defects that cause mutilation, excessive burning, and torture.

Nick Trenticosta, attorney for the New Orleans–based Loyola

Death Penalty Resource Center, filed the claims on Kirkpatrick's behalf on September 5, saying that the execution would violate the "cruel and unusual punishment" clauses of the Louisiana and U.S. constitutions. A week later the Twenty-second Judicial District court delayed the execution.

Lodging charges that executions are sometimes bungled is nothing new. Conventional wisdom, based upon a century of eyewitness accounts, has established that—whether by gas chamber, gallows, firing squad, chemical injection, or electric chair—executions in the United States account for some of the world's most gruesome tales. Equipment failure and human error cause most of the horrors; just plain fate is blamed for others. The May 4, 1990, execution of Jessie Tafero in Florida's electric chair is the most recent example reported. According to the July 20, 1990, issue of *Insight* magazine, witnesses said that "Tafero's head bobbed and his throat produced gurgling sounds for four minutes as the electricity singed his eyebrows and ashes fell from his head." Others present reported that flames, smoke, and sparks shot three to six inches above Tafero's head. After the botched execution, several other executions were postponed as an investigation was called by Governor Robert Martinez.

Such spine-chilling tales are probably the reason why eighteen states have adopted lethal-injection laws since 1976. Just twelve states now retain electrocution laws, and only six have actually carried electrocutions out. Regardless of the method used, only sixteen of the thirty-seven states with death-penalty laws have carried out any executions since 1977.*

Even before Louisiana performed its first execution following the U.S. Supreme Court's reinstatement of capital punishment in 1976, attempts were made to eliminate the electric chair. Beginning in 1981, State Senator Nat Keifer proposed the change to lethal injection as a more humane method and a progressive step. In committee hearings reported by the *Times-Picayune* on June 3, 1981, Keifer said an electrocution "is a horrible, horrible thing" and "we should not sink to the level of the people we are executing and commit violence." Support for the change was also expressed by State Senator Fritz Windhorst, who said that Louisiana should "be as humane as we can" and that lethal injection "minimizes the cruelty in taking a life. . . . It is

---

*As of December 1991, twenty-one states had adopted lethal-injection laws.

quicker, more certain than electrocution." But the 1981 efforts would be rejected by the state House of Representatives, and continued efforts over the next decade failed until the final passage this year of Act 717.

The sponsor of the 1990 legislation was State Senator Don Kelly, D-Natchitoches who as a lawyer dealt with lawsuits involving accidental electrocutions. Arguing that electrocution is "a terribly gross way to carry out the death sentence," he said lethal injection was a more humane way to execute people.

There were some grumbles. "Why should we be concerned about doing it in a humane manner?" asked Representative Peppi Bruneau, R–New Orleans, who said he believes in the "biblical philosophy of retribution." "Shouldn't we be doing it to set an example instead of saying you just fall asleep and go away for killing people?" he added.

Senator Richard Neeson, however, who witnessed the 1985 Louisiana execution of David Dene Martin, described it as "a pretty devastating thing to see." After watching Martin die, Neeson said: "I have always been one who has said that capital punishment is a deterrent to crime. I would have let him go, I would have forgotten about those people who were killed. . . . Looking into that individual's brown eyes, I realized that I didn't know much about the death penalty."

The 1990 Kelly legislation passed by an overwhelming majority of 87 to 3.

The electric chair was first used in New York, on August 6, 1890, to execute William Kemmler, who had killed his mistress with an ax. It was a botched affair that eventually produced an international furor. Not much was known about electricity at the time, but there was a growing clamor to get away from the gruesome, often bungled public hangings of the mid–nineteenth century. Not only were public executions social events, with thousands of people sometimes in attendance, but the hangings did not always come off swift and clean. In clear view of the watchers, including children, the heads of the condemned sometimes separated from their bodies; and some victims twisted and turned in agony, moaning, for as long as eighteen minutes before life left them. Occasionally the rope would break, and the condemned man had to be marched, or carried, back up the steps to the scaffold while a new rope was installed.

Public executions were intended to deter crime, so the more people who witnessed the event, the more effective it was seen to be. The notion that capital punishment was a deterrent to crime ended when the executions became carnivals of bloodlust for some, and social events for others. Sometimes invitations were printed and mailed and concession booths erected; children set up lemonade stands, and some politicians took advantage of the crowds to garner campaign support.

Though in 1834 Pennsylvania became the first state to perform executions in privacy (with the number of witnesses being limited and controlled by state authorities), it was over a hundred years before the nation's last public execution was held, in Owensboro, Kentucky, in 1936—an event that drew a crowd of twenty thousand spectators.

The numerous bungled hangings created a public outcry to end the barbaric "Old West" method of executing people. New York Governor David B. Hill responded in 1886, appointing a committee to find a more humane method. Lethal injection with prussic acid was considered, but rejected following fierce opposition by the medical community. Death by firing squad, seen by a progressive society to be as uncivilized as hanging, was also dismissed. Surprisingly, the solution came not only by accident, but *because* of an accident. The invention of electricity, and its then-primitive technology, resulted in many accidental deaths. Ironically, these accidents not only reflected the awesome potential power of the new technology, but also inspired visions of industry growth and huge profits.

The deaths of workers who came into contact with certain wires sparked an idea in the mind of the inventor of the light bulb, Thomas Edison. It was largely at Edison's urging that the New York State legislature adopted the nation's first "Electrical Death Act," signed into law by Governor Hill on June 4, 1888.

What was not publicly known at the time, however, was the vicious feuding and competition over domination of the new electrical industry between Edison and George Westinghouse. Edison's technical expertise was vested in the direct current (DC) principle, while Westinghouse's prowess was confined to alternating current (AC). The prevailing technology made DC much more expensive to produce, placing Edison at a disadvantage in convincing others that his electricity was better for their needs. Though each of the tycoons leveled various charges at the other, George Westinghouse was publicly adamant about one thing: He was opposed to capital punishment.

When Edison testified before the New York prison commissioners, he insisted that his DC system was harmless. Instead, he told the state officials that Westinghouse's AC system "would kill men like flies." To support that claim, Edison employee Harold P. Brown toured the country demonstrating how effectively AC caused death by electrocuting stray dogs, cats, horses, and a monkey in front of audiences. In one ghastly exhibition, the monkey caught fire.

When prison officials requested the equipment needed for electrical executions, an indignant Westinghouse said: "We regret to inform you that we cannot provide a dynamo for your purposes. Even if we could, it would serve your needs no better than equipment employing Direct Current." He concluded, "The alternating current will kill people, of course. So will gunpowder and dynamite, and whiskey, and lots of other things, but we have a system whereby the deadly electricity can do no harm unless a man is fool enough to swallow a whole dynamo."

In one of the most devious business deals ever arranged, an Edison employee persuaded a South American dealer to purchase an AC dynamo from Westinghouse; the dealer shipped it back to New York, where it found its way to the prison. There it was hooked up to the chair that would execute William Kemmler.

When the switch was pulled on Kemmler one hundred years ago in New York, a reporter for *The New World* newspaper, who witnessed the debacle, described it in part as follows:

> The first execution by electrocution has been a horror. Doctors say the victim did not suffer. Only his maker knows if that is true. To the eye, it looked as though he were in convulsive agony. The current had been passing through his body for 15 seconds when the electrode at the head was removed. Suddenly the breast heaved. There was a straining at the straps which bound him. A purplish foam covered the lips and was spattered over the leather head band. The man was alive.
>
> Warden, physicians, guards . . . everybody lost their wits. There was a startled cry for the current to be turned on again. . . . The rigor of death came on the instant. An odor of burning flesh and singed hair filled the room. For a moment, a blue flame played about the base of the victim's spine. This time the electricity flowed four minutes.
>
> Kemmler was dead. Part of his brain had been baked hard. Some of the blood in his head had been turned to charcoal.

Following the execution it appeared Edison achieved his goal to discredit Westinghouse. The *New York World* headlines stated that old-fashioned hanging was much more deadly than current from a Westinghouse dynamo. And from Pittsburgh, Westinghouse told reporters: "I do not want to talk about it. It was a brutal affair. They could have done a better job with an axe."

Nor was the last word in. Enraged public opinion, fueled by the now-revealed personal battle between the tycoons, was eventually disastrous to Edison. Support swung to Westinghouse, a development that had an awesome impact upon the future of the industry and society in general. As a result, all homes, appliances, and factories in the United States were eventually wired for AC rather than DC currents.

Until 1940, Louisiana's condemned men met the state executioner at the gallows. Between 1918 and 1940, all executions were performed in the parish where the prisoner was convicted. Though the state legislature on many occasions considered adopting the electric chair already in use by other states, the change wasn't made until 1940, when proponents of the chair successfully argued that hangings were gruesome and archaic.

The last official hanging in Louisiana took place in Caldwell Parish on March 7, 1940, when four men were executed for the murder of Frank Gartman following their escape from an Arkansas prison. A Monroe radio station was permitted to cover the event live, and as a large crowd gathered around the Columbia courthouse, William Meharg, William Landers, William Heard, and Floyd Boyce were hanged, in that order.

The state received its portable electric chair, made of oak, in July 1941, along with a truck to carry it and the generator needed to power it. According to Act 14 of 1940, "The operator of the electric chair shall be employed by the manager of the Louisiana State Penitentiary and placed on the penitentiary payroll." The newfangled machinery was to be housed at Angola and driven to each parish as an execution was scheduled. The wait wasn't long. Louisiana's first electrocution would take place in just two months.

On November 30, 1940, Eugene Johnson and Eddie Garrett had broken into the Livingston Parish home of Steven Bench, a fifty-seven-year-old Hungarian farmer, beating him to death with a piece of firewood and stealing $10,000. Later the men were surrounded by Sheriff P. R. Erwin and a posse; Garrett was killed by gunfire. Johnson escaped, only to be captured in Houston and returned for trial. The jury convicted him in April 1941, and on August 27 the Louisiana governor signed his death warrant. Johnson, aged twenty-two, was executed on September 11, 1941. According to records and news reports the state's first electrocution went without a hitch. During the next fifteen years the portable electric chair traveled to parishes across the state fifty-six times.

On one of those trips an event occurred that would significantly contribute to an already growing national movement to abolish the death penalty.

Willie Francis was fifteen years old when he murdered Andrew Thomas, a druggist in St. Martin Parish, and had just turned seventeen when he was strapped into the electric chair on May 2, 1946. The youth became the first known person to walk away from his own electrocution. Witnesses described how his "lips puffed out and he groaned and jumped so that the chair came off the floor." He yelled, "Take it off. Let me breathe." When the application of several jolts did not kill him, Sheriff E. L. "Harold" Resweber contacted Governor Jimmie H. Davis, who was visiting the warden at Angola at the time. Davis granted a reprieve. Francis was helped back to his cell to recuperate from the ordeal. The much-publicized legal effort to save him from a second execution failed and on May 8, 1947, Francis was taken into the same room, strapped to the same chair, and executed.

By then, the death penalty was increasingly rare. Several European nations and eight states had made it illegal. The average annual number of U.S. executions in the 1930s was 167. In the 1950s it was 72. Graphic reports of bungled executions, and a growing number of cases in which executed prisoners were later proved innocent increased the public sentiment against capital punishment. Even in Louisiana the death penalty was used less often. When it was, crowds of people still gathered at courthouses and jails; and executions still caused banner headlines in many newspapers. Finally, in 1956, the state legislature changed the law to require all executions be performed inside the Louisiana State Penitentiary at Angola.

Prison officials constructed an annex to the Red Hat Cellblock. Under the wardenship of Maurice Sigler, Angola's first execution was carried out on May 31, 1957. The death warrant for John Michel, a

Red Hat Cellblock, used from 1935–1973. The Execution Chamber, at right, was used from 1957 to 1961 (Courtesy The Angolite)

black man convicted of raping a white woman during the 1953 Mardi Gras celebration, was the first signed during the administration of Governor Earl K. Long. Ten executions were performed at Red Hat over the next four years.

Eventually Louisiana followed the lead of most other states and stopped executing people. Luis Monge's 1967 death in Colorado's gas chamber was the nation's last execution for a decade, though some states continued to issue death sentences. In a series of cases, the U.S. Supreme Court dismantled the diverse guidelines that states used in imposing death sentences. But, acknowledging that society in general had accepted capital punishment as a means of deterring crime and obtaining retribution against murderers, the high court ruled in 1976 that the death penalty did not violate the Constitution as long as a state provided strict guidelines for a judge and jury to exercise mercy in a murder case. Most states had lacked sufficiently explicit standards for determining who should be executed and who should not. In short order, state legislatures restructured their death-penalty laws to comport with the court rulings, and in 1977 the state of Utah was the first to carry out an execution under the new guidelines. It wasn't long before other states followed suit.

In spite of well-intentioned efforts to eliminate bungled executions, they still plague the nation's criminal-justice system. Mostly, the grisly debacles have been related to use of the electric chair; severe burning and mutilation have occurred during the average one-minute period during which the electricity actually courses through the body. Some experts argue strongly that pain is experienced, at least during the first few moments of the electrocution. The number of botched executions is dwindling as more and more jurisdictions eliminate the electric chair, opting instead for lethal injection. Of the original thirty-one states with electrocution laws, eighteen made the switch to lethal injection after 1976. Still, according to eyewitness and media reports during the 1980s, four of the six states employing the electric chair (Alabama, Florida, Georgia, and Indiana) had experienced serious problems. But Louisiana seemed to have had no problems at all in carrying out nineteen executions in seven years. That was until Sarah Ottinger contacted *The Angolite*.

Ottinger, an attorney temporarily assigned to the Loyola Death Penalty Resource Center and assisting in the case of Frederick Kirkpatrick, asked *The Angolite*'s editors in August 1990 if there had ever been any indications of a botched or bungled execution at Angola. Surprised at the nature of the question, and considering the absence of any such reports by officials, witnesses, or representatives of the news media attending the executions, we readily acknowledged that no such problems existed.

A native of Boston, Sarah Ottinger attended Yale University and later received her law degree from the Northeastern University Law School of Boston. She participated in a law school cooperative program and worked with the Southern Prisoners Defense Committee, where she first came into contact with the Kirkpatrick case. After graduation she joined the Public Defender's Office in Miami. Learning that the Kirkpatrick case was nearing the end of the appeals process, Ottinger came to Louisiana in May, and teamed up with attorney Nick Trenticosta.

On September 5, a 113-page (less exhibits and appendices) document was filed in the Louisiana Twenty-second Judicial District

Court. Ottinger and Trenticosta had attached post-execution evidence, including photographs showing that at least two of Louisiana's executions had resulted in burning, mutilations, and torture. The strength of the Kirkpatrick document lies not only in this visual evidence, or in the exhaustive historical research and varied legal arguments it presents, but also in the affidavits from national experts and eyewitnesses to Louisiana executions. In one affidavit, a world-renowned physiologist declared that those electrocuted suffer extreme pain.

The Angolite reviewed thirty-three color photographs taken of Robert Wayne Williams following his execution in the electric chair

Robert Wayne Williams being escorted to his execution (Courtesy The Angolite)

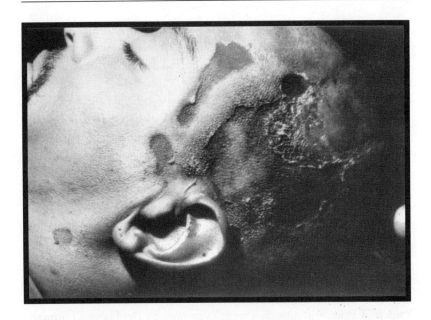

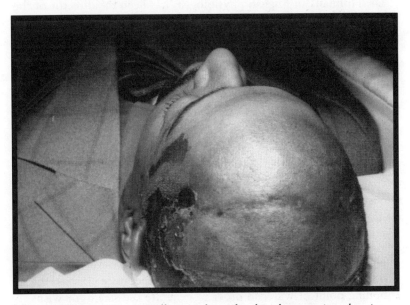

Photos of Robert Wayne Williams taken after his electrocution showing what experts say are first, second, third, and fourth degree burns.
(*Courtesy* The Angolite)

on December 14, 1983. The pictures vividly and graphically depict large areas of what experts say are first-, second-, and third-degree burns. They also show massive discoloration due to burns and blistering.

The Angolite also reviewed twenty-six official autopsy color photos (independent of those filed in the Kirkpatrick case) of nine Florida prisoners executed prior to the botched electrocution of Jesse Tafero on May 4, 1990.

A comparison of the post-execution and postmortem photographs of Jesse Tafero (May 4, 1990); Dennis Adams (May 4, 1989); Theodore Bundy (January 24, 1990); Jeffrey Daugherty (November 7, 1988); Willie Darden (March 3, 1988); Buford White (August 28, 1987); Ronald Straight (May 20, 1986); David Funchess (April 22, 1986); and Daniel Thomas (April 15, 1986) of Florida, with the photographs of Louisiana's Robert Wayne Williams, shows an unmistakable similarity in the degree of mutilation. It was those photos of Robert Wayne Williams that were examined by Dr. Harold Hillman, an expert in electrical burns.

Dr. Hillman, an English physiologist, has been the director of the Unity Laboratory in Applied Neurology at the University of Surrey for the past twenty years. As an expert in physiology and neurology, Dr. Hillman has conducted research on human and animal brains and on resuscitation. He has published over 150 scientific papers and four books. Dr. Hillman is familiar with the methods by which executions by electrocution are carried out in the United States.

When Dr. Hillman examined the Williams photos and studied the autopsies of thirteen men executed in the Florida and Alabama electric chairs between 1983 and 1990, he concluded that "execution by electrocution is intensely painful" because the prisoner retains consciousness long enough to feel pain, and death is never instantaneous. Of the photos, Dr. Hillman said:

> Not only are the burns at the points of contact severe, but the body fluids must have heated up to a temperature close to the boiling point of water in order to generate the steam, or wisps of smoke, which witnesses often note. . . . Much smaller voltages and currents are used in some countries for torture. Statements from victims, and experiments on volunteers in Denmark, have shown that the larger the voltage applied, the more painful the

torture. Victims often faint as a result of the pain. . . . It is generally held by emergency-care doctors, nurses, and first aid personnel that electrocuted patients normally die from asphyxia and cardiac arrest. During asphyxia, a patient feels unable to breathe.

While it is the common perception that the condemned man does not feel the severe burning, boiling body fluids, asphyxiation, cardiac arrest, and pain, Dr. Hillman clearly points out that there is no instantaneous death or even instantaneous loss of consciousness. To accomplish that end, says Hillman, the full force of the electrical current would have to reach the brain, which it does not. Instead, Hillman says, only one-tenth to one-twentieth of the current reaches the brain, while the greater portion of current travels through and over the skin to reach the other electrode. This is borne out by all autopsies on electrocuted convicts. Only minimal damage to the brain is noted, compared to the massive burns to the skin.

Hillman states:

Although it is widely believed that the person being electrocuted loses consciousness and the sensation of pain immediately as the electrocution starts, there is no scientific evidence whatsoever to support this belief. The massive electric current stimulates all the muscles to full contraction. Thus the prisoner cannot react by any further movement, even when the current is turned off for a short period, and the heart is still beating, as has been documented in numerous cases of execution by electrocution. It is usually thought that the failure of the convict to move is a sign that he cannot feel. He cannot move because all his muscles are contracting maximally. Likewise, patients who have been electrocuted, accidentally, can often not detach themselves from the source of the electric shock, because their muscles are paralyzed. Yet they feel pain, if they survive.

While the prisoner maintains consciousness, strapped into the chair, paralyzed yet aware of the gruesome burning of his own body, it is scientifically and medically certain that death is not instantaneous. Death results from cessation of respiration and heart. The recent practice of administering a series of jolts, waiting, and then checking for a pulse makes it more certain than not that death will have ensued by the time the heartbeat is tested. Yet ample documentation exists of earlier executions in which the current had to be reapplied when a doctor stepped in and detected a heartbeat.

A review of the certificates of death issued after each Louisiana execution corroborates Hillman's conclusion. In five executions the "approximate interval between onset and death" was given as four minutes, and in one other it was five minutes. (The remaining certificates of death did not indicate any time period at all.) Dr. Alfred R. Gould, who signed the certificates as coroner of West Feliciana Parish or as attending physician, acknowledged that Robert Wayne Williams, Johnny Taylor, Jr., Elmo Patrick Sonnier, Ernest Knighton, Jr., Robert Lee Willie, and Sterling Richard Rault continued to live three to four minutes after the current was turned off. In fact, numerous such reports were made by Louisiana medical officials following executions dating back to the 1940s.

Unlike other states, Louisiana does not require post-execution autopsies; thus, the conditions of the bodies are not documented at all. This practice appears to be in conflict with Louisiana Revised Statute 33:1563, which says it is the coroner's duty to "either view the body or make an investigation into the cause and manner of death in all cases involving . . . deaths due to electrocution . . . [or] trauma from whatever cause . . . [as well as] deaths in prison." The state of Florida, for example, takes post-execution photographs as part of the autopsy process.

John Hill, a correspondent for Gannett News Service, witnessed the execution of Robert Wayne Williams on December 14, 1983. In a news report filed the following day, Hill said the warden "gave a 'thumbs up' signal. Suddenly Williams's hands and fingers jerked closed; his stomach muscles seemed to contract. There were four distinct jolts of electricity. Smoke and sparks rose from the leg electrode on the first and third wave. But after its first violent contraction, Williams's body showed no voluntary movement."

On May 17, 1990, Dalton Prejean was put to death in Louisiana's electric chair for the murder of a state trooper. Among the pool of reporters witnessing the event was Jonathan Eig, staff writer for the New Orleans *Times-Picayune*, who averred in an affidavit later filed in another case:

At 12:05 A.M., an electrician checked all the connections and turned on the fan. Mr. Prejean's fists were clenched and his chest heaved rapidly. The warden nodded to the executioner and I saw Mr. Prejean jerk violently in response to the first jolt of electricity. He seemed to try to rise from the chair, only to press against the straps.

On the second or third jolt, Mr. Prejean's right fist turned out. On the third jolt, a spark shot from his left leg, in the area of the electrode, followed by a puff of smoke. After the final jolt, Mr. Prejean's body was still. We watched him for five minutes before the coroner and prison doctor approached to examine his body. The prison doctor lifted the hood and checked his eyes. They were half-closed, his face was gray, and his lips were blue. The coroner briefly checked for a heart beat and the prison doctor announced through the microphone, that he declared Mr. Prejean dead. We were escorted out of the witness room.

After Wayne Robert Felde was executed at Angola on March 15, 1988, his sister—a veteran nurse with fifteen years' experience as an emergency-room supervisor, who has seen numerous electrical-burn victims—viewed his body. In an affidavit to Trenticosta and Ottinger, she said she was "shocked at the extent of the burning on Wayne's body." The burns were severe: third-degree burns with sloughing, "meaning the skin had literally come loose from his body and was sliding," she said. Felde's ear was badly burned. "Chunks of skin, about four centimeters in diameter had been burned off the left side of his head, toward the front, revealing the skull bone," she added. The burn to her brother's calf, at the point of contact with the leg electrode, was "gaping and oozing." She stated that the leg was so badly mutilated that "it had been necessary to enclose that portion of his calf in a zipped plastic sleeve, with some sawdustlike material, to absorb and prevent draining of the burn."

In the 1985 case of *Glass* v. *Louisiana,* the U.S. Supreme Court chronicled descriptions by witnesses of electrocutions: "The hands turn red, then white, and the cords of the neck stand out like steel bands." "The prisoner's limbs, fingers, toes and face are severely contorted." "The force of the electric current is so powerful that the prisoner's eyeballs sometimes pop out on his cheeks." "The prisoner often defecates, urinates, and vomits blood and drool." "The body turns bright red as its temperature rises and the flesh swells and his skin stretches to the point of breaking." "Sometimes the prisoner catches fire, particularly if he perspires excessively." "Witnesses hear a sound like bacon frying and the sickly sweet smell of burning flesh permeates the chamber." "In the meantime the prisoner literally boils, the temperature in the brain itself approaches the boiling point of water and when the post-electrocution autopsy is performed, the liver is so hot that doctors said it cannot be touched by the human hand. The body frequently is badly burned and disfigured."

The more brutal aspects of electrocution are withheld from public scrutiny. Unlike the former public executions, contemporary electro-cutions proceed with militarylike precision, before only a handful of witnesses.

The fully clothed prisoner is escorted into the death chamber, his head completely shaved. If he has a final statement, it is read. Witnesses can see into the death chamber through a glass partition, but they are completely separated from any sounds or smells. In a well-rehearsed process, the prisoner's head, chest, arms, and legs are quickly secured to the chair by leather straps. A leatherette cap containing an electrode is placed tightly on his head, while the other electrode is affixed to the calf of one leg. Between the electrodes and skin, sponges dampened in a saline solution are inserted. Last, a hood is dropped, hiding the con-demned man's face. The prison guards leave. All the witnesses can see is a fully clothed man strapped tightly into a large chair with wires trailing away from the electrodes. With the face totally obscured, the only skin witnesses can see is that of the man's hands as they lie on the chair arms. Journalists who've witnessed the executions have written about the apparent simplicity of it all.

While prison officials and others involved in the execution process change with time, there is one official who is always in Angola's death chamber: the state's executioner, Sam Jones. Jones (a pseudonym), a certified electrician as required by law, has carried out all of Louisi-ana's executions since 1983. On a segment of Australian TV's news magazine aired in 1989, Jones was profiled along with Clive Stafford Smith, a defense attorney who has saved over a hundred people from execution. In a unique colloquy Sam Jones made it very clear that Louisiana executions were tidy affairs:

SMITH: What's the longest it's taken you for someone actually to die?

JONES: A wave of one jolt. We hit 'em for one minute and that's it.

SMITH: And what happens, the body starts burning . . .

JONES: No. No physical marks.

SMITH: Oh, that is rubbish. I've seen it. Come on, you put two thousand volts through someone, there are physical marks. Believe me, the body starts burning. It's like what happens to you on the job if you get two thousand volts struck through you. You're crazy if you don't think there isn't any pain. Do you think there's no marks on the body, comes out clean . . .

JONES: I know it ain't no marks on the body because I'm there when they remove them from the chair.

SMITH: Oh, I've been there when it's happened, too, and believe me there are marks and they start excreting all over the place, the bowels . . .

JONES: I don't know where you are going to see all that. But I hadn't seen any of that in eighteen executions.

The matter of burning, pain, and mutilation, however severe, caused by electrocution is nonetheless a secondary factor in light of the intended purpose of execution: the deliberate ending of a life according to the "will of the people" and the "letter of the law." Any contradictions between officials because of evidence of bodily mutilation is, again, a secondary consideration for the very same reasons.

But proponents and opponents of the death penalty do agree on at least one important factor—that the infliction of such punishment, regardless of the method, should be humane and must comport with the evolving standards of decency that mark a maturing society. Fred A. Leuchter, Jr., head of the Boston-based Leuchter Associates, Inc., the nation's only supplier of execution equipment, said: "We should not damage the body more than necessary." Considered an expert in electrocution technology in eleven states, Leuchter told *The Angolite* that he's been consulted following bungled executions and has updated or installed new systems in several states.

"My father used to be superintendent of transportation at a prison, and until I was about seventeen years old," said Leuchter, "I worked with prison inmates and employees. I have a concern for everyone." Once referred to as "Dr. Death" in an *ABC-News* segment because of his line of work, Leuchter insisted that "not only do the prison personnel need to be adequately protected—more important, the inmate should not be tortured." In an interview with *The Atlantic Monthly* (February 1990), Leuchter said he did not feel all of the execution systems existing today are painless. "No execution system should cause pain," he added.

Following his graduation from Boston University, Leuchter designed navigational equipment for the military. He holds a patent for the first electronic sextant and for a photographic device that mapped terrain in Vietnam. His expertise in electrical engineering was tapped by Kirkpatrick's lawyers, Trenticosta and Ottinger. In an affidavit filed with the St. Tammany Parish Court, Leuchter described the electrodes in Louisiana's electric chair as "the most poorly designed . . . I have ever seen in the course of my career."

Noting that most "chairs" used today are old, prone to failure, and improperly designed, Leuchter told *The Angolite:* "Most damage to the body in the form of burns is the result of poor electrical connections." He explained that the original electric chairs were the result of engineering improvements and technical changes made along the way by experts in states that now either no longer execute anyone or have switched to lethal injection. "The new generation of electric chair, and the information used in its operation, have been copied from systems that did not rely on those created by engineers, but by electricians and even inmates," Leuchter said. He stated that some of the nation's original electric chairs were actually constructed by inmates. "Any electrician can hook up a wire," says Leuchter, "but it takes an expert to deal with the electrical complexities of an execution."

In his affidavit in the Kirkpatrick case, Leuchter said in 1987 he had spoken with an Angola warden who informed him that there had been problems with an execution in 1984, when a man had screamed as the electricity was applied, and that the burn at the leg electrode went straight through to the bone. Asked if to his knowledge there have been any other problems, Leuchter told *The Angolite:* "I've heard of some problems, but it's too difficult to get information because no postmortem photographs are taken and there is reluctancy in releasing the necropsy reports."

Leuchter makes both his professional and personal concerns clear. "The persons building [the chair] should meet the responsibility for operating it properly. An inmate to be executed is not just a number. He is a human being and no one has the right to take away his humanity. The state owes it to the inmate to walk in and allow him to go with dignity and without pain."

When *The Angolite* presented Leuchter with the facts of the recent, botched Florida execution of Robert Tafero, he said: "I'm convinced that for six to eight seconds he experienced excruciating pain."

Probably the most damning information comes from nationally recognized electrical engineer, Dr. Theodore Bernstein, who became interested in the history of theories of electrocution through his studies of the effects of electricity and lightning on humans. Recently retired from the faculty of the University of Wisconsin, where his main interests were in the fields of electrical and lightning safety, magnetics, and solid-state circuits, Professor Bernstein has been qualified as an expert in electrical engineering and lightning in over fifteen state and federal courts.

On August 31, 1990, Bernstein traveled to the Louisiana State Penitentiary and inspected the chair's design and electrical equipment. He spent several hours examining and photographing the chair's equipment and circuitry. His findings are revealed in an affidavit filed in the Kirkpatrick case. He concluded, as did Fred Leuchter, that numerous aspects of electrode design "contributed to excessive, completely unnecessary burning of the person being executed." He wrote:

> The buckle on the wet straps is too close to the flesh and acts as an additional conducting path to cause burns at the buckle. The buckle and leather cause arcing of the electrical current to other areas of the flesh, resulting in additional burns. The sponge utilized is too thin and therefore does not spread the current uniformly over a sufficient area, which leads to greater burns. The rough underside of the electrode and the sharp edges of the metal, as constructed, burn right into the skin because of the close spacing permitted by the thin sponge.

"I was surprised," Professor Bernstein told *The Angolite.* "It [the chair] was put together by electricians. It should have been done by electrical engineers."

Following the bungled execution of Horace Franklin Dunkins, twenty-eight, in Alabama's electric chair on July 14, 1989, Bernstein was consulted. The electrical jacks were hooked up improperly and it was believed that no electricity reached the chair at all. At the time, Alabama Prison Commissioner Morris Thigpen said, "I regret very, very much what happened. It was human error. I just hope he was not conscious and did not suffer."

Six years earlier, Alabama attempted to electrocute John Louis Evans III, the state's first execution since 1965. When Evans was placed in the electric chair on April 12, 1983, it took three pulls of the switch to kill him. Ron Tate, an Alabama Corrections Department spokesman, saw Evans's charred, smoking body while it was still strapped to the chair. "It wasn't a pretty sight to see, I'm sure, but it's the only thing we have. I think everybody was looking forward to a nice, little, tidy package deal, but it was altogether different from what all of us expected," said Tate.

When *The Angolite* asked Bernstein to compare the design and electrical defects of Louisiana's chair to those of the chair in Alabama, he said: "It's an accident ready to happen."

Article 1, section 20 of the Louisiana Constitution, following the guarantees of the Eighth Amendment, provides, in part: "No law shall subject any person to euthanasia, to torture, or to cruel, excessive, or unusual punishment." Whether the evidence presented about Louisiana executions will have any effect on our evolving standards of decency, we don't know. But the dignified and humane deaths of thirty-two Angola death row inmates hang in the balance. Already the Louisiana legislature and governor have concluded that lethal injection is a more humane method of performing such executions for those sentenced to death *after* January 1, 1991.

In Florida, the governor suspended executions pending investigation and appropriate alterations or renovations to eliminate "problems" with the state's electric chair.

If that same dignity and humanity are to be belatedly extended to those few condemned sentenced to death *prior* to January 1, 1991, it will take either the executive intervention of the governor for a temporary period, or an action by the Kirkpatrick court, or an amendment to the new law by the state legislature.

[October 1990]

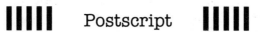 Postscript

The widely publicized and irrefutable photographic evidence, cited in this article, of the physical damage inflicted by Louisiana's electric chair fueled controversy over its continued use. Shortly after "The Horror Show" 's publication, the federal District Court in New Orleans halted the scheduled execution of an inmate until the chair could be examined by experts, and concerns about its design and use could be settled by the court. This marked the first time in its fifty-year history that the constitutionality of the state's electric chair had been questioned in federal court. On January 26, 1991, the court ruled the chair's use constitutional. A month later, while maintaining that there was nothing wrong with the functioning of the electric chair, Annette Viator, chief legal counsel for the Department of Corrections, announced that the DOC would ask the state legislature to consider a measure switching the official method of execution to lethal injection.

On June 25, 1991, the Louisiana legislature amended the state's death-penalty law, mandating that all executions after September 15, 1991, be performed by lethal injection.

On July 22, 1991, Andrew Lee "Flash" Jones became the last person to die in Louisiana's electric chair.

THE DEATHMEN

(CONTINUED)

Ron Wikberg and Wilbert Rideau

The professional executioner has his roots in the advent of civilization. Indeed, the executioner was an outgrowth of mankind's efforts to maintain social order and "justice." As family units expanded into clans and tribes, the corresponding need to establish a governing authority responsible for internal order and the general welfare gave rise to leaders and councils, the first forms of government. As these communities evolved into larger sociopolitical entities, so did the centralization of power and formal authority. In the interest of internal order and the consolidation of societal power, those who held formal authority assumed responsibility for dispensing justice. A private individual's taking of revenge carried the potential of precipitating a blood feud that could threaten the peace and stability of the community. Thus, the power to exact justice was taken from the individual and entrusted to official authorities, who in turn designated certain individuals to act as executioners. The executioner epitomized, with a graphic and awful finality, the enforcement of the will of authority. The creation of an official executioner represented mankind's progress from the law of the jungle to that of civilized order.

Historically, executioners have been popularly perceived as mysterious and sinister figures, slinking about execution chambers, carrying out the despicable task of ending lives in the name of "authority" and "justice." They have served as society's bogeymen, either feared, hated, or held in awe. History shows that many executioners were vile, loathsome personalities who, as often as not, were criminals opting to perform their duties in order to save their own skins. Others, however, were affable, law-abiding persons who, for varying reasons, chose the role of executioner because that was what they wanted to do.

The appeal of the job varied with times and circumstances, and at times officials found it extremely difficult to find people to serve as executioners. For instance, being an executioner would have made you the most hated man in Quebec in 1751, so no volunteers could be found. Officials were forced to impose the job upon slaves or men condemned to death.

According to the Amherst papyri, which make an accounting of state criminals in Egypt circa 1500 B.C., the guilty chose their own method of death and carried it out themselves. In China, Egypt, and Assyria, too, malefactors were ordered to act as their own executioners, being forced to take poison.

Because of the difficulty in getting individuals to serve as executioners, the job was often offered to criminals. In the thirteenth century, the English royal burgh of Wigtown passed a law that the executioner had to be a criminal sentenced to death, whose sentence was deferred as long as he carried out the public hangman's duties. When he became too old and could no longer do the job, he himself was hanged. It would be centuries before a better deal was offered criminals who became executioners. Records show that in early seventeenth-century England, a man named Derrick was sentenced to death, but pardoned by the Earl of Essex and employed to hang twenty-three others. Derrick decided to stay on after his quota was up, remaining the official executioner for nearly half a century.

There were similar policies in the Scandinavian countries. In the small Swedish town of Arboga in 1470, a thief standing on the gallows awaiting the noose was offered the job of hangman. The attending public, having pity on the man, agreed to the offer, and the thief was pardoned. A red-hot iron was then used to brand his body with the marks of both thief and executioner. Two centuries later, in 1608, the Swedish thief Mickel Matsson, from Gronso, was asked by the court if he would become executioner in the community of Uppsala in exchange for not being hanged. Matsson agreed and was led to the gallows, where both his ears were cut off, a method used at the time to identify executioners. Many communities chose to identify their executioners by disfigurement; others merely demanded that they wear distinctively marked clothing.

The desire to save one's own skin by becoming executioner sometimes meant that a criminal had to execute members of his own family. Crosland, a well-known executioner during the days of Charles II, hanged both his father and brother. Convicted of horse stealing, all three were sentenced to hang, but the judges offered to pardon the one who would be willing to hang the other two. The father and elder son refused, but the youngest, John Crosland, agreed. History records that he did the job admirably and was appointed official hangman for Derby and several surrounding communities, a position he held until old age.

Some hanged their kin without having been condemned themselves. Roger Gray, a seventeenth-century English executioner, hanged his own brother, then wrote to his nephew: "I am much afflicted to be the conveyancer of such news unto you as cannot be very welcome. Your father died eight days since, but the most generously I ever saw a man. I will say this of him, everywhere; for I myself trussed him up."

One of Ireland's more colorful deathmen, Tom Galvin, made extra money during his retirement by showing curiosity-seekers the ropes he had used to hang many of his nearest relatives. Selling pieces of the rope or some relic of the condemned to spectators following popular executions was a common way for executioners to make money. In some places, the executioner was permitted to take any and all of the personal property of the condemned.

Animals, and even the witnessing public, were used as executioners in England and Scotland during the fourteenth and fifteenth centuries, when both jurisdictions used the "Halifax Gibbet" and the "Scottish Maiden." These devices allowed a long rope to be attached to a pin holding a blade above the condemned's head. When the rope was pulled, releasing the pin, the blade would swiftly behead the criminal. In instances of theft of an animal, the rope was sometimes affixed to the animal, which at some point walked away and pulled the pin. In other cases that had aroused community sentiment, the rope was thrown into the crowd of spectators. Sometimes, feeling sympathy for the condemned, they refused to approach the rope, thus forcing the executioner to do the job himself. The Gibbet was last used in 1650; the Maiden was discontinued in 1750.

In Germany, when soldiers were convicted of certain crimes, they were executed by their colleagues. The condemned would be turned loose in the forest, where his fellow soldiers hunted him, running him to ground and spearing him to death. It was a special honor for the man who speared him first. In other instances the condemned soldier was compelled to run a gauntlet while his fellow militiamen beat him to death with clubs and sticks.

Early executioners had to be a macho lot. Not only did many methods of capital punishment demand physical strength, but executioners often had to protect themselves from the angry spectators.

For centuries condemned men, women, and children were decapitated by ax or sword. Herr Randell, Germany's executioner as late as 1901, was an expert with the sword who beheaded criminals usually with a single sweep. Germany also provided history with the world's oldest executioner, one Reichardt, who in 1931, at the age of eighty, executed Kurt Tetzner at Regenburg. During his term the elderly Reichardt killed sixty people.

Burning at the stake was the penalty generally reserved for women convicted of treason, murder, or witchcraft. While demanding little physical prowess, the execution of women occasionally brought bursts of ire and threats against the executioner from spectators. After the condemned was tied to the stake and faggots of firewood were heaped at her feet, a rope with a slipknot was placed around the neck, the other end being held by the executioner a distance away. Before the fire was lighted the executioner, as a general rule, strangled the woman by pulling on the rope, unless prompted not to do so by an excited crowd. That is what happened to Catherine Hayes after she was convicted of murdering her husband. The executioner released the rope before strangulation occurred, and Hayes was burned alive for the crowd's enjoyment. Thus, on occasion, the executioner was also a showman, conducting the execution so as to provide his audience a form of morbid entertainment. Some executioners became quite adept at gauging the mood of large crowds; sometimes the executioner's own life depended on it.

In "Boddel og Galgefugl" a Swedish writer described what any angry crowd could do following a botched execution:

A woman by the name of Johanne had been sentenced to die because she had been the mistress of her brother-in-law, and she was to be executed with the sword. . . . Master Anders Aalborg should perform the beheading. When the poor Johanne should die . . . he bungled the first blow and merely cut a small ring into the neck so that the woman fell over and gave a pitiful scream; and thereafter he gave her five or six blows and still could not decapitate her. Then fear took hold of the executioner and he threw the sword of justice away, shouted in mortal fear 'Mercy! Mercy!' and fled away. But the furious mob of people . . . set out after him and he was beaten brutally and killed.

In England and France, executioners were servants picked by lords of the manor. They were called hereditary hangmen, whose families were rewarded with a plot of land and a home. Their duties were passed from generation to generation.

In France in 1688, Charles Henri Sanson would become the first in a long line of Sansons to be appointed royal executioner. For 159 years the Sansons handed the "seal of executioner" from father to son. Prior to the French Revolution in 1789, the methods of execution varied: decapitation by sword for the nobility, and hanging, burning at the stake, or drawing and quartering for common criminals. Following Dr. Joseph-Ignace Guillotin's invention of the "guillotine," Sanson executed 2,794 people between 1792 and 1795, including King Louis XVI and Marie Antoinette in 1793. During the Reign of Terror following the revolution, Sanson beheaded as many as fifty people a day.

The Sanson reign would end in 1847, when Henri-Clement Sanson was officially dismissed from his position for having pawned France's guillotine in order to pay personal debts. France maintained death-penalty laws until they were abolished under the administration of President François Mitterrand in 1981.

For centuries, official records of European executions and executioners were kept rarely or not at all. Not so in England, however, where documents and records were painstakingly kept, including that of William Calcraft, who not only became the "London Executioner," but also served a longer term as executioner than anyone else in English history. Formerly a shoemaker, watchman, butler, and hawker, Calcraft served from 1829 to 1874, carrying out England's last public execution, that of author Michael Barrett, in 1868.

In 1879, Englishman William Marwood was appointed official hangman; building upon Calcraft's technical expertise, he invented what was called the long drop, a method that quickened death by breaking the neck. Though he was hangman for only four years, Marwood's reforms made death by hanging more humane.

In 1935, John Laurence wrote in *The History of Capital Punishment:*

> The story of a nation's crime is national history. The scaffold has made and altered history. If capital punishment had been as rigorously taboo in the twenty centuries of the Christian era as has been the encouragement of education, it is not a matter of doubt that the history of the world would not be what it is. The rope has done more than break men's necks. It has numbed the brains of the living, and men's thoughts have remained inarticulate from fear of the freely falling knife and the headsman's axe.

Though England and her colonies, as well as France, at one time employed numerous executioners, England too, eventually opted for hereditary deathmen. The foremost of these were the Pierrepoint family, father, uncle, and son. For fifty-six years the Pierrepoints, beginning with Henry Albert Pierrepoint in 1900, in in served as England's official executioners. In the ten years he held that position, Henry executed 105 people in thirty-eight prisons in five different British colonies. Sensitive people sometimes see such men as a bloodthirsty villains and believe they are haunted by the ghosts of their victims. But the elder Pierrepoint told one interviewer: "Well, I have executed over a hundred persons. But I've never seen a ghost yet." Henry's brother, Thomas, became assistant executioner and took over after Henry's retirement in 1910. Thomas retired at age seventy-five having served the Crown for forty-two years.

His nephew, Albert's son, also named Albert Pierrepoint, inherited the position at twenty-seven, having served since 1927 as an assistant at forty executions under the tutelage of his uncle. Until his retirement in 1956, Albert Pierrepoint trained German and Austrian executioners in the craft of hanging. After World War II, he helped execute over two hundred war criminals, performing as many as twenty-seven hangings in one twenty-four-hour period.

In his autobiography, *Executioner Pierrepoint,* Albert surprised the world by announcing that he was a staunch opponent of the death penalty:

I operated, on behalf of the State, what I am convinced was the most humane and the most dignified method of meting out death to a delinquent—however justified or unjustified the allotment of death may be—and on behalf of humanity I trained other nations to adopt the British system of execution. . . . It is a fact which is no source of pride to me at all—it is simple history—that I have carried out the execution of more judicial sentences of death (outside the field of politics) than any executioner in any British record or archive. That fact is the measure of my experience. The fruit of my experience has this bitter aftertaste: that I do not now believe that any one of the hundreds of executions I carried out has in any way acted as a deterrent against future murder. Capital Punishment, in my view, achieved nothing except revenge.

. . .

I now sincerely hope that no man is ever called upon to carry out another execution in my country. I have come to the conclusion that executions solve nothing, and are only an antiquated relic of a primitive desire for revenge which takes the easy way and hands over the responsibility for revenge to other people. . . . I conceived an early ambition, implanted by my father. My belief is still, as I look back on the obstacles I met, and the dangers I have surmounted, that I was sent on this earth to do this work and that the same power told me I should leave it. I had an ambition, I have it no longer. All the desire is quite gone.

England's last execution was carried out on August 23, 1964, and Parliament abolished capital punishment in 1965.

Though the United States used hanging as its primary method of execution for nearly two centuries, early America also utilized drowning, burning at the stake, and decapitation. Executions, for a very long time, were primarily local affairs, carried out by local authorities who either assigned the task of executing the condemned to the chief local law officer or retained the services of a professional executioner. There is little available evidence to indicate how American executioners acquired their expertise other than through trial and error, at the cost of many botched executions.

The call for more humane executions led the state of New York to adopt electrocution in 1888. Its use would spread throughout the nation, but it would always be a uniquely American method of execution. According to Amnesty International, the United States is the only nation that has ever used the electric chair to execute people.

Lewis E. Lawes, Sing Sing prison's warden from 1905 to 1930, supervised over 150 electrocutions. In *Twenty Thousand Years in Sing Sing,* Lawes wrote: "When the official executioner [John Hubert] suddenly resigned without notice, and the position of executioner was advertised, hundreds of applications were received from men and women." Lawes said some applicants were actually against capital punishment, but were jobless and had families to support. Ex-servicemen described their killing experiences at the war front. "I'll take the job if there's no publicity attached to it," wrote one applicant. "These fellows knew what they were doing when they set out to kill. Why then should I have any compunction about doing the same to them? I'll take the job, and do it with vigor and efficiency," said another.

Hubert was eventually replaced by Robert Elliott, who later became widely known as "America's Chief Executioner." Elliott wound up carrying out that duty for the states of New York, New Jersey, Pennsylvania, and Massachusetts, executing hundreds of people in the electric chair.

During the first quarter of the twentieth century, there was a growing trend to shift the responsibility of execution from sheriffs and contracted private executioners to prison and state correctional officials. In 1923, Alabama passed a law discontinuing the practice of executing people in the county where they had been tried; from then on, all executions were to be carried out at the state prison. The law designated the warden the official executioner and granted him immunity from any possible charge of murder for executing the condemned. This was the way of the future.

On April 22, 1983, John Evans III was strapped into the Alabama electric chair, which had been built by inmates in 1927. When the signal came, Holman Prison warden J. D. White pulled the switch. It took three pulls to kill Evans, leaving him charred and smoking, and stirring a nationwide controversy. Evans's execution had been handled by a "death watch" team of prison security officers headed by the warden. By 1990, most of the nation's executions were handled by such teams. So it came to pass that the most despicable of tasks, historically given to criminals and professional executioners to perform because citizens refused to do it, had finally been given to regular citizens—prison personnel.

Retired Alabama prison employee Murray Daniels told *Playboy* magazine in 1986: "It ain't no joy to kill nobody." Daniels, then seventy-two, had conducted several executions. "We didn't want to do it. That was our living. Had to do what the bossman said. I'm not proud of it. It was bread to me. If I couldn't 'a done what the bossman wanted, he'd get somebody else. It ain't no show to kill a man. You kill a man and make a big show of it, all you done is kill a hog."

Other executioners who have spoken or written about their life's work have similarly expressed the importance of showing the condemned some dignity. In his autobiography, Albert Pierrepoint wrote:

> I will not deny that on occasions I have been emotionally involved in the fate of a condemned person because of what I have previously read or heard about the crime, or the circumstances of the trial, or popular agitation for or against the prisoners which has erupted afterwards. . . . As the executioner, it has fallen to me to make the last confrontation with all the condemned. It is I who have looked them in the eyes. . . . And it is at that moment, with their eyes on mine, and all the official witnesses huddled in a corner behind them, that I have known that any previous emotional involvement I may have had is to be regretted. There is only a final relationship which matters: in Christianity this is my brother or sister to whom something dreadful must be done, and I have tried always to be gentle with them, and to give them what dignity I could in their death.

From 1941, when Louisiana switched to electrocution, until 1961, Grady Jarratt was the official executioner. Prior to 1957, when executions were transferred to the State Penitentiary at Angola, the Texas native traveled from parish to parish to carry out his deadly duties. Legal responsibility for executions was then vested in the sheriff of each parish, but the truck-mounted generator and portable electric chair were under the authority of Angola prison officials. At the designated time, the chair and the executioner would meet at the parish where the execution was scheduled.

"The truck had an inmate electrician, a prison chief electrician, and either a security officer or captain that would go along," said corrections veteran Hilton Butler, who began his prison career at Angola in 1952 and recalls accompanying the electric chair with Captain E. Foster on several occasions in the 1950s. (Much later, Butler became warden of Angola and carried out eleven executions during his administration.)

On May 20, 1949, just eight years after Louisiana began using the electric chair, Grady Jarratt traveled to Opelousas to execute Matthew "Mack" Cook and Joe Cook, brothers who had killed a prominent local and raped his young female companion. As Jarratt pulled the switch on Matthew, he said: "Good-bye, Mack!" "Wham!" Butler recalled, "that's the way he did them all. The last thing he said to them was, 'Good-bye, whatever their name was.' Then he pulled the lever."

Thomas Hill, a former Angola employee, described Grady Jarratt as a pleasant and professional person who often greeted execution witnesses, shook their hands, and chatted. He didn't mind people seeing him or knowing who he was. In fact, when Jarratt pulled the switch, he was in plain view of everyone present. "We did executions on Thursday night, which would be early Friday morning. Usually Jarratt would come in two days ahead of time and go through the chair with a fine-toothed comb. I mean everything had to be right up to snuff. Even the leather. He would take it in his hands and ply it. If it had a crack in it, then we'd have to make a new one. He was very, very particular," said Hill.

The 1961 execution of Jesse James Ferguson was the last Jarratt performed for Louisiana. A moratorium on capital punishment ensued.

When Louisiana reinstituted the death penalty in 1976, it also revived the need for official executioners. But many of the men who possessed the expertise, former professional executioners, had died or had grown old and retired from the killing business without having trained another generation to replace them. While other states simply assigned the responsibility to their corrections officials, Louisiana wanted its own public executioner, not a member of any law enforcement or correctional agency. Grady Jarratt had died during the moratorium and there were no professional executioners to be found, but Louisiana's problem was quickly solved when a Baton Rouge electrician volunteered his services. "I heard that the executioner they had here died in Texas," Sam Jones explained to *The Angolite*. "Somebody told me. So I took a regular civil service application and filled it out, put my phone number on it, and they contacted me." Then-warden Frank Blackburn hired him, giving him the alias "Sam Jones," after the governor who oversaw Louisiana's switch from hanging to electrocution decades before.

Why be an executioner? "I believed in it," Jones explained. "I never was the kind of person to say so-and-so ought to do something. If I felt that strong about it, I'd do it myself." He emphasized that the money he's paid has little to do with his being executioner. On the contrary, he said that it actually costs him money. "I go in the hole on these executions," he said. "Sometimes it costs me $800 to fly and

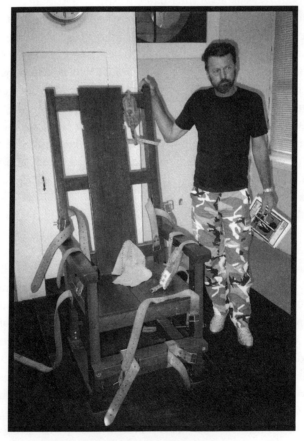

Sam Jones, state executioner of Louisiana,
1983–1991 (Courtesy The Angolite)

I only get $400 and I usually hand that to my kids and they use it in their church, or whatever."

Sam acknowledged that not only has he never been a victim of crime, but neither has his family nor anyone close to them. Yet he identifies with the victims of crime and publicly proffers the rationale that he performs executions for them because somebody has to speak for them. Asked if he really feels that he does speak for crime victims, he told *The Angolite:* "Yeah, I feel I do, because they don't have anyone else speaking for 'em. They just become a number [in the system]." Sam did not know that every facet of Louisiana's system of justice—courts, Pardon Board, Parole Board, and even the governor's office—provides for input from the victim.

Sam had no professional expertise as an executioner when he was hired, but it didn't matter. Louisiana was willing to allow him to learn the art of execution through on-the-job-training, trial and error. In 1984 he recalled his first execution, that of Robert Wayne Williams in 1983, for Baton Rouge's *Morning Advocate* reporter Melinda Shelton: "Everybody has their doubts when they do something for the first time and, sure, I had mine. The first time I was nervous because it was the first time. I didn't doubt I could do it, but I didn't know what to expect. I had no previous experience, and I'd never seen one [an execution] before."

Jones has since acquired definite opinions about execution, one being that the condemned feels no pain. "I've been shocked before," he told *Playboy* in 1986, "but I didn't feel any pain. Been hit with 480 and I didn't feel anything. I never experienced no pain getting shocked. Neither do they. It goes in the top of the head and out the left leg. There're two phases. It comes in through the head and out the leg, just like an element in a toaster."

The Angolite showed Sam several color post-execution photos of Robert Wayne Williams, asking if he had seen the burns on Williams's body before. (Two of the photos are reproduced on page 293.) There was a long pause while he studied the pictures. "No, I've never seen that," he said, shaking his head. "That's the first time I've seen that. I didn't see that on him when they had him in the chair. It may have come up later. I don't know what happens to 'em, what procedure the body goes through after they're electrocuted." Asked if he had seen similar burns on any of the other eighteen men he has executed, he answered: "No. I don't remember seeing it on 'em. As soon as they take 'em out of the chair, they put 'em in a body bag and they're gone. . . . I don't remember seeing it on Wayne."

Though Sam has said publicly that electrocutions are humane and really too easy for the condemned, he would not want to be electrocuted. Asked if he could envision himself in circumstances in which he could commit a crime and kill someone, he acknowledged: "That could happen to anybody. Nobody know what the future brings." *The Angolite* then asked him which method of execution he would personally prefer if he had to be executed. "Well, I don't know that much about the others," he answered. "I know electrical and the lethal injection. I went to New Jersey up there and went through that with them. But, if I had my rathers, I'd guess I'd want the needle." Why? "I just figure it would be easier on me," he said. "All it do is put you to sleep."

During his first several years as executioner, Sam insisted on working under his alias and not being photographed. More recently, he has started allowing himself to be photographed and has even appeared on television.

He was asked how allowing his face to be photographed protected his anonymity. "People don't recognize you," he explained. "I've been sitting in a lounge before and be on TV and the barmaid serve me a drink and not even know who she's serving a drink to. And I've never had nobody walk up to me and say, 'You're so-and-so.' "

Sam differs greatly from past executioners not only in his readiness to court fame, but also in his role as executioner. In the past, executioners were generally responsible for the entire execution scenario. For instance, Grady Jarratt would check out the execution site a couple of days early to make sure that everything was in proper working order. He greeted witnesses and officials and dealt with the condemned face-to-face, executing him in full view of everyone.

Sam, on the other hand, avoids all contact with the witnesses and others present. He discreetly arrives at the death house shortly before the execution, and waits behind the wall adjacent to the electric chair while the shackled prisoner enters the death chamber and is strapped into the chair by prison security officers. Through a small rectangular window in the wall, he observes the ritual and waits for the warden's nod—the signal for him to push the button that sends thousands of volts of electricity burning through the condemned. He departs just as secretly as he arrived. *The Angolite* asked Sam if he personally checks the chair and electrical apparatus to be used in the execution. "No," he said, "Angola takes care of that." Unlike most executioners throughout history, Sam is not asked to do very much. His sole duty has been reduced to pushing a button, something a child, an animal, or even a machine could do—though Louisiana's requirement that the executioner be a certified electrician implies a larger responsibility.

While many professional executioners of the past spoke of dignity and even possible redemption for the condemned, there is no room in Sam's execution philosophy for dignity, and he does not believe the condemned are redeemable. His appearance on Australian television last year provided much insight. Asked how he saw the condemned, he replied: "They trash, simple as that. That's all they are. Pure trash. If they was any good, they wouldn't be in that spot where they at. I don't care whether they male or female, black or white, or green or pink. It makes me no difference. None at all. When I strap them in the chair and the warden gives me the nod, I'll push the button. I don't care who it is." Even if it was his grandson, he said. Asked about the reaction of the condemned when they're brought into the death chamber, he stated: "You can tell they's scared. They got fear in their eyes and all that, but most of them, they keep up the macho image. They all say they goin' home. I don't know where they goin' but I'm sending 'em there."

Speaking of the American justice system, Sam Jones told *The Angolite,* "Takes too long. Too long a procedure." Stays of execution frustrate him. "They're getting too many stays," he explained. "It's too complicated and too involved. Why should it take forever? The man committed the crime. He should pay for it. Sitting on death row for ten years is not solving anything. It's not helping him." Asked if speeding up the process might result in mistakes, Sam said: "It's possible to make mistakes in anything, but I don't believe they do that nowadays. No."

[February 1991]

‖‖‖   Postscript   ‖‖‖

Sam Jones performed his last electrocution in Louisiana on July 22, 1991. Corrections authorities informed *The Angolite* editors that, regardless of how executions are conducted in the future, the services of "Sam Jones" would no longer be needed, bringing his tenure as official state executioner to an end.

BIBLIOGRAPHY

|||||

THE FARRAR LEGACY

Interviews

Jim Amoss, editor, New Orleans *Times-Picayune*
Margaret A. Bolton (Farrar's great-niece)
Terri Carbo, deputy clerk of court, Louisiana Supreme Court, New Orleans
Professor Mark Carleton, "Politics and Punishment" (Louisiana State University Press, 1972), Baton Rouge, Louisiana
Andrew Dunn, supervisor of Identification Department, Louisiana State Penitentiary, Angola, Louisiana
Will Menary, Keeper of Records, Howard Tilton Library, Tulane University, New Orleans
Warren Woodfork, superintendent of city police, New Orleans Police Department

Other information is taken from the unpublished *History of Angola*, by Roger S. Thomas, assistant warden for treatment, Louisiana State Penitentiary, Angola, Louisiana; from materials available in the Louisiana Section of the New Orleans Library; and from *State* v. *Canton, 59 Southern 202 (1912) in *Louisiana Supreme Court Reports* (West Publishing Company).

THE LEGEND OF LEADBELLY

Asch, Moses and Alan Lomax, editors. *The Leadbelly Songbook.* New York: Oak Publications, 1962.
Carleton, Mark T. *Politics and Punishment.* Baton Rouge: LSU Press, 1971.
DeMichael, Don. "Leadbelly." Columbia Records.
Ramsey, Frederic, Jr. "Leadbelly's Legacy." *Saturday Review of Literature,* January 28, 1950.

"The Fight over Leadbelly's Bones." New Orleans *States Item,* October 10, 1974.

"He's Dead and Tired of Being Worried." New Orleans *States Item,* October 11, 1974.

Hogan, William. "King of the 12-String Guitar." *San Francisco Chronicle,* December 3, 1971.

"Legendary Figure." *Dallas Times Herald,* December 25, 1974.

Millstein, Gilbert. "Very Good Night." *New York Times Magazine,* October 15, 1950.

New Orleans *States Item,* June 4, 1968.

New Orleans *Times-Picayune,* January 23, 1975.

Ramsey, Frederic, Jr. "The Lyre of Leadbelly & Django." *Saturday Review,* December 15, 1959.

Shaw, Arnold. *The World of Soul: The Black Contribution to Pop Music.* Regenery, 1970.

Time, May 24, 1976.

THE HORROR SHOW

Interviews

Elva J. Carter, librarian, East Baton Rouge Parish Library
Rosetta Williams (mother of Robert Williams)

Other Sources

"Although on the Decrease, Will It Ever be Abolished?" *Morning Advocate* (Baton Rouge), Jan. 15, 1961.

Bernstein, Theodore. "A Grand Success." *IEEE Spectrum,* vol. 10, no. 2 (Feb. 1973).

———. "Theories of the Causes of Death from Electricity." *Medical Instrumentation,* vol. 9, no. 6 (Nov.–Dec. 1975).

"Debating a Fate Worse Than Death." *Insight,* July 2, 1990.

"Execution That Jolted World." *The Buffalo* (New York) *News,* May 2, 1982.

"Ferguson Walked Calmly into Death House in 1961." Baton Rouge *Morning Advocate,* Dec. 14, 1983.

Garrison, Webb. "The Execution That Changed Your Life." *Detective,* January 1972.

Gray, Ian, and Moira Stanley. *A Punishment in Search of a Crime: Americans Speak Out Against the Death Penalty.* New York: Avon Books, 1989.

"House Body Okays Death Penalty Halt." Baton Rouge *State Times*, June 11, 1968.

"Inmate Challenges Louisiana Executions." *Dallas Morning News,* Sept. 16, 1990.

Jones, G.R.N. "Judicial Electrocution." *The Lancet,* vol. 335 (March 24, 1990), p. 713.

"Killer Offers a Cryptic Message as Death Closes In." New Orleans *Times-Picayune,* March 16, 1988.

Kirkpatrick v. *Whitley.* "Petition for Post-Conviction Relief to Vacate Judgment and Sentence; Writ of Habeas Corpus; Motion for Stay of Execution and Evidentiary Hearing," filed by Nick Trenticosta, attorney, Loyola Death Penalty Resource Center, New Orleans. Docket No. 96597, 22nd Judicial District Court, St. Tammany Parish, Louisiana.

MacDonald, Carlos F. "The Infliction of the Death Penalty by Means of Electricity." *The New York Medical Journal.* vol. 55 (May 7, 1892).

"Pros, Cons on Capital Punishment Weighed." New Orleans *Times-Picayune,* May 20, 1973.

Report of the (Massachusetts) *Legislative Council Committee on Capital Punishment,* October 3, 1962.

Reynolds, Terry S., and Theodore Bernstein. "The Damnable Alternating Current." *Proceedings of the IEEE,* vol. 64, no. 9 (Sept. 1976).

Reynolds, Terry S., and Theodore Bernstein. "Edison and 'The Chair.' *IEEE Technology and Society Magazine,* vol. 8, no. 1 (March 1989).

Thomas, Roger. *"History(s) of Angola."* Unpublished manuscript.

"Time to Die: Jeff Killer Is Executed." New Orleans *Times-Picayune.* February 29, 1984.

THE DEATHMEN (CONTINUED)

Black, Charles L. *Capital Punishment: The Inevitability of Caprice and Mistake.* New York: W. W. Norton & Co., 1974.

Camus, Albert. "Reflections on the Guillotine." In *Resistance, Rebellion and Death.* New York: Alfred A. Knopf, 1961.

Carter, Elva J., librarian, East Baton Rouge Parish Library, Baton Rouge, Louisiana.

Criminal Justice Newsletter. New York and Washington, D.C.: Pace Publications, December 3, 1990.

Death Row, U.S.A. New York: NAACP Legal Defense Fund, 1990.

Encyclopedia of American Crime. New York: Facts on File.

Gardner, M. R. "Executions and Indignities: An Eighth Amendment Assessment of Methods of Inflicting Capital Punishment."

Gettinger, Stephen H. *Sentenced to Die.* New York: Macmillan, 1979.

Gordon, Irving L. *American History: A Review Text.* New York: AMSCO, 1983.

Greene, Johnny. "The Executioner." *Playboy,* vol. 33 (March 1986).

Guinness Book of World Records. New York: Sterling Publishing Co., Inc., 1989.

Hitchens, Christopher. "Minority/Report." *The Nation,* Aug. 29, 1987.

Ingle, Joseph B. *Last Rights.* New York: Abingdon, 1990.

Johnson, R. "This Man Has Expired." *Commonweal,* January 13, 1989.

Laurence, John. *The History of Capital Punishment.* New York: Citadel Press, 1960, 1983.

Lawes, Lewis E. *Twenty Thousand Years in Sing Sing.* New York: Ray Long & Richard R. Smith, 1932.

Lilly, J. Robert, Ph.D., Department of Sociology; Northern Kentucky University, Highland Heights, Kentucky.

Meltsner, Michael. *Cruel and Unusual.* New York: Random House, 1973.

"Official Executions, Then and Now." New Orleans *Times-Picayune,* Aug. 1, 1990.

People, June 5, 1989.

Pierrepont, Albert. *Executioner Pierrepoint.* London: Harrap, 1974.

"Report of the Commission to Investigate and Report the Most Humane and Practical Method of Carrying into Effect the Sentence of Death in Capital Cases 3." Transmitted to the Legislature of the State of New York, January 17, 1888.

Sheridan, Leo W. *I Killed for the Law* The Career of Robert Elliot. New York: Stackpole Sons, 1938.

Thomas, Roger. *History of Angola* (Unpublished manuscripts).

Trachtman, Paul. *The Gunfighters.* New York: Time-Life Books, 1981.

Truzzi, Marcello, ed., *Sociology of Everyday Life.* New York: Prentice Hall, 1968.

U.S. News & World Report, July 17, 1989.

U.S. Supreme Court Reports (West Publishing Company), dicta from various cases, in particular *Glass* v. *Louisiana,* 105 S. Ct. 2159 (1985) and *Francis* v. *Resweber,* 67 S. Ct. 381 (1964).

INDEX

IIIII